The Political Economy of Slavery
■ Studies in the Economy and Society
of the Slave South

Eugene D. Genovese ■ The
Political Economy of Slavery
■ Studies in the Economy &
Society of the Slave South

Pantheon Books ✖ A DIVISION
OF RANDOM HOUSE, NEW YORK

SECOND PRINTING, JUNE 1966

© Copyright, 1965, 1964, 1961, by Eugene Genovese

All rights reserved under International and Pan-American Copyright Conventions. Published in New York by Pantheon Books, a division of Random House, Inc., and simultaneously in Toronto, Canada, by Random House of Canada Limited. Manufactured in the United States of America.

LIBRARY OF CONGRESS CATALOG CARD NUMBER: 65-14583

THE AUTHOR WISHES TO THANK THE FOLLOWING, FOR PERMISSION TO REPRINT:

Agricultural History Society—"Livestock in the Slave Economy" by Eugene D. Genovese. Reprinted from *Agricultural History*, Vol. 36.

Harcourt, Brace & World, Inc.—From "The Hollow Men" by T. S. Eliot, in *Collected Poems of T. S. Eliot, 1909–1962.*

The Journal of Southern History—"Significance of the Slave Plantation for Southern Economic Development" by Eugene D. Genovese. Copyright 1962 by The Southern Historical Association.

Oxford University Press, Inc.—From *The Prince* by Machiavelli (Vincent-Ricci translation).

Phylon, The Atlanta University Review of Race and Culture—"The Negro Laborer in Africa and the Slave South" by Eugene D. Genovese. Copyright 1960 by Phylon, the Atlanta University Review of Race and Culture.

Prentice-Hall, Inc.—From *The Economic Growth of the United States, 1790–1860,* by Douglass C. North. Copyright © 1961.

Charles Scribner's Sons—From *The Emergence of Lincoln,* Vol. 1, by Allan Nevins.

Textile History Review (*Cotton History Review*)—"Cotton, Slavery, and Soil Exhaustion" by Eugene D. Genovese.

FOR MY PARENTS,
Dominick and Lena Genovese,
WHO MADE IT POSSIBLE

Preface

These studies have had a long history, longer than I sometimes care to recall, having begun as an undergraduate honors paper at Brooklyn College almost fifteen years ago. Arthur C. Cole, whose kindness and wise counsel I still vividly recall, suggested that I investigate the agricultural reform movement in the Old South. The suggestion appalled me—with typical undergraduate modesty I had proposed to do a paper on "Southern Thought from Late Colonial Times to the Civil War"—but embarrassment and confidence in the old professor's judgment caused me to yield. When I moved on to Columbia University, I carried a growing interest in the subject with me. Eventually, although the story had some strange turnings, a doctoral dissertation on the same subject emerged.

Some of these studies grew out of that dissertation; others sprung from allied projects. It was clear from the beginning that Southern agriculture could not be studied apart from politics and social structure. Fortunately, neither Professor Cole nor Professor Dumas Malone ever thought that the subject could be treated in any other way, and I escaped having to waste my time doing "pure" economic history. (How astonishing that an age which finds pure women both contaminated and boring so ardently seeks pure economists.) My inclination to study the slave economy as one aspect of a social process received special encouragement from Frank Tannenbaum, whose writings and lectures on Latin America set a high standard. To all of these men I am deeply indebted, as I am to Richard B. Morris, who assumed responsibility for my dissertation when Professor Malone retired and who piloted me through some rough seas.

To David Donald, who was teaching at Columbia University when I studied there, I owe a special debt. His criticisms of my work have always been hard, but his generous support, especially at some difficult junctures in the ensuing years, has been inestimable. He has always retained grave reservations about my method and conclusions, and like Professors Cole, Malone, Tannenbaum, and Morris, hardly shares my philosophical standpoint. Yet, in the best tradition of the academic community, which is nonetheless too often violated by petty men, they always tried to help me find my own road instead of trying to drag me down theirs.

A number of friends helped in a variety of ways at various stages, and I hope that they will accept a general acknowledgment, for I am well aware of how much I owe to others. I have been especially indebted, however, to Ann J. Lane, who read most of these essays at different stages and offered indispensable criticisms of style and content, and to Mr. André Schiffrin of Pantheon Books, who persuaded me to make a number of changes that have improved the manuscript immensely.

Six of these studies appeared previously in journals, as noted in the acknowledgments, and are reprinted by permission of those journals. These have benefited from suggestions of the respective editors, especially the one from *Agricultural History*, which was then so splendidly edited by Fred Kohlmeyer and has since passed into the able hands of James Shideler. All have been rewritten. "The Slave South: An Interpretation" has been enlarged and revised substantially; "The Negro Laborer in Africa and the Slave South" has also been altered considerably; the others have had rough spots removed, additions and deletions made, and some errors corrected in the face of criticism from scholars, whose assistance is acknowledged in the footnotes.

The other four studies appear for the first time. The two unpublished papers on the industrialists and industry were read by Robert Starobin, whose forthcoming dissertation on slave labor in industry will no doubt tell us much we need to know. His skeptical reaction and thoughtful questions did not change my mind but did lead to some necessary rethinking. The final paper, "The Origins of Slavery Expansionism," was read to the departmental faculty seminar at Rutgers University, where it led to a lively exchange among my colleagues. Their reactions helped me to see the limits of my argument and, I hope, to put it in proper perspective.

E. D. G.

Contents

LIST OF ABBREVIATIONS

Agr. Hist.	*Agricultural History*
AHR	*American Historical Review*
AHQ	*Alabama Historical Quarterly*
DBR	*De Bow's Review*
GHQ	*Georgia Historical Quarterly*
HMM	*Hunt's Merchants' Magazine*
JEBH	*Journal of Economic and Business History*
JEH	*Journal of Economic History*
JMH	*Journal of Mississippi History*
JNH	*Journal of Negro History*
JPE	*Journal of Political Economy*
JSH	*Journal of Southern History*
LHQ	*Louisiana Historical Quarterly*
MHR	*Missouri Historical Review*
MVHR	*Mississippi Valley Historical Review*
NCHR	*North Carolina Historical Review*
PSQ	*Political Science Quarterly*
QJE	*Quarterly Journal of Economics*
SAQ	*South Atlantic Quarterly*
SCHGM	*South Carolina Historical and Genealogical Magazine*
	(The word "Genealogical" is no longer in the title, but for convenience the same abbreviation is used for both the earlier and later volumes.)
SEJ	*Southern Economic Journal*

SHQ   *Southwestern Historical Quarterly*

SQR   *Southern Quarterly Review*

THR   *Textile History Review* (The early volumes were called *Cotton History Review*, but for convenience the same abbreviation is used.)

VMHB   *Virginia Magazine of History and Biography*

The Political Economy of Slavery ■ Studies in the Economy & Society of the Slave South ■ *Plantation slavery had in strictly business aspects at least as many drawbacks as it had attractions. But in the large it was less a business than a life; it made fewer fortunes than it made men.*

■ ULRICH BONNELL PHILLIPS

Introduction

⬚ *One*

These studies fall under the rubric of "the political economy of slavery," not "the economics of slavery," because they are concerned less with economics or even economic history as generally understood than with the economic aspect of a society in crisis. They argue that slavery gave the South a social system and a civilization with a distinct class struc‑ture, political community, economy, ideology, and set of psychological patterns and that, as a result, the South in‑creasingly grew away from the rest of the nation and from the rapidly developing sections of the world. That this civilization had difficulty in surviving during the nineteenth century—a bourgeois century if any deserves the name—raises only minor problems. The difficulty, from this point of view, was neither economic, nor political, nor moral, nor ideological; it was all of these, which constituted manifesta‑tions of a fundamental antagonism between modern and premodern worlds.

The premodern quality of the Southern world was im‑parted to it by its dominant slaveholding class. Slavery has existed in many places, side by side with other labor sys‑tems, without producing anything like the civilization of the South. Slavery gave the South a special way of life because it provided the basis for a regional social order in which the slave labor system could dominate all others. Southern slavery was not "mere slavery"—to recall Louis

Hartz's luckless term—but the foundation on which rose a powerful and remarkable social class: a class constituting only a tiny portion of the white population and yet so powerful and remarkable as to try, with more success than our neo-abolitionists care to see, to build a new, or rather to rebuild an old, civilization.

The first of these studies, "The Slave South: An Interpretation," sketches the main features of antebellum Southern civilization, which it describes as having been moving steadily into a general crisis of society as a whole and especially of its dominant slaveholding class.[1] The slaveholders' economic and political interests, as well as ideological and psychological commitments, clashed at many points with those of Northern and European capitalists, farmers, and laborers. The successful defense of slavery presupposed an adequate rate of material growth, but the South could not keep pace with an increasingly hostile North in population growth, manufacturing, transportation, or even agricultural development. The weaknesses of Southern agriculture were especially dangerous and galling to the regime— dangerous because without adequate agricultural progress other kinds of material progress were difficult to effect; galling because Southerners prided themselves on their rural society and its alleged virtues.

Part Two examines the agricultural base of the Southern economy and especially labor productivity, soil exhaustion, the quantity and quality of livestock, crop diversification, and the movement for agricultural reform. These studies attempt to demonstrate that the efforts of Southerners to develop a sound agricultural economy within the slave system were yielding meager results and had little hope of success as measured by the general and political needs of the slaveholders.

Part Three consists of three studies that take up some of the more important impediments to industrialization: the retardation of demand, the ambiguous position of the industrialists in a slaveholding society, and the relationship of the slaveholding planters to industrial development. These subjects do not exhaust the list of impediments, and none of the studies pretends to exhaust its particular subject. They are submitted in the hope that they demonstrate the partial and restricted nature of industrial advance under the slaveholders' regime.

Part Four begins with a paper on "The Origins of Slavery Expansionism," which may serve as a conclusion for the book as a whole. It tries to demonstrate that the South had a great stake in the struggle over the Western territories, which tore the country apart between the Mexican War and the secession crisis. This paper is followed by a discussion of the profitability of slavery in relation to the theme of the other studies.

❊ *Two*

The War for Southern Independence, from the viewpoint of these studies, arose naturally from the long process of the development of the slaveholders' regime. Since this viewpoint is not generally accepted, it would be proper to give some account of the contending interpretations. Historians fall into two broad camps: the traditionalists have seen the war as an irrepressible or inevitable conflict, whereas the revisionists have seen it as an unnecessary bloodbath that could have been prevented by good will or statesmanship. Until about thirty years ago the lines were firmly drawn.

In recent decades a great shift has occurred. The revisionists have scored a series of stunning victories over their opponents and forced them to abandon most of their ground. They have done hard digging into source materials, whereas since the appearance of Arthur C. Cole's admirable *The Irrepressible Conflict* (1934) the traditionalists have largely contented themselves with writing nice essays. Originally, the traditionalist argument posited a wide area of antagonism between the North and South, viewing slavery as a moral issue but also as the basis of intense material differences. Their notion of material differences contained two debilitating tendencies: it centered on narrow economic issues like the tariff, which hardly added up to a reasonable cause for a bloody war; and it assumed, in accordance with a rigid theoretical model, a slavery-engendered soil exhaustion and territorial expansionism which empirical research did not establish.

The revisionists have offered a great many monographs which argue that slavery did not necessarily prevent soil reclamation and agricultural adjustment; they have investigated the conditions for Southern expansionism and concluded that slavery neither needed nor had prospects for additional territory. As a result of their work, the traditional or irrepressible-conflict interpretation has come to rest almost entirely on moral grounds: the conscience of the nation could not tolerate forever the barbarism of slavery. The question of a profound material antagonism has thereby virtually been laid to rest.

If we had to choose between the two positions narrowed to embrace the moral question alone, it would be difficult to avoid choosing some variation of the revisionist, especially since such neo-revisionist historians as Allan Nevins and David Donald have avoided the more naive formulations of earlier writers and offered attractive alternatives. In effect, they each deny that North and South represented hostile civilizations and stress the inability of American institutional structure to cope with problems and disagreements that were in themselves negotiable. Against such an interpretation, continued harping on the moral issue becomes trying. Moral issues do have their place, as do the irrational actions with which they are sometimes associated, but to say that slavery was merely an immoral way to command labor and that it produced no special society is to capitulate before the revisionists' thrust. They maintain simply and forcefully that time and good will would have removed slavery had a holier-than-thou attitude not prevailed in the North and had there not been so much room for the demagogy of scheming politicians in both sections. The best that the recent traditionalists have been able to offer as a reply is the assertion that Southern immorality proved too profitable to be dispensed with. This is no answer. The notion that the values of the South's ruling class, which became the values of the South as a whole, may be dismissed as immoral is both dubious and unenlightening, but we may leave this point aside. If the commitment of the slaveholders to slavery was merely a matter of dollars and cents, a national effort could have paid them to become virtuous. The answer, I suppose, is that the North could not be expected to pay to free slaves when it believed slaveholding immoral in the first place. As a matter of fact, it could have, and there is not much evidence of such highmindedness in the North outside of a small band of abolitionists. Either the revisionists are essentially right or the moral question existed as an aspect of something much deeper.

I begin with the hypothesis that so intense a struggle of moral values implies a struggle of world views and that so intense a struggle of world views implies a struggle of worlds—of rival social classes or of societies dominated by rival social classes. In investigating this hypothesis I have rejected the currently fashionable interpretation of slavery as simply a system of extra-economic compulsion designed to sweat a surplus out of black labor. Slavery was such a system, but it was much more. It supported a plantation community that must be understood as an integrated social system, and it made this community the center of Southern life. It extruded a class of slaveholders with a special ideology and psychology and the political and economic power to impose their values on society as a whole. Slavery may have been immoral to the world at large, but to these men, notwithstanding their doubts and inner conflicts, it increasingly came to be seen as the very foundation of a proper social order and therefore as the essence of morality in human relationships. Under the circumstances the social conflict between North and South took the form of a moral conflict. We need not deny the reality of the moral issue to appreciate that it represented only one aspect of a many-sided antagonism. These studies seek to explore the material foundations of that irrepressible antagonism.

Let us make our bows to the age. I do not believe in inevitability in the everyday meaning of the word, nor in a mechanical determinism that leaves no place for man's will, nor in sin. I do say that the struggle between North and South was irrepressible. From the moment that slavery passed from being one of several labor systems into being the basis of the Southern social order, material and ideological conflict with the North came into being and had to grow worse.[2] If this much be granted, the question of inevitability becomes the question of whether or not the slaveholders would give up their world, which they identified quite properly with slavery itself, without armed resistance. The slaveholders' pride, sense of honor, and commitment to their way of life made a final struggle so probable that we may safely call it inevitable without implying a mechanistic determinism against which man cannot avail.

I have attempted to demonstrate that the material prerequisites for the slaveholders' power were giving way before internal and external pressures; that the social system was breaking on immanent contradictions; that the economy was proving incapable of adapting itself to reforms while slavery existed; that slavery was naturally generating territorial expansion; and that therefore secession and the risk of war were emerging as a rational course of action. I have, in other words, tried to rebuild the case on which a materialist interpretation of an irrepressible conflict may rest. In doing so, I realize that much of the argument is an extension and refinement of arguments presented as long as a century ago, and I cannot avoid feeling that the book falls within González Prada's definition of sociology—the art of saying old things in new ways and the science of affirming contradictions.

The studies are presented with full awareness that the issues sooner or later become those of ideology and psychology. Not every material interest is worth defending to the death, and it is not obvious that any should be. In this book I can only suggest a starting point for a discussion of the slaveholders' ideology and psychology; but even if I or someone much more able could offer a volume, it would not be possible to array sufficient scientific evidence to close the debate between traditional and revisionist historians. A good revisionist could accept every one of the empirical findings in the studies presented here and rework his interpretation to account for them in a manner worthy of respect. The ultimate issues are those of history as social process and the place of men within it. No amount of research or argument on the origins of the War for Southern Independence could alone convert anyone to a position on those questions. The work of the revisionist historians has forced every honest opponent of theirs to rethink his position many times and to try to raise its level of analysis. If these studies do as much for them, the time and labor they represent will have been well spent.

N O T E S

1 The generalizations presented in this first study require considerable elaboration and defense, which the following studies only begin to offer. I do, however, plan to submit several volumes after this one. In my study of George Fitzhugh, *The Logical Outcome of the Slaveholders' Philosophy*, which is almost finished, I shall develop the ideological side of the argument. Also well under way is a study of rebelliousness and docility in the Negro slave, *Sambo & Nat Turner*, which will treat an important part of the story that had to be neglected here. Finally, I expect to submit, in what form I am not yet sure, extensive studies of the planters and the middle- and lower-class whites.

2 If I may pick a quarrel with Leon P. Litwack's admirable *North of Slavery* (Chicago, 1961), I cannot understand the statement that abolition in the North came about as a result of ideological rather than economic factors. The lack of a large class of slaveholders, as distinct from a class of businessmen and professionals who owned some slaves, resulted in a lack of deep ideological commitment and economic interest, not to mention psychological dependence. To try to weigh economic against ideological factors seems to me a fruitless pursuit. In this setting the moral attack on slavery, which needs no elaborate explanation in the world of the nineteenth century—only its absence would require explanation—met little resistance from those who benefited from the system.

PART ONE ❧ THE SETTING

What kills spontaneous fictions, what recalls the impassioned fancy from its improvisation, is the angry voice of some contrary fancy. Nature, silently making fools of us all our lives, never would bring us to our senses; but the maddest assertions of the mind may do so, when they challenge one another. Criticism arises out of the conflict of dogmas.

■ GEORGE SANTAYANA

Scepticism and Animal Faith

One ■ The Slave South:
An Interpretation

❧ *The Problem*

The uniqueness of the antebellum South continues to challenge the imagination of Americans, who, despite persistent attempts, cannot divert their attention from slavery. Nor should they, for slavery provided the foundation on which the South rose and grew. The master-slave relationship permeated Southern life and influenced relationships among free men. A full history would have to treat the impact of the Negro slave and of slaveless as well as slaveholding whites, but a first approximation, necessarily concerned with essentials, must focus on the slaveholders, who most directly exercised power over men and events. The hegemony of the slaveholders, presupposing the social and economic preponderance of great slave plantations, determined the character of the South. These men rose to power in a region embedded in a capitalist country, and their social system emerged as part of a capitalist world. Yet, a nonslaveholding European past and a shared experience in a new republic notwithstanding, they imparted to Southern life a special social, economic, political, ideological, and psychological content.

To dissolve that special content into an ill-defined agrarianism or an elusive planter capitalism would mean to sacrifice

13

concern with the essential for concern with the transitional and peripheral. Neither of the two leading interpretations, which for many years have contended in a hazy and unreal battle, offers consistent and plausible answers to recurring questions, especially those bearing on the origins of the War for Southern Independence. The first of these interpretations considers the antebellum South an agrarian society fighting against the encroachments of industrial capitalism; the second considers the slave plantation merely a form of capitalist enterprise and suggests that the material differences between Northern and Southern capitalism were more apparent than real. These two views, which one would think contradictory, sometimes combine in the thesis that the agrarian nature of planter capitalism, for some reason, made coexistence with industrial capitalism difficult.

The first view cannot explain why some agrarian societies give rise to industrialization and some do not. A prosperous agricultural hinterland has generally served as a basis for industrial development by providing a home market for manufactures and a source of capital accumulation, and the prosperity of farmers has largely depended on the growth of industrial centers as markets for foodstuffs. In a capitalist society agriculture is one industry, or one set of industries, among many, and its conflict with manufacturing is one of many competitive rivalries. There must have been something unusual about an agriculture that generated violent opposition to the agrarian West as well as the industrial Northeast.

The second view, which is the more widely held, emphasizes that the plantation system produced for a distant market, responded to supply and demand, invested capital in land and slaves, and operated with funds borrowed from banks and factors. This, the more sophisticated of the two interpretations, cannot begin to explain the origins of the conflict with the North and does violence to elementary facts of antebellum Southern history.

✄ *Slavery and the Expansion of Capitalism*

The proponents of the idea of planter capitalism draw heavily, wittingly or not, on Lewis C. Gray's theory of the genesis of the plantation system. Gray defines the plantation as a "capitalistic type of agricultural organization in which a considerable number of unfree laborers were employed under a unified direction and control in the production of a staple crop."[2] Gray considers the plantation system inseparably linked with the international development of capitalism. He notes the plantation's need for large outlays of capital, its strong tendency toward specialization in a single crop, and its commercialism and argues that these appeared with the industrial revolution.

In modern times the plantation often rose under bourgeois auspices to provide industry with cheap raw materials, but the consequences were not always harmonious with bourgeois society. Colonial expansion produced three sometimes overlapping patterns: (1) the capitalists of the advanced country simply invested in colonial land—as illustrated even today by the practice of the United Fruit Company in the Caribbean; (2) the colonial planters were largely subservient to the advanced countries—as illustrated by the British West Indies before the abolition of slavery; and (3) the planters were able to win independence and build a society under their own direction—as illustrated by the Southern United States. In alliance with the North, the planter-dominated South broke away from England, and political conditions in the new republic allowed it considerable freedom for self-development. The plantation society that had begun as an appendage of British capitalism ended as a powerful, largely autonomous civilization with aristocratic pretensions and possibilities, although it remained tied to the capitalist world by bonds of commodity production. The essential element in this distinct civilization was the slaveholders' domination, made possible by their command of labor. Slavery provided the basis for a special Southern economic and social life, special problems and tensions, and special laws of development.

❧ *The Rationality and Irrationality of Slave Society*

Slave economies normally manifest irrational tendencies that inhibit economic development and endanger social stability. Max Weber, among the many scholars who have discussed the problem, has noted four important irrational features.[3] First, the master cannot adjust the size of his labor force in accordance with business fluctuations. In particular, efficiency cannot readily be attained through the manipulation of the labor force if sentiment, custom, or community pressure makes separation of families difficult. Second, the capital outlay is much greater and riskier for slave labor than for free.[4] Third, the domination of society by a planter class increases the risk of political influence in the market. Fourth, the sources of cheap labor usually dry up rather quickly, and beyond a certain point costs become excessively burdensome. Weber's remarks could be extended. Planters, for example, have little opportunity to select specifically trained workers for special tasks as they arise.

There are other telling features of this irrationality. Under capitalism the pressure of the competitive struggle and the bourgeois spirit of accumulation direct the greater part of profits back into production. The competitive side of Southern slavery produced a similar result, but one that was modified by the pronounced tendency to heavy consumption. Economic historians and sociologists have long noted the high propensity to consume among landed aristocracies. No doubt this difference has been one of degree. The greater part of slavery's profits also find their way back into production, but the method of reinvestment in the two systems is substantially different. (Capitalism largely directs its profits into an expansion of plant and equipment, not labor; that is, economic progress is qualitative.) Slavery, for economic reasons as well as for those of social prestige, directs its reinvestments along the same lines as the original investment—in slaves and land; that is, economic progress is quantitative.)

In the South this weakness proved fatal for the slaveholders. They found themselves engaged in a growing conflict with Northern farmers and businessmen over such issues as tariffs, homesteads, internal improvements, and the decisive question of the balance of political power in the Union. The slow pace of their economic progress, in contrast to the long strides of their rivals to the north, threatened to undermine their political parity and result in a Southern defeat on all major issues of the day. The qualitative leaps in the Northern economy manifested themselves in a rapidly increasing population, an expanding productive plant, and growing political, ideological, and social boldness. The slaveholders' voice grew shriller and harsher as they contemplated impending disaster and sought solace in complaints of Northern aggression and exploitation.

Just as Southern slavery directed reinvestment along a path that led to economic stagnation, so too did it limit the volume of capital accumulated for investment of any kind. We need not reopen the tedious argument about the chronology of the plantation, the one-crop system, and slavery. (While slavery existed, the South had to be bound to a plantation system 'and an agricultural economy based on a few crops.) As a result, the South depended on Northern facilities, with inevitably mounting middlemen's charges.)Less obvious was the capital drain occasioned by the importation of industrial goods. While the home market remained backward, Southern manufacturers had difficulty producing in sufficient quantities to keep costs and prices at levels competitive with Northerners) The attendant dependence on Northern and British imports intensified the outward flow of badly needed funds.

Most of the elements of irrationality were irrational only from a capitalist standpoint. The high propensity to consume luxuries, for example, has always been functional (socially if not economically rational) in aristocratic societies, for it has provided the ruling class with the façade necessary to control the middle and lower classes. Thomas R. Dew knew what he was doing when he defended the high personal expenditures of Southerners as proof of the superiority of the slave system.[5] Few Southerners, even few slaveholders, could afford to spend lavishly and effect an aristocratic standard of living, but those few set the social tone for society. One wealthy planter with a great house and a reputation for living and entertaining on a grand scale could impress a whole community and keep before its humbler men the shining ideal of plantation magnificence. Consider Pascal's observation that the habit of seeing the king accompanied by guards, pomp, and all the paraphernalia designed to command respect and inspire awe will produce those reactions even when he appears alone and informally. In the popular mind he is assumed to be naturally an awe-inspiring being.[6] In this manner, every dollar spent by the planters for elegant clothes, a college education for their children, or a lavish barbecue contributed to the political and social domination of their class. We may speak of the slave system's irrationality only in a strictly economic sense and then only to indicate the inability of the South to compete with Northern capitalism on the latter's grounds. The slaveholders, fighting for political power in an essentially capitalist Union, had to do just that.

Capitalist and Pseudo-Capitalist Features of the Slave Economy

The slave economy developed within, and was in a sense exploited by, the capitalist world market; consequently, slavery developed many ostensibly capitalist features, such as banking, commerce, and credit. These played a fundamentally different role in the South than in the North. Capitalism has absorbed and even encouraged many kinds of precapitalist social systems: serfdom, slavery, Oriental state enterprises, and others. It has introduced credit, finance, banking, and similar institutions where they did not previously exist. It is pointless to suggest that therefore nineteenth-century India and twentieth-century Saudi Arabia should be classified as capitalist countries. We need to analyze a few of the more important capitalist and pseudo-capitalist features of Southern slavery and especially to review the barriers to industrialization in order to appreciate the peculiar qualities of this remarkable and anachronistic society.[7]

The defenders of the "planter-capitalism" thesis have noted the extensive commercial links between the plantation and the world market and the modest commercial bourgeoisie in the South and have concluded that there is no reason to predicate an antagonism between cotton producers and cotton merchants. However valid as a reply to the naive arguments of the proponents of the agrarianism-versus-industrialism thesis, this criticism has unjustifiably been twisted to suggest that the presence of commercial activity proves the predominance of capitalism in the South.[8] Many precapitalist economic systems have had well-developed commercial relations, but if every commercial society is to be considered capitalist, the word loses all meaning. In general, commercial classes have supported the existing system of production. As Maurice Dobb observes,[9] their fortunes are bound up with those of the dominant producers, and merchants are more likely to seek an extension of their middlemen's profits than to try to reshape the economic order.

We must concern ourselves primarily with capitalism as a social system, not merely with evidence of typically capitalistic economic practices. In the South extensive and complicated commercial relations with the world market permitted the growth of a small commercial bourgeoisie. (The resultant fortunes flowed into slaveholding, which offered prestige and economic and social security in a planter-dominated society.) Independent merchants found their businesses dependent on the patronage of the slaveholders. The merchants either became planters themselves or assumed a servile attitude toward the planters. The commercial bourgeoisie, such as it was, remained tied to the slaveholding interest, had little desire or opportunity to invest capital in industrial expansion, and adopted the prevailing aristocratic attitudes.

The Southern industrialists were in an analogous position, although one that was potentially subversive of the political power and ideological unity of the planters. The preponderance of planters and slaves on the countryside retarded the home market. The Southern yeomanry, unlike the Western, lacked the purchasing power to sustain rapid industrial development.[10] The planters spent much of their money abroad for luxuries. The plantation market consisted primarily of the demand for cheap slave clothing and cheap agricultural implements for use or misuse by the slaves. Southern industrialism needed a sweeping agrarian revolution to provide it with cheap labor and a substantial rural market, but the Southern industrialists depended on the existing, limited, plantation market. Leading industrialists like William Gregg and Daniel Pratt were plantation-oriented and proslavery. They could hardly have been other.

The banking system of the South serves as an excellent illustration of an ostensibly capitalist institution that worked to augment the power of the planters and retard the development of the bourgeoisie. Southern banks functioned much as did those which the British introduced into Latin America, India, and Egypt during the nineteenth century. Although the British banks fostered dependence on British capital, they did not directly and willingly generate internal capitalist development. They were not sources of industrial capital but "large-scale clearing houses of mercantile finance vying in their interest charges with the local usurers."[11]

The difference between the banking practices of the South and those of the West reflects the difference between slavery and agrarian capitalism. In the West, as in the Northeast, banks and credit facilities promoted a vigorous economic expansion. During the period of loose Western banking (1830–1844) credit flowed liberally into industrial development as well as into land purchases and internal improvements. Manufacturers and merchants dominated the boards of directors of Western banks, and landowners played a minor role. Undoubtedly, many urban businessmen speculated in land and had special interests in underwriting agricultural exports, but they gave attention to building up agricultural processing industries and urban enterprises, which guaranteed the region a many-sided economy.[12]

The slave states paid considerable attention to the development of a conservative, stable banking system, which could guarantee the movement of staple crops and the extension of credit to the planters. Southern banks were primarily designed to lend the planters money for outlays that were economically feasible and socially acceptable in a slave society: the movement of crops, the purchase of land and slaves, and little else.

Whenever Southerners pursued easy-credit policies, the

damage done outweighed the advantages of increased production. This imbalance probably did not occur in the West, for easy credit made possible agricultural and industrial expansion of a diverse nature and, despite acute crises, established a firm basis for long-range prosperity. Easy credit in the South led to expansion of cotton production with concomitant overproduction and low prices; simultaneously, it increased the price of slaves.

Planters wanted their banks only to facilitate cotton shipments and maintain sound money. They purchased large quantities of foodstuffs from the West and, since they shipped little in return, had to pay in bank notes. For five years following the bank failures of 1837 the bank notes of New Orleans moved at a discount of from 10 to 25 per cent. This disaster could not be allowed to recur. Sound money and sound banking became the cries of the slaveholders as a class.

Southern banking tied the planters to the banks, but more important, tied the bankers to the plantations. The banks often found it necessary to add prominent planters to their boards of directors and were closely supervised by the planter-dominated state legislatures. In this relationship the bankers could not emerge as a middle-class counterweight to the planters but could merely serve as their auxiliaries.

The bankers of the free states also allied themselves closely with the dominant producers, but society and economy took on a bourgeois quality provided by the rising industrialists, the urban middle classes, and the farmers who increasingly depended on urban markets. The expansion of credit, which in the West financed manufacturing, mining, transportation, agricultural diversification, and the numerous branches of a capitalist economy, in the South bolstered the economic position of the planters, inhibited the rise of alternative industries, and guaranteed the extension and consolidation of the plantation system.

If for a moment we accept the designation of the planters as capitalists and the slave system as a form of capitalism, we are then confronted by a capitalist society that impeded the development of every normal feature of capitalism. The planters were not mere capitalists; they were precapitalist, quasi-aristocratic landowners who had to adjust their economy and ways of thinking to a capitalist world market. Their society, in its spirit and fundamental direction, represented the antithesis of capitalism, however many compromises it had to make. The fact of slave ownership is central to our problem. This seemingly formal question of whether the owners of the means of production command labor or purchase the labor power of free workers contains in itself the content of Southern life. The essential features of Southern particularity, as well as of Southern backwardness, can be traced to the relationship of master to slave.

✂ *The Barriers to Industrialization*

If the planters were losing their economic and political cold war with Northern capitalism, the failure of the South to develop sufficient industry provided the most striking immediate cause. Its inability to develop adequate manufactures is usually attributed to the inefficiency of its labor force. No doubt slaves did not easily adjust to industrial employment, and the indirect effects of the slave system impeded the employment of whites.[13] Slaves did work effectively in hemp, tobacco, iron, and cotton factories but only under socially dangerous conditions. They received a wide variety of privileges and approached an elite status. Planters generally appreciated the potentially subversive quality of these arrangements and looked askance at their extension.

Slavery concentrated economic and political power in the

hands of a slaveholding class hostile to industrialism. The slaveholders feared a strong urban bourgeoisie, which might make common cause with its Northern counterpart. They feared a white urban working class of unpredictable social tendencies. In general, they distrusted the city and saw in it something incongruous with their local power and status arrangements.[14] The small slaveholders, as well as the planters, resisted the assumption of a heavy tax burden to assist manufacturers, and as the South fell further behind the North in industrial development more state aid was required to help industry offset the Northern advantages of scale, efficiency, credit relations, and business reputation.

Slavery led to the rapid concentration of land and wealth and prevented the expansion of a Southern home market. Instead of providing a basis for industrial growth, the Southern countryside, economically dominated by a few large estates, provided only a limited market for industry. Data on the cotton textile factories almost always reveal that Southern producers aimed at supplying slaves with the cheapest and coarsest kind of cotton goods. Even so, local industry had to compete with Northern firms, which sometimes shipped direct and sometimes established Southern branches.

William Gregg, the South's foremost industrialist, understood the modest proportions of the Southern market and warned manufacturers against trying to produce exclusively for their local areas. His own company at Graniteville, South Carolina, produced fine cotton goods that sold much better in the North than in the South. Gregg was an unusually able man, and his success in selling to the North was a personal triumph. When he had to evaluate the general position of Southern manufacturers, he asserted that he was willing to stake his reputation on their ability to compete with Northerners in the production of *"coarse cotton fabrics."*[15]

Some Southern businessmen, especially those in the border

states, did good business in the North. Louisville tobacco and hemp manufacturers sold much of their output in Ohio. Some producers of iron and agricultural implements sold in nearby Northern cities. This kind of market was precarious. As Northern competitors rose and the market shrank, Southern producers had to rely on the narrow and undependable Southern market.[16] Well before 1840 iron-manufacturing establishments in the Northwest provided local farmers with excellent markets for grain, vegetables, molasses, and work animals. During the antebellum period and after, the grain growers of America found their market at home. America's rapid industrial development offered farmers a magnificently expanding urban market, and not until much later did they come to depend to any important extent on exports.

To a small degree the South benefited in this way. By 1840 the tobacco-manufacturing industry began to absorb more tobacco than was being exported, and the South's few industrial centers provided markets for local grain and vegetable growers. Since the South could not undertake a general industrialization, few urban centers rose to provide substantial markets for farmers and planters. Southern grain growers, except for those close to the cities of the free states, had to be content with the market offered by planters who preferred to specialize in cotton or sugar and buy foodstuffs. The restricted rations of the slaves limited this market, which inadequate transportation further narrowed. It did not pay the planters to appropriate state funds to build a transportation system into the back country, and any measure to increase the economic strength of the back-country farmers seemed politically dangerous to the aristocracy of the Black Belt. The farmers of the back country remained isolated, self-sufficient, and politically, economically, and socially backward. Those grain-growing farmers who could compete with producers in the Upper South and the Northwest for the plantation market lived within the Black Belt. Since the planters did not have to buy from these local producers, the economic relationship greatly strengthened the political hand of the planters.

The General Features of Southern Agriculture

The South's greatest economic weakness was the low productivity of its labor force. The slaves worked indifferently. They could be made to work reasonably well under close supervision in the cotton fields, but the cost of supervising them in more than one or two operations at a time was prohibitive. Slavery prevented the significant technological progress that could have raised productivity substantially. Of greatest relevance, the impediments to technological progress damaged Southern agriculture, for improved implements and machines largely accounted for the big increases in crop yields per acre in the Northern states during the nineteenth century.

Slavery and the plantation system led to agricultural methods that depleted the soil. The frontier methods of the free states yielded similar results, but slavery forced the South into continued dependence upon exploitative methods after the frontier had passed further west. It prevented reclamation of worn-out lands. The plantations were much too large to fertilize easily. Lack of markets and poor care of animals by slaves made it impossible to accumulate sufficient manure. The low level of capital accumulation made the purchase of adequate quantities of commercial fertilizer unthinkable. Planters could not practice proper crop rotation, for the pressure of the credit system kept most available land in cotton, and the labor force could not easily be assigned to the required tasks without excessive costs of supervision. The general inefficiency of labor thwarted most attempts at improvement of agricultural methods.

The South, unable to feed itself, faced a series of dilemmas in its attempts to increase production of nonstaple crops and to improve its livestock. An inefficient labor force and the backward business practices of the dominant planters hurt. When planters did succeed in raising their own food, they also succeeded in depriving local livestock raisers and grain growers of their only markets. The planters had little capital with which to buy improved breeds and could not guarantee the care necessary to make such investments worth while. Livestock raisers also lacked the capital, and without adequate urban markets they could not make good use of the capital they had.

Thoughtful Southerners, deeply distressed by the condition of their agriculture, made a determined effort to remedy it. In Maryland and Virginia significant progress occurred in crop diversification and livestock improvement, but this progress was contingent on the sale of surplus slaves to the Lower South. These sales provided the income that offset agricultural losses and made possible investment in fertilizers, equipment, and livestock. The concomitant reduction in the size of the slave force facilitated supervision and increased labor productivity and versatility. Even so, the income from slave sales remained an important part of the gross income of the planters of the Upper South. The reform remained incomplete and could not free agriculture from the destructive effects of the continued reliance on slave labor.

The reform process had several contradictions, the most important of which was the dependence on slave sales. Surplus slaves could be sold only while gang-labor methods continued to be used in other areas. By the 1850s the deficiencies of slavery that had forced innovations in the Upper South were making themselves felt in the Lower South. Increasingly, planters in the Lower South explored the possibilities of reform. If the deterioration of agriculture in the Cotton Belt had proceeded much further, the planters would have had to stop buying slaves from Maryland and Virginia and look for markets for their own surplus slaves. Without the acquisition of fresh lands there could be no general reform of Southern agriculture. The Southern economy was moving steadily into an insoluble crisis.

❧ *The Ideology of the Master Class*

The planters commanded Southern politics and set the tone of social life. Theirs was an aristocratic, antibourgeois spirit with values and mores emphasizing family and status, a strong code of honor, and aspirations to luxury, ease, and accomplishment. In the planters' community, paternalism provided the standard of human relationships, and politics and statecraft were the duties and responsibilities of gentlemen. The gentleman lived for politics, not, like the bourgeois politician, off politics.

The planter typically recoiled at the notions that profit should be the goal of life; that the approach to production and exchange should be internally rational and uncomplicated by social values; that thrift and hard work should be the great virtues; and that the test of the wholesomeness of a community should be the vigor with which its citizens expand the economy. The planter was no less acquisitive than the bourgeois, but an acquisitive spirit is compatible with values antithetical to capitalism. The aristocratic spirit of the planters absorbed acquisitiveness and directed it into channels that were socially desirable to a slave society: the accumulation of slaves and land and the achievement of military and political honors. Whereas in the North people followed the lure of business and money for their own sake, in the South specific forms of property carried the badges of honor, prestige, and power. Even the rough parvenu planters of the Southwestern frontier—the "Southern Yankees"—strove to accumulate wealth in the modes acceptable to plantation society. Only in their crudeness and naked avarice did they differ from the Virginia gentlemen. They were a generation removed from the refinement that follows accumulation.

Slavery established the basis of the planter's position and power. It measured his affluence, marked his status, and supplied leisure for social graces and aristocratic duties. The older bourgeoisie of New England in its own way struck an aristocratic pose, but its wealth was rooted in commercial and industrial enterprises that were being pushed into the background by the newer heavy industries arising in the West, where upstarts took advantage of the more lucrative ventures like the iron industry. In the South few such opportunities were opening. The parvenu differed from the established planter only in being cruder and perhaps sharper in his business dealings. The road to power lay through the plantation. The older aristocracy kept its leadership or made room for men following the same road. An aristocratic stance was no mere compensation for a decline in power; it was the soul and content of a rising power.

Many travelers commented on the difference in material conditions from one side of the Ohio River to the other, but the difference in sentiment was seen most clearly by Tocqueville. Writing before the slavery issue had inflamed the nation, he remarked that slavery was attacking the Union "indirectly in its manners." The Ohioan "was tormented by wealth," and would turn to any kind of enterprise or endeavor to make a fortune. The Kentuckian coveted wealth "much less than pleasure or excitement," and money had "lost a portion of its value in his eyes."[17]

Achille Murat joined Tocqueville in admiration for Southern ways. Compared with Northerners, Southerners were frank, clever, charming, generous, and liberal.[18] They paid a price for these advantages. As one Southerner put it, the North led the South in almost everything because the Yankees had quiet perseverance over the long haul, whereas the Southerners had talent and brilliance but no taste for sustained labor. Southern projects came with a flash and died just as suddenly.[19] Despite such criticisms from within the ranks, the leaders of the South clung to their ideals, their faults, and their conviction of superiority. Farmers, said Edmund Ruffin, could not expect to achieve a cultural level above that of the "boors who reap rich harvests from the fat soil of Belgium." In the Northern states, he added with some justification, a farmer could rarely achieve the ease, culture, intellect, and refinement that slavery made possible.[20] The prevailing attitude of the aristocratic South toward itself and its Northern rival was ably summed up by William Henry Holcombe of Natchez: "The Northerner loves to make money, the Southerner to spend it."[21]

At their best, Southern ideals constituted a rejection of the crass, vulgar, inhumane elements of capitalist society. The slaveholders simply could not accept the idea that the cash nexus offered a permissible basis for human relations. Even the vulgar parvenu of the Southwest embraced the plantation myth and refused to make a virtue of necessity by glorifying the competitive side of slavery as civilization's highest achievement. The slaveholders generally, and the planters in particular, did identify their own ideals with the essence of civilization and, given their sense of honor, were prepared to defend them at any cost.

This civilization and its ideals were antinational in a double sense. The plantation offered virtually the only market for the small nonstaple-producing farmers and provided the center of necessary services for the small cotton growers. Thus, the paternalism of the planters toward their slaves was reinforced by the semipaternal relationship between the planters and their neighbors. The planters, in truth, grew into the closest thing to feudal lords imaginable in a nineteenth-century bourgeois republic. The planters' protestations of love for the Union were not so much a desire to use the Union to protect slavery as a strong commitment to localism as the highest form of liberty. They genuinely loved the Union so long as it alone among the great states of the world recognized that localism had a wide variety of rights. The Southerners' source of pride was not the Union, nor the nonexistent Southern nation; it was the plantation, which they raised to a political principle.

⚏ *The Inner Reality of Slaveholding*

The Southern slaveholder had "extraordinary force." In the eyes of an admirer his independence was "not as at the North, the effect of a conflict with the too stern pressure of society, but the legitimate outgrowth of a sturdy love of liberty."[22] This independence, so distinctive in the slaveholders' psychology, divided them politically from agrarian Westerners as well as from urban Easterners. Commonly, both friendly and hostile contemporaries agreed that the Southerner appeared rash, unstable, often irrational, and that he turned away from bourgeois habits toward an aristocratic pose.

Americans, with a pronounced Jeffersonian bias, often attribute this spirit to agrarians of all types, although their judgment seems almost bizarre. A farmer may be called "independent" because he works for himself and owns property; like any grocer or tailor he functions as a petty bourgeois. In Jefferson's time, when agriculture had not yet been wholly subjected to the commanding influences of the market, the American farmer perhaps had a considerable amount of independence, if we choose to call self-sufficient isolation by that name, but in subsequent days he has had to depend on the market like any manufacturer, if not more so. Whereas manufacturers combine to protect their economic interests, such arrangements have proved much more difficult, and until recently almost impossible, to effect among farmers. In general, if we contrast farmers with urban capitalists, the latter emerge as relatively the more independent. The farmer yields constantly to the primacy of nature, to a direct, external force acting on him regardless of his personal worth; his independence is therefore rigorously circumscribed. The capitalist is limited by the force of the market, which operates indirectly and selectively. Many capitalists go under in a crisis, but some emerge stronger and surer of their own excellence. Those who survive the catastrophe do so (or so it seems) because of superior ability, strength, and management, not because of an Act of God.

The slaveholder, as distinct from the farmer, had a private source of character making and mythmaking—his slave. Most obviously, he had the habit of command, but there was more than despotic authority in this master-slave relationship. The slave stood interposed between his master and the object his master desired (that which was produced); thus, the master related to the object only mediately, through the slave. The slaveholder commanded the products of another's labor, but by the same process was forced into dependence upon this other.[23]

Thoughtful Southerners such as Ruffin, Fitzhugh, and Hammond understood this dependence and saw it as arising from the general relationship of labor to capital, rather than from the specific relationship of master to slave. They did not grasp that the capitalist's dependence upon his laborers remains obscured by the process of exchange in the capitalist market. Although all commodities are products of social relationships and contain human labor, they face each other in the market not as the embodiment of human qualities but as things with

a seemingly independent existence. Similarly, the laborer sells
his labor-power in the way in which the capitalist sells his
goods—by bringing it to market, where it is subject to the
fluctuations of supply and demand. A "commodity fetishism"
clouds the social relationship of labor to capital, and the worker
and capitalist appear as mere observers of a process over which
they have little control.[24] Southerners correctly viewed the
relationship as a general one of labor to capital but failed to
realize that the capitalist's dependence on his laborers is hidden,
whereas that of master on slave is naked. As a Mississippi
planter noted:

> I intend to be henceforth stingy as far as unnecessary
> expenditure—as a man should not squander what another
> accumulates with the exposure of health and the wearing
> out of the physical powers, and is not that the case with
> the man who needlessly parts with that which the negro
> by the hardest labor and often undergoing what we in
> like situation would call the greatest deprivation . . .[25]

This simultaneous dependence and independence contributed to that peculiar combination of the admirable and the
frightening in the slaveholder's nature: his strength, gracious-
ness, and gentility; his impulsiveness, violence, and unsteadi-
ness. The sense of independence and the habit of command
developed his poise, grace, and dignity, but the less obvious
sense of dependence on a despised other made him violently
intolerant of anyone and anything threatening to expose the
full nature of his relationship to his slave. Thus, he had a far
deeper conservatism than that usually attributed to agrarians.
His independence stood out as his most prized possession, but
the instability of its base produced personal rashness and
directed that rashness against any alteration in the status quo.
Any attempt, no matter how well meaning, indirect, or harm-
less, to question the slave system appeared not only as an

attack on his material interests but as an attack on his self-esteem at its most vulnerable point. To question either the morality or the practicality of slavery meant to expose the root of the slaveholder's dependence in independence.

❇ The General Crisis of the Slave South

The South's slave civilization could not forever coexist with an increasingly hostile, powerful, and aggressive Northern capitalism. On the one hand, the special economic conditions arising from the dependence on slave labor bound the South, in a colonial manner, to the world market. The concentration of landholding and slaveholding prevented the rise of a prosperous yeomanry and of urban centers. The inability to build urban centers restricted the market for agricultural produce, weakened the rural producers, and dimmed hopes for agricultural diversification. On the other hand, the same concentration of wealth, the isolated, rural nature of the plantation system, the special psychology engendered by slave ownership, and the political opportunity presented by the separation from England, converged to give the South considerable political and social independence. This independence was primarily the contribution of the slaveholding class, and especially of the planters. Slavery, while it bound the South economically, granted it the privilege of developing an aristocratic tradition, a disciplined and cohesive ruling class, and a mythology of its own.

Aristocratic tradition and ideology intensified the South's attachment to economic backwardness. Paternalism and the habit of command made the slaveholders tough stock, determined to defend their Southern heritage. The more economically debilitating their way of life, the more they clung to it. It was this side of things—the political hegemony and aristocratic ideology of the ruling class—rather than economic factors that prevented the South from relinquishing slavery voluntarily.

As the free states stepped up their industrialization and as the westward movement assumed its remarkable momentum, the South's economic and political allies in the North were steadily isolated. Years of abolitionist and free-soil agitation bore fruit as the South's opposition to homesteads, tariffs, and internal improvements clashed more and more dangerously with the North's economic needs. To protect their institutions and to try to lessen their economic bondage, the slaveholders slid into violent collision with Northern interests and sentiments. The economic deficiencies of slavery threatened to undermine the planters' wealth and power. Such relief measures as cheap labor and more land for slave states (reopening the slave trade and territorial expansion) conflicted with Northern material needs, aspirations, and morality.[26] The planters faced a steady deterioration of their political and social power. Even if the relative prosperity of the 1850s had continued indefinitely, the slave states would have been at the mercy of the free, which steadily forged ahead in population growth, capital accumulation, and economic development. Any economic slump threatened to bring with it an internal political disaster, for the slaveholders could not rely on their middle and lower classes to remain permanently loyal.[27]

When we understand that the slave South developed neither a strange form of capitalism nor an undefinable agrarianism but a special civilization built on the relationship of master to slave, we expose the root of its conflict with the North. The internal contradictions in the South and the external conflict with the North placed the slaveholders hopelessly on the defensive with little to look forward to except slow strangulation. Their only hope lay in a bold stroke to complete their political independence and to use it to provide an expansionist solution for their economic and social problems. The ideology and psychology of the proud slaveholding class made surrender or resignation to gradual defeat unthinkable, for its fate, in its own eyes at least, was the fate of everything worth while in Western civilization.

N O T E S

1 For a succinct statement of the first view see Frank L. Owsley, "The Irrepressible Conflict," in Twelve Southerners, *I'll Take My Stand* (New York, 1930), p. 74. One of the clearest statements of the second view is that of Thomas P. Govan, "Was the Old South Different?" *JSH*, XXI (Nov. 1955), 448.

2 *History of Agriculture in the Southern United States to 1860* (2 vols.; Gloucester, Mass., 1958), I, 302.

3 *The Theory of Social and Economic Organization* (New York, 1947), pp. 276 ff. The term "rational" is used in its strictly economic sense to indicate that production is proceeding in accordance with the most advanced methods to maximize profits.

4 This simple observation has come under curious attack. Kenneth M. Stampp insists that the cost of purchasing a slave forms the equivalent of the free worker's wage bill. See *The Peculiar Institution* (New York, 1956), pp. 403 ff. The initial outlay is the equivalent of part of the capitalist's investment in fixed capital and constitutes what Ulrich B. Phillips called the "overcapitalization of labor" under slavery. The cost of maintaining a slave is only a small part of the free worker's wage bill, but the difference in their productivity is probably greater than the difference in their cost under most conditions.

5 *The Pro-Slavery Argument* (Charleston, S.C., 1852), p. 488.

6 Blaise Pascel, *Pensées* (Modern Librarby ed.; New York, 1941), p. 105.

7 This colonial dependence on the British and Northern markets did not end when slavery ended. Sharecropping and tenantry produced similar results. Since abolition occurred under Northern guns and under the program of a victorious, predatory outside bourgeoisie, instead of under internal bourgeois auspices, the colonial bondage of the economy was preserved, but the South's political independence was lost.

8 Govan, *JSH*, XXI (Nov. 1955), 448.

9 *Studies in the Development of Capitalism* (New York, 1947), pp. 17 f. In the words of Gunnar Myrdal: "Trade by itself . . . rather tends to have backwash effects and to strengthen the forces maintaining stagnation or regression." *Rich Lands and Poor* (New York, 1957), p. 53.

10 An attempt was made by Frank L. Owsley and his students to prove that the Southern yeomanry was strong and prosperous. For a summary treatment see *Plain Folk of the Old South* (Baton Rouge, La., 1949). This view was convincingly refuted by Fabian Linden, "Economic Democracy in the Slave South: An Appraisal of Some Recent Views," *JNH*, XXXI (April 1946), 140–89.

11 Paul A. Baran, *The Political Economy of Growth* (New York, 1957), p. 194.

12 The best introduction to this period of Western banking is the unpublished doctoral dissertation of Carter H. Golembe, "State Banks and the Economic Development of the West, 1830–1844," Columbia University, 1952, esp. pp. 10, 82–91. *Cf.* Bray Hammond, "Long and Short Term Credit in Early American Banking," *QJE*, XLIX (Nov. 1934), esp. p. 87.

13 Slavery impeded white immigration by presenting Europeans with an aristocratic, caste-ridden society that scarcely disguised its contempt for the working classes. The economic opportunities in the North were, in most respects,

far greater. When white labor was used in Southern factories, it was not always superior to slave labor. The incentives offered by the Northern economic and social system were largely missing; opportunities for acquiring skills were fewer; in general, productivity was much lower than in the North.

14 Richard C. Wade's recent *Slavery in the Cities* (New York, 1964) provides new support for these conclusions.

15 William Gregg, *Essays on Domestic Industry* (first published in 1845; Graniteville, S.C., 1941), p. 4. Original emphasis.

16 Consider the experience of the locomotive, paper, and cotton manufacturers as reported in: Carrol H. Quenzel, "The Manufacture of Locomotives and Cars in Alexandria in the 1850's," *VMHB*, LXII (April 1954), 182 ff; Ernest M. Lander, Jr., "Paper Manufacturing in South Carolina before the Civil War," *NCHR*, XXIX (April 1952), 225 ff; Adelaide L. Fries, "One Hundred Years of Textiles in Salem," *NCHR*, XXVII (Jan. 1950), 13.

17 Alexis de Tocqueville, *Democracy in America* (2 vols.; New York, 1945), I, 364.

18 Achille Murat, *America and the Americans* (Buffalo, 1851), pp. 19, 75.

19 J. W. D. in the *Southern Eclectic*, II (Sept. 1853), 63–66.

20 *Address to the Virginia State Agricultural Society* (Richmond, Va., 1853), p. 9.

21 Diary dated Aug. 25, 1855, but clearly written later. Ms. in the University of North Carolina.

22 William M. Sanford (?), *Southern Dial*, I (Nov. 1857), 9.

23 *Cf.* G. W. F. Hegel, *The Phenomenology of Mind* (2 vols.; London, 1910), I, 183 ff.

24 *Cf.* Karl Marx, *Capital* (3 vols.; New York, 1947), I, 41–55.

25 Everard Green Baker Diary, Feb. 13, 1849, in the University of North Carolina. The entry was unfinished.

26 These measures met opposition from powerful sections of the slaveholding class for reasons that cannot be discussed here. The independence of the South would only have brought the latent intraclass antagonisms to the surface.

27 The loyalty of these classes was real but unstable. For our present purposes let us merely note that Lincoln's election and federal patronage would, if Southern fears were justified, have led to the formation of an antiplanter party in the South.

PART TWO ❧ VIRGIN LAND AND SERVILE LABOR

What these men of slow voices and leisurely bearing and great capacity for intimate personal relationships and inbred fondness for power stood for at Washington was not slavery alone, not cotton and rice and sugar-cane alone, not agriculture alone, but the whole social organism, the whole civilization . . .

■ WILLIAM GARROTT BROWN
The Lower South in American History

Two ■ The Low Productivity of Southern Slave Labor: Causes and Effects

The economic backwardness that condemned the slaveholding South to defeat in 1861–1865 had at its root the low productivity of labor, which expressed itself in several ways. Most significant was the carelessness and wastefulness of the slaves. Bondage forced the Negro to give his labor grudgingly and badly, and his poor work habits retarded those social and economic advances that could have raised the general level of productivity. Less direct were limitations imposed on the free work force, on technological development, and on the division of labor.

Although the debate on slave productivity is an old one, few arguments have appeared during the last hundred years to supplement those of contemporaries like John Elliott Cairnes and Edmund Ruffin. Cairnes made the much-assailed assertion that the slave was so defective in versatility that his labor could be exploited profitably only if he were taught one task and kept at it. If we allow for exaggeration, Cairnes's thesis is sound. Most competent observers agreed that slaves worked badly, without interest or effort. Edmund Ruffin, although sometimes arguing the reverse, pointed out that whereas at one time cheap, fertile farmland required little skill, soil exhaustion had finally created conditions demanding the intelligent participation of the labor force.[1] Ruffin neither developed his idea nor drew the appropriate conclusions. The systematic education and training of the slaves would have been politically dangerous. The use of skilled workers would increasingly have required a smaller slave force, which would in turn have depended on expanding markets for surplus slaves and thus could not have been realized in the South as a whole. Other Southerners simply dropped the matter with the observation that the difference in productivity between free and slave labor only illustrated how well the Negroes were treated.[2]

Ample evidence indicates that slaves worked well below their capabilities. In several instances in Mississippi, when cotton picking was carefully supervised in local experiments, slaves picked two or three times their normal output. The records of the Barrow plantation in Louisiana reveal that inefficiency and negligence resulted in two-thirds of the punishments inflicted on slaves, and other contemporary sources are full of corroborative data.[3]

However much the slaves may have worked below their capacity, the limitations placed on that capacity were probably even more important in undermining productivity. In particular, the diet to which the slaves were subjected must be judged immensely damaging, despite assurances from contemporaries and later historians that the slave was well fed.

The slave usually got enough to eat, but the starchy, high-energy diet of cornmeal, pork, and molasses produced specific hungers, dangerous deficiencies, and that unidentified form of malnutrition to which the medical historian Richard H. Shryock draws attention.[4] Occasional additions of sweet potatoes or beans could do little to supplement the narrow diet. Planters did try to provide vegetables and fruits, but not much land could be spared from the staples, and output remained minimal.[5] Protein hunger alone—cereals in general and corn in particular cannot provide adequate protein—greatly reduces the ability of an organism to resist infectious diseases. Even increased consumption of vegetables probably would not have corrected the deficiency, for as a rule the indispensable amino acids are found only in such foods as lean meat, milk, and eggs. The abundant pork provided was largely fat. Since the slave economy did not and could not provide sufficient livestock, no solution presented itself.[6]

In the 1890s a dietary study of Negro field laborers in Alabama revealed a total bacon intake of more than five pounds per week, or considerably more than the three and one-half pounds that probably prevailed in antebellum days. Yet, the total protein found in the Negroes' diet was only 60 per cent of that deemed adequate.[7] Recent studies show that individuals with a high caloric but low protein intake will deviate from standard height-weight ratios by a disproportionate increase in weight.[8] The slave's diet contained deficiencies other than protein; vitamins and minerals also were in short supply. Vitamin deficiencies produce xerophthalmia, beriberi, pellagra, and scurvy and create what one authority terms "states of vague indisposition [and] obscure and ill-defined disturbances."[9]

There is nothing surprising in the slave's appearance of good health: his diet was well suited to guarantee the appearance of good health and to provide the fuel to keep him going in the fields, but it was not sufficient to ensure either sound bodies or the stamina necessary for sustained labor. We need not doubt the testimony of William Dosite Postell, who presents evidence of reasonably good medical attention to slaves and of adequate supply of food bulk. Rather, it is the finer questions of dietary balance that concern us. At that, Postell provides some astonishing statistics that reinforce the present argument: 7 per cent of a sample of more than 8,500 slaves from Georgia, Mississippi, Alabama, and Louisiana above the age of fifteen were either physically impaired or chronically ill.[10] As W. Arthur Lewis writes of today's underdeveloped countries: "Malnutrition and chronic debilitating disease are probably the main reason why the inhabitants . . . are easily exhausted. And this creates a chain which is hard to break, since malnutrition and disease cause low productivity, and low productivity, in turn, maintains conditions of malnutrition and disease."[11]

The limited diet was by no means primarily a result of ignorance or viciousness on the part of masters, for many knew better and would have liked to do better. The problem was largely economic. Feeding costs formed a burdensome part of plantation expenses. Credit and market systems precluded the assignment of much land to crops other than cotton and corn. The land so assigned was generally the poorest available, and the quality of foodstuffs consequently suffered. For example, experiments have shown that the proportion of iron in lettuce may vary from one to fifty milligrams per hundred, according to soil conditions.

The slave's low productivity resulted directly from inadequate care, incentives, and training, and from such other well-known factors as the overseer system, but just how low was it? Can the productivity of slave labor, which nonstatistical evidence indicates to have been low, be measured? An examination of the most recent, and most impressive, attempt at measurement suggests that it cannot. Alfred H. Conrad and John R. Meyer have arranged the following data to demonstrate the movement of "crop value per hand per dollar of slave price" during the antebellum period: size of the cotton crop, average price, value of crop, number of slaves aged ten to fifty-four, crop value per slave, and price of prime field hands.[12] Unfortunately, this method, like the much cruder one used by Algie M. Simons in 1911 and repeated by Lewis C. Gray, does not remove the principal difficulties.

First, the contribution of white farmers who owned no slaves or who worked in the fields beside the few slaves they did own, cannot be separated from that of the slaves. The output of slaveless farmers might be obtained by arduous digging in the manuscript census returns for 1850 and 1860, but the output of farmers working beside their slaves does not appear to lend itself to anything better than baseless guessing. There is also no reason to believe that slaves raised the same proportion of the cotton crop in any two years, and we have little knowledge of the factors determining fluctuations.

Second, we cannot assume that the same proportion of the slave force worked in the cotton fields in any two years. In periods of expected low prices slaveholders tried to deflect part of their force to food crops. We cannot measure the undoubted fluctuations in the man-hours applied to cotton. The Conrad-Meyer results, in particular, waver; they show a substantial increase in productivity before the Civil War, but the tendency to assign slaves to other crops in periods of falling prices builds an upward bias into their calculations for the prosperous 1850s. It might be possible to circumvent the problem by calculating for the total output instead of for cotton, but to do so would create even greater difficulties, such as how to value food grown for plantation use.[13]

Not all bad effects of slavery on productivity were so direct. Critics of slaveholding have generally assumed that it created a contempt for manual labor, although others have countered with the assertion that the Southern yeoman was held in high esteem. True, the praises of the working farmer had to be sung in a society in which he had the vote, but an undercurrent of contempt was always there. Samuel Cartwright, an outspoken and socially minded Southern physician, referred scornfully to those whites "who make negroes of themselves" in the cotton and sugar fields.[14] Indeed, to work hard was "to work like a nigger." If labor was not lightly held, why were there so many assurances from public figures that no one need be ashamed of it?[15]

There were doubtless enough incentives and enough expressions of esteem to allow white farmers to work with some sense of pride; the full impact of the negative attitude toward labor fell on the landless. The brunt of the scorn was borne by those who had to work for others, much as the slave did. The proletarian, rural or urban, was free and white and therefore superior to one who was slave and black, but the difference was minimized when he worked alongside a Negro for another man. So demoralized was white labor that planters often preferred to hire slaves because they were better workers.[16] How much was to be expected of white labor in a society that, in the words of one worried editor, considered manual labor "menial and revolting"?[17]

The attitude toward labor was thus composed of two strains: an undercurrent of contempt for work in general and the more prevalent and probably more damaging contempt for labor performed for another, especially when considered "menial" labor. These notions undermined the productivity of those free workers who might have made important periodic contributions, and thus seriously lowered the level of productivity in the economy. Even today a tendency to eschew saving and to work only enough to meet essential needs has been observed in underdeveloped countries in which precapitalist social structure and ideology are strong.[18]

⛞ Technological Retardation

Few now doubt that social structure has been an important factor in the history of science and technology or that capitalism has introduced the greatest advances in these fields. For American agricultural technology, the craftsman, the skilled worker, and the small producer—all anxious to conserve labor time and cut costs—may well have provided the most significant technological thrust. Specifically, the great advances of the modern era arose from a free-labor economy that gave actual producers the incentives to improve methods and techniques.[19] In nineteenth-century America, writes one authority, "the farmers . . . directed and inspired the efforts of inventors, engineers, and manufacturers to solve their problems and supply their needs . . . [and] the early implements were in many cases invented or designed by the farmers themselves."[20]

If workers are to contribute much to technology, the economy must permit and encourage an increasing division of labor, for skilled persons assigned to few tasks can best devise better methods and implements. Once an initial accumulation of capital takes place, the division of labor, if not impeded, will result in further accumulation and further division. Such extensive division cannot readily develop in slave economies. The heavy capitalization of labor, the high propensity to consume, and the weakness of the home market seriously impede the accumulation of capital. Technological progress and division of labor result in work for fewer hands, but slavery requires all hands to be occupied at all times. Capitalism has solved this problem by a tremendous economic expansion along varied lines (qualitative development), but slavery's obstacles to industrialization prevent this type of solution.

In part, the slave South offset its weakness by drawing upon the technology of more progressive areas. During the first half of the nineteenth century the North copied from Europe on a grand scale, but the South was limited even in the extent to which it could copy and was especially restricted in possibilities for improving techniques once they had been acquired. The regions in which transference of technical skills has always been most effective have been those with an abundance of trained craftsmen as well as of natural resources.[21] In the North a shortage of unskilled labor and a preoccupation with labor-saving machinery stimulated the absorption of advanced techniques and the creation of new ones. In the South the importation of slaves remedied the labor shortage and simultaneously weakened nonslave productive units. The availability of a "routinized, poorly educated, and politically ineffectual rural labor force" of whites as well as Negroes rendered, and to some extent still renders, interest in labor-saving machinery pointless.[22]

Negro slavery retarded technological progress in many ways: it prevented the growth of industrialism and urbanization; it retarded the division of labor, which might have spurred the creation of new techniques; it barred the labor force from that intelligent participation in production which has made possible the steady improvement of implements and machines; and it encouraged ways of thinking antithetical to the spirit of modern science. These impediments undoubtedly damaged Southern agriculture, for improved equipment largely accounted for the dramatic increases in crop yields per acre in the North during the nineteenth century.[23] The steady deterioration of American soil under conditions imposed by commercial exploitation, we now know, has been offset primarily by gains accruing from increased investment in technological improvements. Recent studies show that from 1910 to 1950 output per man-hour doubled only because of the rapid improvements in implements, machinery, and fertilizer.[24]

Southern farmers suffered especially from technological backwardness, for the only way in which they might have compensated for the planters' advantage of large-scale operation would have been to attain a much higher technological level. The social pressure to invest in slaves and the high cost of machinery in a region that had to import much of its equipment made such an adjustment difficult.

Large-scale production gave the planter an advantage over his weaker competitors within the South, but the plantation was by no means more efficient than the family farm operating in the capitalist economy of the free states. Large-scale production, to be most efficient under modern conditions, must provide a substitute for the incentives possessed by the individual farmer. The experience of Soviet agriculture, with its politically induced collectivization, has again demonstrated that the prerequisite for efficient large-scale commodity production is a level of industrial technology as is only now being attained even in the most advanced countries.[25]

The Division of Labor

Although few scholars assert that the Southern slave plantations were self-sufficient units, most assume a fair degree of division of labor in their work force. The employment of skilled artisans usually receives scant attention. An examination of the plantation manuscripts and data in the manuscript census returns shows, however, considerable sums paid for the services of artisans and laborers and a low level of home manufactures.

As Tryon has shown, the Confederacy could not repeat the achievements of the colonies during the Revolutionary War, when family industry supplied the war effort and the home front. Although household manufacturing survived longer in the slave states than in other parts of the country, slave labor proved so inefficient in making cloth, for example, that planters preferred not to bother. In those areas of the South in which slavery predominated, household manufactures decreased rapidly after 1840, and the system never took hold in the newer slave states of Florida, Louisiana, and Texas.[26] Whereas in the North its disappearance resulted from the development of much more advanced factory processes, in the South it formed part of a general decline in skill and technique.

An examination of the manuscript census returns for selected counties in 1860 bears out these generalizations. It also shows that the large plantations, although usually producing greater totals than the small farms, did poorly in the production of home manufactures. In Mississippi's cotton counties the big planters (thirty-one or more slaves) averaged only $76 worth of home manufactures during the year, whereas other groups of farmers and planters showed much less. In the Georgia cotton counties the small planters (twenty-one to thirty slaves) led other groups with $127, and the big planters produced only half as much. Fifty-eight per cent of the big planters in the Mississippi counties examined recorded no home manufactures at all, and most agriculturalists in the Georgia counties produced none. In Virginia the same results appeared: in tobacco counties the big planters led other groups with $56 worth of home manufactures, and in the tidewater and northern wheat counties the big planters led with only $35.[27]

The Richmond *Dispatch* estimated in the 1850s that the South spent $5,000,000 annually for Northern shoes and boots.[28] Although the figure cannot be verified, there is no doubt that Southerners bought most of their shoes in the North. One of the bigger planters, Judge Cameron of North Carolina, owner of five plantations and 267 slaves in 1834, had to purchase more than half the shoes needed for his Negroes despite his large establishment and a conscientious attempt to supply his own needs.[29] Most planters apparently did not even try to produce shoes or clothing. When a planter with about thirty slaves in Scotland Neck, North Carolina, made arrangements to have clothing produced on his estate, he hired an outsider to do it.[30] Yet, until 1830 shoes were produced in the United States by tools and methods not essentially different from those used by medieval serfs,[31] and not much equipment would have been needed to continue those methods on the plantations. Even simple methods of production were not employed on the plantations because the low level of productivity made them too costly relative to available Northern shoes. At the same time, the latter were more expensive than they ought to have been, for transportation costs were high, and planters had little choice but to buy in the established New England shoe centers.

Plantation account books reveal surprisingly high expenditures for a variety of tasks requiring skilled and unskilled labor.[32] A Mississippi planter with 130 slaves paid an artisan $320 for labor and supplies for a forty-one-day job in 1849. Other accounts show that Governor Hammond spent $452 to have a road built in 1850; another planter spent $108 for repair of a carriage and $900 for repair of a sloop in 1853, as well as $175 for repair of a bridge in 1857; a third spent $2,950 for the hire of artisans in 1856 on a plantation with more than 175 slaves.[33]

The largest payments went to blacksmiths. A Panola, Mississippi, planter listed expenditures for the following in 1853: sharpening of plows, mending of shovels, and construction of plows, ox-chains, hooks, and other items. In 1847 a Greensboro, Alabama, planter, whose books indicate that he was business-like and efficient, spent about $140 for blacksmiths' services on his large plantation of seventy-five slaves.[34] One South Carolina planter with forty-five slaves had an annual black-smith's account of about $35, and expenditures by other planters were often higher.[35]

Even simple tasks like the erection of door frames sometimes required the services of hired carpenters, as in the case of a Jefferson County, Mississippi, planter in 1851.[36] If buildings, chimneys, or slave cabins had to be built, planters generally hired free laborers or slave artisans.[37] Skilled slaves had unusual privileges and incentives, but there was not much for them to do on a single plantation. Rather than allow a slave to spend all his time acquiring a skill for which there was only a limited need, a planter would hire one for short periods. Even this type of slave specialization brought frowns from many planters, who considered the incentives and privileges subversive of general plantation discipline.

If it paid to keep all available slaves in the cotton fields during periods of high prices, the reverse was true during periods of low prices. At those times the factors forcing a one-crop agriculture and the low productivity of nonfield labor wrought devastating results. The South's trouble was not that it lacked sufficient shoe or clothing factories, or that it lacked a diversified agriculture, or that it lacked enough other industrial enterprises; the trouble was that it lacked all three at the same time. The slight division of labor on the plantations and the slight social division of labor in the region forced the planters into dependence on the Northern market. As a result, the cost of cotton production rose during periods of low as well as high cotton prices. Even during the extraordinary years of the Civil War, when Southerners struggled manfully to feed and clothe themselves, the attempt to produce home manufactures met with only indifferent results.[38] These observations merely restate the problem of division of labor in the slave South: the low level of productivity, caused by the inefficiency of the slaves and the general backwardness of society, produced increasing specialization in staple-crop production under virtually colonial conditions.

❧ Farm Implements and Machinery

"There is nothing in the progress of agriculture," the United States Agricultural Society proclaimed in 1853, "more encouraging than the rapid increase and extension of labor-saving machinery."[39] The South did not profit much from these technological advances, nor did it contribute much to them.[40]

The most obvious obstacle to the employment of better equipment was the slave himself.[41] In 1843 a Southern editor sharply rebuked planters and overseers for complaining that Negroes could not handle tools. Such a complaint was, he said, merely a confession of poor management, for with proper supervision Negro slaves would provide proper care.[42] The editor was unfair. Careful supervision of unwilling laborers would have entailed either more overseers than most planters could afford or a slave force too small to provide the advantages of large-scale operation. The harsh treatment that slaves gave equipment shocked travelers and other contemporaries, and neglect of tools figured prominently among the reasons given for punishing Negroes.[43] In 1855 a South Carolina planter wrote in exasperation:

> The wear and tear of plantation tools is harassing to every planter who does not have a good mechanic at his nod and beck every day in the year. Our plows are broken, our hoes are lost, our harnesses need repairing, and large demands are made on the blacksmith, the carpenter, the tanner, and the harnessmaker. [*sic*][44]

The implements used on the plantations were therefore generally much too heavy for efficient use. The "nigger hoe," often found in relatively advanced Virginia, weighed much more than the "Yankee hoe," which slaves broke easily. Those used in the Southwest weighed almost three times as much as those manufactured in the North for Northern use.[45] Curiously, in many cases equipment was too light for adequate results. Whereas most planters bought extra-heavy implements in the hope that they would withstand rough handling, others resigned themselves and bought the cheapest possible.[46]

We do not know the proportion of Southern implements made by local blacksmiths, but the difference in quality between them and Northern goods was probably not so great as one might think. Local blacksmiths made wretched goods, but those made in the North especially for the Southern market fell well below national standards. J. D. Legare, editor of the *Southern Cabinet*, visited Northern implement factories and was "struck" by the inferior grade of goods sent South. The materials and workmanship did not approach standards set for goods destined for Northern markets. The reason for the double standard, as Legare admitted, was that planters demanded inexpensive items.[47] We have little information on implements produced in the North for the Southern market. John Hebron Moore quite plausibly suggests that a few unscrupulous Northern manufacturers gave the rest a bad reputation by misrepresentations and other unethical practices.[48] Misrepresentations aside, frequent complaints suggest that the implements were often inferior to those designated for the North. M. W. Philips demonstrated that Northern plows lasted three times as long as local Mississippi products,[49] but the question at issue is not the quality of Northern equipment but the quality of that which Southerners could and would buy.

In 1857 an agricultural journal carried a special report by a former editor who had visited the South Carolina state fair and had inspected plows made by Southern manufacturers. He described the instruments as poor, of indifferent quality and crude construction, adding that most Southern producers had advanced only to the point at which James Small of Berwickshire had left the plow in 1740.[50]

Good plows in 1857 sold for fifteen or twenty dollars, although perhaps some of those selling for five or ten dollars were adequate. "A low estimate of the investment in implements necessary to the operation of an average Northern farm was $500."[51] Cultivators and harrows cost from five to twenty dollars; a grist mill from fifteen to thirty dollars; a treadmill horsepower from eighty-five to 150 dollars; a seed drill sixty dollars; and a reaper-mower 135 dollars. Planters, M. W. Philips noted, usually refused to buy anything except the cheapest of essential items. "We of the South have a jaundiced eye. Everything we view looks like gold—costly."[52]

Plows such as those generally in use in Arkansas were valued at five dollars, and of greater significance, an average cotton-producing unit of one hundred acres was said to have only fifteen dollars' worth of equipment other than plows.[53] A

Mississippi planter valued his thirty "indifferent" plows at seventy-five dollars; even if he had made a liberal allowance for depreciation, he was clearly using the poorest kind of equipment.[54] As an indication of the quality of the work done by local blacksmiths, one planter spent a total of five dollars for ten turning plows in 1853.[55] Gray claims that most Southern plows were worth only three to five dollars. There is little reason to question either his estimate or his opinion that they probably did not last more than a year or so.[56]

Most planters in Mississippi, wrote Philips, thought they could use one kind of plow for every possible purpose.[57] The weakness was doubly serious, for the one kind was usually poor. The most popular plow in the Lower South—at least, well into the 1840s—was the shovel plow, which merely stirred the surface of the soil to a depth of two or three inches.[58] Made of wrought iron, it was "a crude and inefficient instrument which, as commonly employed, underwent no essential improvement throughout its long career."[59] It was light enough for a girl to carry and exemplified the "too light" type of implement used on the plantations.

In the 1850s the shovel plow slowly gave way in the South to a variety of light moldboard plows, which at least were of some help in killing and controlling weeds. Good moldboard plows should have offered other advantages, such as aid in burying manure, but those in the South were not nearly so efficient as those in the North.[60] In 1830, Connecticut manufacturers began to produce large numbers of Cary plows, exclusively for the Southern market. These light wooden plows with wrought-iron shares were considered of good quality. Unfortunately, they required careful handling, for they broke easily, and they could not penetrate more than three or four inches below the surface. During the 1820s Northern farmers had been shifting to cast-iron plows that could cover 50 per cent more acreage with 50 per cent less animal- and manpower.[61] When cast-iron plows did enter the South, they could not be used to the same advantage as in the North, for they needed the services of expert blacksmiths when, as frequently happened, they broke.[62]

Twenty years after the introduction of the cultivator in 1820, Northern farmers considered it standard equipment, especially in the cornfields, but cultivators, despite their tremendous value, were so light that few planters would trust them to their slaves. Since little wheat was grown below Virginia, the absence of reapers did not hurt much, but the backwardness of cotton equipment did. A "cotton planter" (a modified grain drill) and one man could do as much work as two mules and four men,[63] but it was rarely used. Similarly, corn planters, especially the one invented by George Brown in 1853, might have saved a good deal of labor time, but these were costly, needed careful handling, and would have rendered part of the slave force superfluous. Since slaveholding carried prestige and status, and since slaves were an economic necessity during the picking season, planters showed little interest.[64]

The cotton picker presents special technical and economic problems. So long as a mechanical picker was not available a large labor force would have been needed for the harvest; but in 1850 Samuel S. Rembert and Jedediah Prescott of Memphis did patent a mule-drawn cotton picker that was a "simple prototype of the modern spindle picker."[65] Virtually no progress followed upon the original design until forty years later, and then almost as long a span intervened before further advances were made. The reasons for these gaps were in part technical, and in part economic pressures arising from slavery and sharecropping. Although one can never be sure about such things, the evidence accumulated by historians of science and technology strongly suggests that the social and economic impediments to technological change are generally more powerful than the specifically technical ones. The introduction of a cotton picker would have entailed the full mechanization of farming processes, and such a development would have had to be accompanied by a radically different social order. Surely, it is not accidental that the mechanical picker has in recent decades taken hold in the Southwest, where sharecropping has been weak, and has moved east slowly as changes in the social organization of the countryside have proceeded. Even without a mechanical picker the plantations might have used good implements and a smaller labor force during most of the year and temporary help during the harvest. In California in 1951, for example, 50 per cent of the occasional workers needed in the cotton fields came from within the county and 90 per cent from within the state. Rural and town housewives, youths, and seasonal workers anxious to supplement their incomes provided the temporary employees.[66] There is no reason to believe that this alternative would not have been open to the South in the 1850s if slavery had been eliminated.

A few examples, which could be multiplied many times, illustrate the weakness of plantation technology. A plantation in Stewart County, Georgia, with a fixed capital investment of $42,660 had only $300 invested in implements and machinery. The Tooke plantation, also in Georgia, had a total investment in implements and machinery of $195, of which a gin accounted for $110. Plantations had plows, perhaps a few harrows and colters, possibly a cultivator, and in a few cases a straw cutter or corn and cob crusher. Whenever possible, a farmer or planter acquired a gin, and all had small tools for various purposes.[67]

The figures reported in the census tabulations of farm implements and machinery are of limited value and must be used carefully. We have little information on shifting price levels, and the valuations reported to the census takers did not conform to rigorous standards. The same type of plow worth five dollars in 1850 may have been recorded at ten dollars in 1860, and in view of the general rise in prices something of the kind probably occurred.[68]

Even if we put aside these objections and examine investments in selected counties in 1860, the appalling state of plantation technology is evident. Table 1 presents the data from the manuscript returns for 1860. Of the 1,969 farmers and planters represented, only 160 (or 8 per cent) had more than $500 invested in implements and machinery. If we assume that a cotton gin cost between $100 and $125, the figures for the cotton counties suggest that all except the planters (twenty or more slaves) either did without a gin or had little else. Note that an increase in the slave force did not entail significant expansion of technique. As the size of slaveholdings increased in the cotton counties, the investments in implements increased also, but in small amounts. Only units of twenty slaves or more showed tolerably respectable amounts, and even these were poor when one considers the size of the estates.[69]

Gray has suggested that the poor quality of Southern implements was due only in part to slave inefficiency. He lists as other contributing factors the lack of local marketplaces for equipment, the ignorance of the small farmers and overseers, prejudice against and even aversion to innovations, and a shortage of capital in the interior.[70] Each of these contributing factors itself arose from the nature of slave society. The weakness of the market led to a lack of marketplaces. The social structure of the countryside hardly left room for anything but ignorance and cultural backwardness, even by the standards of nineteenth-century rural America. The social and economic pressures to invest in slaves and the high propensity to consume rendered adequate capital accumulation impossible. The psychological factor—hostility to innovation—transcended customary agrarian conservatism and grew out of the patriarchal social structure.

The attempts of reformers to improve methods of cultivation, diversify production, and raise more and better livestock were undermined at the outset by a labor force without versatility or the possibility of increasing its productivity substantially. Other factors must be examined in order to understand fully why the movement for agricultural reform had to be content with inadequate accomplishments, but consideration of the direct effects of slave labor alone tells us why so little could be done.

TABLE I

Median Value of Farm Implements and Machinery
in Selected Counties, 1860[a]

Sample Counties	Number of Slaves on Farms and Plantations[b]							
	0	1-4	5-9	10-20	21-30	31-60	61-100	100+
Virginia Tobacco Counties (Amelia, Buckingham)	$40	$ 50	$ 50	$100	$150	$ 320	$ 925	
Virginia Tidewater (Gloucester, Charles City)	30	35	70	150	200	500	725	
Virginia Northern Wheat Counties (Fauquier, Prince William)	60	100	150	300	425	1200	1350	
Georgia Upland (Walker, Gordon)	10	75	100	215	450	300		
Georgia Cotton (Dougherty, Thomas)	25	75	135	200	350	400	500	
Mississippi Cotton (De Soto, Marshall)	50	100	150	300	500	700	1000	1200

[a] Calculated from the manuscript census returns for 1860; see note 27.
[b] The number of persons in each group was as follows:

	0	1-4	5-9	10-20	21-30	31-60	61-100
Virginia Tobacco:		67	45	45	52	23	20	6
Virginia Tidewater:		41	26	31	24	12	9
Virginia Northern Wheat:		175	59	62	62	19	7
Georgia Upland:		364	37	27	17	4	3
Georgia Cotton:		43	19	18	21	13	22
Mississippi Cotton:		204	83	89	92	47	45	5

N O T E S

1 Cairnes, *The Slave Power* (London, 1863), p. 46; Ruffin, *The Political Economy of Slavery* (Washington, D.C., 1857), p. 4; *Farmer's Register*, III (1863), 748–49. The best introduction to the subject is still Ulrich B. Phillips, *American Negro Slavery* (New York, 1918), Chap. XVIII.

2 See *SQR*, XIX (Jan. 1851), 221. Ruffin sometimes also argued this way.

3 Charles Sackett Sydnor, *Slavery in Mississippi* (New York, 1933), p. 16; E. A. Davis (ed.), *Plantation Life in the Florida Parishes of Louisiana: The Diary of B. H. Barrow* (New York, 1943), pp. 86 ff.

4 "Medical Practice in the Old South," *SAQ*, XXIX (April 1930), 160–61. See also Felice Swados, "Negro Health on Ante-Bellum Plantations," *Bulletin of the History of Medicine*, X (Oct. 1941), 460–61; and Eugene D. Genovese, "The Medical and Insurance Costs of Slaveholding in the Cotton Belt," *JNH*, XLV (July 1960), 141–55.

5 "Probably at no time before the Civil War were fruits and vegetables grown in quantities sufficient to provide the population with a balanced diet," writes John Hebron Moore, *Agriculture in Ante-Bellum Mississippi* (New York, 1958), p. 61. At that, slaves undoubtedly received a disproportionately small share of the output.

6 *Infra*, Chapter V.

7 W. O. Atwater and Charles D. Woods, *Dietary Studies with Reference to the Negro in Alabama in 1895 and 1896* (Washington, D.C., 1897). Adequate animal proteins plus corn probably would have sufficed to prevent nutritional deficiencies. See C. A. Elvehjem, "Corn in Human Nutrition," *Proceedings of the Fourth Annual Meeting of the Research Institute* (Washington, D.C., 1955), p. 83.

8 See J. Masek, "Hunger and Disease" in Josué de Castro (ed.), *Hunger and Food* (London, 1958).

9 Josué de Castro, *The Geography of Hunger* (Boston, 1952), p. 48.

10 *The Health of Slaves on the Southern Plantations* (Baton Rouge, La., 1951), esp. pp. 159 ff.

11 *The Theory of Economic Growth* (Homewood, Ill., 1955), p. 33.

12 "The Economics of Slavery in the Ante Bellum South," *JPE*, LXVI (April 1958), 95–130, esp. Table 17. Reprinted in Conrad and Meyer, *The Economics of Slavery and Other Econometric Studies* (Chicago, 1964).

13 Other questions are also raised by the Conrad-Meyer price data; cotton statistics were not kept with the degree of accuracy required for sophisticated analysis. In any event, the authors have not demonstrated a significant increase in productivity at all. They show no increase for the depressed 1840s, but 20% for the 1850s. These results emerge from a certain carelessness in rounding off figures. Crop value per hand per dollar of slave price is indexed at .05 for 1840; .05 for 1850; and .06 for 1860. But if we carry out the arithmetic two more decimal places we get .0494 (1840), .0538 (1850), and .0562 (1860)—i.e., a 9% increase for the depressed 1840s and only 4% for the 1850s. These results are implausible and, in any case, contradict their own conclusions.

14 J. D. B. De Bow, *Industrial Resources of the Southern and Western States* (3 vols.; New Orleans, 1852–53), III, 62.

15 "Let no man be ashamed of labor; let no man be ashamed of a hard hand or a sunburnt face." William W. Holden, *Address Delivered Before the Duplin County Agricultural Society* (Raleigh, N.C., 1857), p. 7.

16 Cornelius O. Cathey, *Agricultural Developments in North Carolina, 1783–1860* (Chapel Hill, N.C., 1956), pp. 54–55.

17 *Southern Cultivator*, V (Jan. 1847), 141.

18 *Cf.* S. Daniel Neumark, "Economic Development and

Economic Incentives," *South African Journal of Economics*, March 1958, pp. 55–63. For a discussion of this question as related to Greek slavery see Karl Polanyi's brilliant essay on Aristotle in Polanyi *et al.*, *Trade and Market in the Early Empires* (Glencoe, Ill., 1957), p. 77.

19 Edgar Zilsel, "The Sociological Roots of Science," *American Journal of Sociology*, XLVII (Jan. 1942), 557 ff.

20 Fowler McCormick, *Technological Progress in American Farming* (Washington, D.C., 1940), p. 9.

21 H. J. Habakkuk, "The Historical Experience on the Basic Conditions of Economic Progress," in Léon H. Dupriez (ed.), *Economic Progress* (Louvain, 1955), pp. 149–69.

22 James H. Street, *The New Revolution in the Cotton Economy* (Chapel Hill, N.C., 1957), p. 34.

23 Leo Rogin, *The Introduction of Farm Machinery . . . in the United States During the Nineteenth Century* (Berkeley, Cal., 1931), Chap. I.

24 Cited by Ronald L. Mighell, *American Agriculture: Its Structure and Place in the Economy* (New York, 1955), pp. 7–8.

25 Paul A. Baran, *Political Economy of Growth*, pp. 267 ff, 278–83, insists that collectivization was justified because the only alternative to it in a country lacking enough urban purchasing power to support high food prices would dry up rural sources of capital accumulation by heavier peasant consumption. He adds that the U.S.S.R. had to force the pace of industrialization for political and military reasons and that grain deliveries to cities had to be guaranteed. Maurice Dobb, *Soviet Economic Development Since 1917* (New York, 1948) presents similar arguments. These arguments, however valid, do not contradict the observation that collectivization removed a good part of the peasants' incentives without providing them with implements and machines. Collectivization may, from the point of view of the regime, have been necessary and urgent, but a big price had to be paid for it. For a summary of experiences with

large-scale farming elsewhere see Lewis, *Theory of Economic Growth*, pp. 134 ff.

26 Rolla M. Tryon, *Household Manufactures in the United States, 1640–1860* (Chicago, 1917), pp. 5, 184 ff, 295–98, 371.

27 Specialists who wish to consult the sampling and computing methods used here may see my unpublished dissertation, "The Limits of Agrarian Reform in the Slave South," Columbia University, 1959, appendices.

28 De Bow, *Industrial Resources*, II, 130.

29 Cameron Papers, CXIII, University of North Carolina.

30 Simmons Jones Baker Account Book, miscellaneous notes, University of North Carolina.

31 Blanche Evans Hazard, *The Organization of the Boot and Shoe Industry in Massachusetts before 1875* (Cambridge, Mass., 1921), p. 3.

32 The use of white labor for ditching is frequently cited, but the size of the expenditures has not generally been appreciated. One planter paid $170 in 1852, another $250 in 1859. Such sums were not trifles, especially for small planters. See Moses St. John R. Liddell Papers, 1852, Louisiana State University; entry of Feb. 8, 1859, Leonidas Pendleton Spyker Diary, also at L.S.U.

33 Haller Nutt Papers, 1849, Duke University; James H. Hammond Account Book, 1850, Library of Congress; Stephen D. Doar Account Books, 1853, 1857, Library of Congress; Charles Bruce Plantation Accounts, 1856, Library of Congress.

34 Everard Green Baker Papers, I, University of North Carolina; Iverson L. Graves Papers, XV, University of North Carolina; Henry Watson Papers, 1847, Duke University. Graves spent $20 to sharpen and repair tools during four months of 1853.

35 De Bow, *Industrial Resources*, I, 161. One planter with 50 slaves spent about $75 in eight months. Killona Plantation Journals, I, 60 ff, Department of Archives and History,

Jackson, Mississippi. See also William McKinley Book, p. 17, and Robert Withers Books, I, 46, at the University of North Carolina; and James Sheppard Papers, April 9, 1849, at Duke University.

36 Entry of Jan. 4, 1851, Duncan G. McCall Plantation Journal and Diary, Duke University. The plantation had 75 slaves.

37 *Ibid.*, Jan. 6, 1851; Spyker Diary, Jan. 15, 1857. Spyker, with more than 100 slaves, spent more than $200 for the services of a mason. A letter to Mrs. Howell Cobb (1846) indicates that Negro cabins were generally built by hired labor at up to $250 per cabin. Ulrich B. Phillips, *Plantation and Frontier Documents: 1649–1863* (2 vols.; Cleveland, 1909), II, 38.

38 Mary Elizabeth Massey, *Ersatz in the Confederacy* (Columbia, S.C., 1952), Chap. I and *passim.*

39 *Journal of the United States Agricultural Society*, I (1853), 132.

40 Cathey, commenting on the agitation for improved implements in North Carolina in the 1850s, says that, surprisingly, none of those demanded were produced on a large scale within the state and no local inventor profited much from his efforts. *Agricultural Developments*, p. 68. In view of the small market the result is no surprise, unless undue attention is paid to the statements of agricultural reformers or to the illusory valuations that sometimes appeared in census returns.

41 The familiar generalization that slaves so mistreated equipment that planters were reluctant to purchase good implements has received fresh support from Moore's *Agriculture in Ante-Bellum Mississippi*, p. 41.

42 *Southern Planter* (Richmond, Va.), III (Sept. 1843), 205–6.

43 See "Instructions to Overseer," James H. Hammond Plantation Book, 1832–39.

44 *Farmer and Planter*, VI (Feb. 1855), 43.

45 C. G. Parsons, *Inside View of Slavery* (Boston, 1855), p.

94; Clarence H. Danhof, "Agriculture" in Harold F. Williamson (ed.), *The Growth of the American Economy* (2nd ed.; New York, 1957), pp. 133–53.

46 On the coastal plain of the Southeast during the twentieth century the persisting lack of capital has caused reliance on harrows and plows that are too light for most purposes.

47 *Southern Cabinet*, I (Sept. 1840), 531–36.

48 *Agriculture in Ante-Bellum Mississippi*, p. 168.

49 *Ibid.*, p. 166.

50 *Farmer and Planter*, VIII (Nov. 1857), 245.

51 Danhof in Williamson, *Growth of the American Economy*, p. 150.

52 *Farmer and Planter*, II (March 1851), 19.

53 *DBR*, XII (Jan. 1852), 72.

54 Valuation figures for 1847, Sheppard Papers.

55 Expenditures for Feb.–May 1855, Graves Papers, XV.

56 Gray, *History of Agriculture*, II, 796.

57 *American Cotton Planter*, II (March 1854), 244.

58 *Southern Cabinet*, I (April 1840), 199; Danhof in Williamson, *Growth of the American Economy*, pp. 141–42.

59 Rogin, *Introduction of Farm Machinery*, p. 54.

60 On the advantages of the moldboard plow for weeding and burying manure see E. John Russell, *Soil Conditions and Plant Growth* (8th ed., rev. by E. W. Russell; London, 1950), pp. 578 ff. These plows were in general use in New England as early as 1840. M. H. Chevalier, "Les Charrues anciennes de l'Amérique et de l'Océanie," Société des Ingénieurs Civils de France, *Mémoires et compte rendu des travaux*, LXXIII (1920), 71. In recent years agronomists have challenged the usefulness of deep plowing, arguing that it does more harm than good. The literature is vast, but the issue still unresolved. A firm conclusion about the methods used by antebellum planters must therefore wait. It is significant, however, that the planters' failure to plow

deep was due not to any special knowledge or experience but to their lack of proper equipment.

61 Rogin, *Introduction of Farm Machinery*, pp. 8–9, 30–31. The Cary plow was also called the Dagon, Degen, Connecticut, and various other names.

62 Avery O. Craven maintains that in Maryland and Virginia farmers and planters used excellent equipment after 1840. See his *Soil Exhaustion as a Factor in the Agricultural History of Virginia and Maryland, 1606–1860* (Urbana, Ill., 1926), p. 152. This equipment was excellent only when measured by the standards of that in use further south.

63 Danhof in Williamson, *Growth of the American Economy*, p. 143; *American Cotton Planter*, XII (April 1858), 115. Grain drills sold for about $100 in the South, according to the *Farmer and Planter*, II (Nov. 1851), 161. See also *DBR*, VI (Feb. 1848), 133.

64 George F. Lemmer says that tobacco and hemp growers in Missouri failed to keep pace with grain growers in the use of improved implements and machinery because tobacco and hemp machinery did not improve much. See his "Farm Machinery in Ante-Bellum Missouri," *MHR*, XL (July 1946), 469, 479. I should suggest that it was not accidental that hemp and tobacco were slave crops and grain a free crop. The pressure for labor-saving machinery in the hemp and tobacco regions was slight.

65 Street, *New Revolution*, p. 92.

66 *Ibid.*, p. 197.

67 David Hillhouse Memorandum Book, p. 25, Alexander Robert Lawton Papers, University of North Carolina. For the Tooke Plantation see Ralph B. Flanders, "Two Plantations and a County in Ante-Bellum Georgia," *GHQ*, XII (March 1928), 4. See also Cameron Papers, CXIII; Hairston Plantation Book, 1857, University of North Carolina; 1849 inventory in Killock Plantation Books, VII, and Newstead Plantation Diary, 1861, both in the University of North Carolina; Andrew Flinn Plantation Book, 1840, University of South Carolina; Plantation and Account Book, 1851, pp.

1, 83 in the Eli J. Capell and Family Papers, Louisiana State University; Joseph M. Jaynes Plantation Account Books, p. 15, Duke University.

68 Commodity prices rose from 23% to 35% from 1849 to 1857, and then slumped somewhat following the crisis. In 1859 prices were from 10% to 16% higher than they had been in 1849. See Snyder-Tucker and Warren-Pearson indices in Bureau of the Census (comp.), *Historical Statistics of the United States* (Washington, D.C., 1949), pp. 232–33.

69 "The averages of Southern states were high not only because sugar-refining and cotton-ginning machinery were expensive but, more important, because the larger plantations were almost congeries of farms. The value of farm machinery per acre of improved land is a better index. For representative Southern states, the figures are Virginia $0.82; North Carolina $0.90; Alabama $1.16; Mississippi $1.74; and Louisiana $6.80. For representative Northern states the figures are Massachusetts $1.80; Ohio $1.38; New York $2.03; and Pennsylvania $2.14." Paul W. Gates, *The Farmer's Age, 1815–1860* (New York, 1960), p. 291.

70 *History of Agriculture*, II, 794.

Three ■ The Negro Laborer in Africa and the Slave South

Kenneth M. Stampp's *The Peculiar Institution* challenges effectively the traditional view that enslavement in America raised the Negro from savagery to civilization.[1] Drawing upon anthropological data, he shows that Africans brought to the United States as slaves had been removed from societies far more advanced than most of our historians have appreciated. Unfortunately, he pays only passing attention to that aspect of the traditional view bearing most directly on the economics of slavery in general and the productivity of black labor in particular.

The Negro slave worked badly, according to some leading historians, not because he was a slave but because he was a Negro. This argument has taken two forms: (1) the Negro has certain unfortunate biological traits, such as a migratory instinct or an easygoing indolence;[2] and (2) the Negro came from a lower culture in Africa and had to be disciplined to labor.[3] The first argument does not require refutation here; the negative findings of genetics and anthropology are conclusive and well known.[4] The second argument raises serious economic and social questions. In the words of Lewis C. Gray:

The great body of Negroes came to America ignorant savages. Care was requisite to prevent them from injuring themselves with the implements employed. It was necessary to teach them the simplest operations with hand tools and to instruct them in the elementary methods of living—how to cook, put on their clothing and care for their houses . . . Under competent supervision the Negro acquired peculiar skill in picking and hoeing cotton and other simple routine operations of field labor.[5]

Ulrich B. Phillips defends slavery as a historically progressive institution that assembled the working population in a more productive pattern than had existed previously. He then implies that enslavement in America civilized the Negro and disciplined him to labor. Probably, ancient slavery often did play the role Phillips suggests, but to accept that generalization by no means commits one to the corollary drawn for American Negro slavery. Phillips gives no evidence but refers to the views of the sociologist Gabriel Tarde, who, we are told, "elaborated" on Thomas R. Dew's idea that enslavement domesticated men much as animals had been domesticated previously.[6]

An examination of Tarde's discussion shows that it offers little support to Phillips. The idea of reducing men to slavery, Tarde suggests, probably arose after the successful domestication of animals, and in both cases the subjected were tamed, transformed into beasts of burden, and made productive for others. Tarde's ideas should be considered within the context of his theory of imitation, according to which an enslaved people learns from its conquerors, whereas the latter do not deign to absorb the ways of their victims.[7] This idea is in itself dubious—how much richer is Hegel's analysis of "Lordship and Bondage" in his *Phenomenology of Mind,* in which the interaction of master and slave is so brilliantly explored—but if it has any relevance to the problem at hand, it merely suggests that the Negro in America came into contact with a higher culture. Who, outside the ranks of the most dogmatic cultural relativists, would argue with such a generalization? On the central question of labor productivity Tarde's thesis is valid only if we assume that the Negro had to be brought to America to acquire the habit of systematic agricultural labor. Phillips never puts the matter quite that baldly, but his analysis rests on this proposition.

Phillips' interpretation of African life has had a profound effect upon students of American Negro slavery, but it depends on the now discredited work of Joseph Alexander Tillinghast and Jerome Dowd. According to Tillinghast, African Negroes were "savages," subject to the "unfathomable . . . mysterious force" of heredity. The West African population before the European conquest supposedly had no cereals and survived on a bare subsistence of vegetable roots. Tillinghast, Dowd, and others upon whose work Phillips draws have applied untenable methods, made dubious assumptions, and produced work that anthropologists today consider of little or no value.[8] One might be inclined to pardon Phillips and those who have followed him for trusting the judgment of anthropologists were it not that the arguments contain hopeless contradictions, and were it not that even during the nineteenth century some scholars were perceptive enough to warn that anthropologists and other social scientists often fell victim to the racial prejudices permeating European and American life.[9] By the time of Phillips' death and during the period in which Craven and Gray were writing, impressive new work on African society was coming off the presses.

The first contradiction in the Tillinghast-Phillips interpretation is the fact of importation, for if the African had not been disciplined to agricultural labor why was he brought here at all? The "domestication" of savages is no easy matter, and only a small percentage of the enslaved usually survive. Europeans first brought Negroes from Africa because they were accustomed to agricultural labor, whereas many of the previously enslaved Indians were not and tended to collapse under the pressure.[10]

Second, in order to show that Africans were backward, Tillinghast and Phillips say that slavery was common among them. And so it was![11] There is no better proof that African society had "domesticated" its own population before the white man volunteered to assume responsibility. West African peoples like the Ashanti and Dahomey had, in addition to successful labor systems, elaborate military structures, legal arrangements, and commercial relations.[12] A re-examination of the economic structure of West Africa and of its implications for American slavery is therefore in order.

There are other objections to Phillips' argument. He assumes that the Negro, once brought here, retained many African traits, which hampered his productivity. So prominent an anthropologist as Melville J. Herskovits, who certainly does not share Phillips' biases or general conclusions, attempts to prove that the Negro has preserved a large part of his African heritage to the present day.[13] This contention has come under heavy and successful fire from E. Franklin Frazier, who shows that Herskovits' evidence illuminates Brazilian rather than North American experience. American Negroes had contempt for newly imported Africans and set out to "Americanize" them forthwith. As Frazier says, the array of isolated instances of African survivals only indicates how thoroughly American slavery wiped out African social organization, habits, and ways of thought.[14] If we are to avoid baseless racist and mystical assumptions, we shall have to know just what traits the Negro supposedly brought from Africa and kept for generations and just how they affected his productivity. We have received no such data, and nothing in Herskovits' work, which deals with a different set of problems, lends support to the Phillips-Gray-Craven school. We must conclude, therefore, that the assertion of special traits does nothing more than to restate the original notion of a Negro undisciplined to agricultural labor until brought here.

Phillips has to assume that the poor work habits of slaves amounted to mere negligence or even stupidity, but they often reflected an awareness of economic value and a penchant for sabotage. Side by side with ordinary loafing and mindless labor went deliberate wastefulness, slowdowns, feigned illnesses, self-inflicted injuries, and the well-known abuse of livestock and equipment, which itself probably arose within a complex psychological framework.[15] Viewed as such, Phillips' easy notion of ignorant savages making a mess of things falls to the ground.

Most Negroes brought from Africa to North America doubtless came from the West Coast. The Dahomey, famous as slave raiders, rarely went more than two hundred miles inland, and most of their victims lived much closer to the coast.[16] The West African peoples undoubtedly had mature systems of agriculture. The Dahomey even had a plantation system; all these peoples—Dahomey, Ashanti, Yoruba, to mention a few of the outstanding—had significant division of labor. They carried on and carefully regulated a system of trade; craft guilds existed widely; and a class structure had begun to emerge.[17]

The Yoruba, Nupe, and Fulani had absorbed Moslem culture, and when the Fulani overran northern Nigeria, they carried Moslem scholars with them. Before the Fulani conquest, the Nupe of Nigeria had developed an urban civilization partly under Moslem influence.[18] This influence undoubtedly had a positive effect on Negro technical and economic life, but most of the indigenous peoples did not need outsiders to teach them the fundamentals of agrarian life. "West African societies," writes the outstanding authority on

Islam in Africa, "had already achieved fully developed techniques and economic organization before Islam made its appearance. Its influence was most evident in the commercial sphere which in the Sudan belt was wholly taken over by Moslems."[19]

The development of mining provides some clues to the economic level of West Africa. Gold and iron mining flourished at least as early as the fourteenth century, and the Arabs drew upon the area for gold. The tales of wonderful metals and metalwork attracted the Portuguese and led to their initial explorations. The peoples of Ghana and Nigeria used iron hoes and other agricultural implements, and the Yoruba of southern Nigeria enjoyed a reputation for fine work in copper and tin.[20] Diamond writes: "Iron hoes were, of course, essential to the Dahomean economy, and were perhaps the most important products manufactured in the young state. Therefore, the blacksmiths were revered by the people, as were all craftsmen who did good work."[21]

In contrast to Tillinghast's picture of indolent, berry-picking natives, the proverbs, aphorisms, and customs of the West African peoples indicate that they were accustomed to hard work. Sayings included: "Poverty is the elder of laziness"; "He who stays in bed when he is able to work will have to get up when he cannot"; and "Dust on the feet is better than dust on the behind."[22] Prestige accrued to those who worked hard, fast, and well and was therefore a powerful motivating force. These facts, now taken for granted by anthropologists, are not so surprising when one considers that even in the most primitive societies there is hard work to do. One works, as Herskovits says, because everyone works, because one must work to live, and because it is the tradition to work. The Dahomey, who were among the more advanced of the African peoples, had a reputation for industriousness, held hard work praiseworthy, and practiced crop rotation and agricultural diversification.[23]

The most puzzling aspect of Phillips' position is his awareness of slavery among the West Africans. He remarks that slavery was "generally prevalent" and adds that, according to Mungo Park, the slaves in the Niger Valley outnumbered the free men by three to one at the end of the eighteenth century.[24] Phillips never seems to realize that the existence of African slavery shatters his insistence that the Negroes had not been habituated to agricultural labor. Tillinghast and Dowd, for their part, set the bad example, for in the same books in which they assure us that the Negroes were the laziest of food gatherers they announce that these same Negroes had slaves, debt peons, and private property.[25]

The Dahomey had large crown-owned plantations worked by slave gangs under the direction of overseers whose business was to maximize output. Debt peonage was a well-established institution.[26] Among the Nupe, slaves did a great deal of agricultural labor and reportedly numbered in the thousands by the time of the British conquest. The more primitive tribes of northern Nigeria had been conquered and enslaved by the Nupe before the beginning of the nineteenth century.[27] The Ashanti had an elaborate system of family land ownership and imposed a light *corvée* on those of low status. The tribes of the Ashanti hinterland practiced slavery, debt peonage, and systematic agriculture. The Ashanti defeated one of these tribes, the Dagomba, at the end of the seventeenth century and obligated it to produce two thousand slaves annually.[28] The Ibo of southeastern Nigeria, slave traders as well as a source of slaves, produced several important crops with servile labor.[29] During the eighteenth and early nineteenth centuries the great West African peoples—the Yoruba, Dahomey, and Fulani—fought continually for control of southwestern Nigeria, and each in turn enslaved thousands during the wars.[30]

African slavery was far removed from New World slavery in many respects and perhaps ought not to be considered under the same rubric. The Ashanti economy in which slaves participated strove, for example, toward autarky. The system of land tenure placed a brake on individual accumulation of land, and status therefore rested primarily on political and social rather than economic criteria. However surprisingly, masters had no power over the economic surplus produced by their slaves, who worked for themselves. In the words of A. Norman Klein:

> The productivity of "slave" labor was never applied to the process of economic accumulation. Nor could it be. To be a slaveowner was not to be a member of a special group deriving its income from the outputs of the chattel. There simply was no mechanism for accumulation from slave labor. The only stratum in Ashanti society which stood to gain from the productivity of "slave" labor was the slave stratum itself. By assuring, in Ashanti law, that the general rule for personal property applied to its "slaves" it nipped in the bud the formation of any such vested interests. That rule of personal property may be stated: No individual may be deprived of the results of his own economic endeavor. The primary function of "slavery" in Ashanti society was not in production but in social status.

Of the slaves in this strange system, Klein writes:

> His main liabilities stemmed from his being non-kin and unaffiliated. This meant that the *odonko* stood outside and was isolated from the closed network of matrilineally derived rights and obligations. His humanity was valued less than that of a lineage member. To be someone's personal property entailed becoming thingified, depersonalized, treated as a commodity. This last was, in fact, his hallmark. . . . His gravest concern arose from the possibility of being ritually dispatched at the next funeral service.[31]

The term "slavery" applied to West African societies could easily mislead us, for the slaves held therein functioned in the economy without special disadvantage. Apart from the gloomy possibility of ritual execution, the worst a slave suffered was to have to endure as a pariah who could be shifted from one household to another by sale. Since no mechanism for economic exploitation existed, no impassable barriers to freedom did either. The ease with which a slave might be adopted into the family as a free man varied markedly in time and place but remained noticeable. Because of certain peculiarities of property inheritance in a matrilineal society, there were even special advantages in taking a slave for a wife. Two conclusions emerge: West Africans had disciplined themselves to agricultural labor; and the transfer of a slave from an African to a European master meant a profound change in the nature and extent of his obligations.

The absence of slavery, in any form, among some of the coastal peoples does not imply that agriculture was undeveloped or that hard work was lacking. The Bobo, for example, who were probably an important source of slaves for the United States, refused to hold slaves but had a reputation for being conscientious laborers.[32]

Angola and the Congo supplied numerous slaves to South America and some to North America. These peoples, too, came from societies resting on agricultural foundations. The Bantu-speaking peoples of southwestern Africa practiced slavery, although to what extent we do not know. The more primitive and undeveloped peoples, including some cannibals, did not supply slaves from among their own but did act as slave catchers for the Europeans.[33]

For a general statement of the economic level of precolonial West Africa we may turn to the distinguished former premier of Senegal, whose credentials as a student of African history and culture are not in question. Writes Mamadou Dia

in his essay on "L'Économie africaine avant l'intervention
européenne":

> The traditional African economy does not deserve to be
> treated disdainfully as a primitive economy, based on
> static structures, with technical routines incapable of
> adapting themselves to new situations. Everything proves,
> on the contrary, that this agricultural economy showed
> evidence of a strong vitality with possibilities for creating
> or assimilating techniques appropriate to assure its sur-
> vival.[34]

The African economy was nevertheless much less developed
than that of the European world, and we may assume that the
productivity of the Negro was well below that of the white
man of Western Europe. We need not rush to accept the
grotesque exaggerations about the level of West African
society that currently are flooding the literature. Emancipation
would not have suddenly accomplished the miracle of raising
the productivity of the Southern Negro to the level of, say,
the Northern farmer. Since the Negro was accustomed to
agricultural work in Africa as well as in the South, the task
of raising his productivity should not have been difficult. In a
friendly society, with adequate incentives, the Negro laborer's
efficiency should have improved quickly. There is no scientific
basis for any other assumption.

That the Negro worked hard in African agriculture does
not prove that his economic faculties did not decline once he
was separated from his homeland. Frank Wesley Pitman writes
that Negroes taken to the West Indies knew how to tend
their own gardens and care for livestock but were totally un-
prepared for the work expected of them in the sugar fields.[35]
By what process, it may be wondered, does a man prepare
himself to be driven in a slave gang? Yet we know that even
the slave plantation was known in Africa, and Herskovits has

shown that American slavery represented a distorted continuation of the various forms of collective labor common to Africa.[36]

The brutality of American slavery confronted the African—even the African who had been a slave in his homeland—with something new. Under its mildest forms Southern slavery had to be much harsher than its African counterpart. With the partial exception of the Dahomey, African slavery was patriarchal. Even slaves from a conquered tribe were sometimes assimilated into the new culture. A slave might buy his freedom and become a free man in a new homeland. There was little racial antipathy, although it was by no means unknown. In the South the Negro received a series of hard blows. He worked under more stringent conditions, was torn from his culture, family life, and system of values, and found himself in a society that offered no adequate substitutes. If the Negro was "culturally" unattuned to hard work, this condition reflected not his African background but a deterioration from it.

To say that the Negro suffered from a cultural dislocation that may have affected his economic propensities is not to imply that, after all, the Negro slave proved a poor worker because he was a Negro. Enslavement itself, especially the enslavement of a people regarded as racially inferior and unassimilable, produces such dislocations. Once slavery passes from its mild, patriarchal stage, the laborer is regarded less and less as a human being and more and more as a beast of burden, particularly when he is a foreigner who can be treated as a biological inferior. Even in patriarchal societies, slavery facilitates the growth of large-scale production, which corrodes the older comradeship between master and slave. The existence of slavery lays the basis for such a development, especially where markets are opened and institutional barriers to commercialization removed. Such a course may not be inevitable, but slavery does establish a powerful tendency toward large-scale exploitation of men and resources. The rise of the plantation system in Dahomey serves as an illustration, although the economic structure was unusual and cannot be regarded as a mature, commercially oriented slave system. Thus slavery, no matter how patriarchal at first, will, if permitted to grow naturally, break out of its modest bounds and produce an economy that will rip the laborer from his culture and yet not provide him with a genuine replacement.

Even if we judge the problem of the slave South to have been the presence of a culturally dislocated labor force, we should not be justified in asserting that the difficulty lay with the Negro as a Negro. Rather, the cause of the process of dislocation and the deterioration of his work habits was slavery itself. Slavery, once it becomes a large-scale enterprise, reverses its earlier contribution to the productivity of the laborer and undermines the culture, dignity, efficiency, and even the manhood of the enslaved worker.

NOTES

1 Stampp, *The Peculiar Institution*, Chap. I.

2 Alfred Holt Stone, *Studies in the American Race Problem* (New York, 1908), pp. 145, 790–93.

3 Gray, *History of Agriculture*, Vol. I, Chap. XX; Phillips, *American Negro Slavery*, pp. 278 ff, 344; and *Life and Labor in the Old South* (Boston, 1948), pp. 188 ff; Craven, *Soil Exhaustion*, p. 163.

4 See, *e.g.*, Otto Klineberg, *Race Differences* (New York,

1935). Recent work has not altered his major conclusions, which are based on psychological, genetic, and other data.

5   *History of Agriculture*, I, 467.

6   Phillips, *American Negro Slavery*, p. 344 and n. 1; generally Chaps. I and XVIII.

7   Gabriel Tarde, *The Laws of Imitation*, tr. Elsie Clews Parsons (New York, 1903), pp. 278 f, also p. 221 and *passim*.

8   Joseph Alexander Tillinghast, *The Negro in Africa and America* ("Publications of the American Economic Association," 3rd Series, III, No. 2; New York, 1902), pp. 2 f, 18 f; *cf.* Jerome Dowd, *The Negro Races* (New York, 1907), Vol. I. For a thorough and convincing critique of these works see Melville J. Herskovits, *The Myth of the Negro Past* (New York, 1941), Chaps. I and II, esp. pp. 55–61.

9   Consider, *e.g.*, N. G. Chernyshevsky's stinging rebuke to Western scientists in his splendid essay "An Essay on the Scientific Conception of Certain Problems of World History: Part One—Races," *Selected Philosophical Essays* (Moscow, 1953), pp. 199–220. The essay was written in 1887 and appeared in Russia a year later.

10 The experience of the Indians within the present limits of the United States is well known. Even more impressive is the evidence from Latin America, where a sustained effort to enslave Indians was successful only where they had previously developed an agricultural society. In other cases, the experience paralleled that of Bahia, Brazil, where 40,000 Indians were enslaved in 1563 but only about 3,000 survived the next twenty years. See João Dornas Filho, *A Escravidão no Brasil* (Rio de Janeiro, 1939), p. 40.

11 We know little about indigenous African slavery, but most reliable anthropological and historical works refer to its existence.

12 C. G. Seligman, *Races of Africa* (3rd ed.; London, 1957), p. 58.

13 See his *Myth of the Negro Past*, esp. p. 16.

14 E. Franklin Frazier, *The Negro in the United States* (New York, 1949), pp. 6–11. I think Frazier goes too far. Certain influences did remain. We cannot explore them here, but they would not support the Phillips thesis anyway.

15 *Cf.* Raymond and Alice Bauer, "Day to Day Resistance to Slavery," *JNH*, XXVII (Oct. 1942), 401 f, 407.

16 Herskovits, *Myth of the Negro Past*, pp. 61 f.

17 Seligman, *Races of Africa*, pp. 51–54; Melville J. Herskovits, *Economic Anthropology* (New York, 1952), esp. Chaps. VI and VIII; Rosemary Arnold, "A Port of Trade; Whydah on the Guinea Coast," Chap. VIII of Polanyi *et al.*, *Trade and Market in the Early Empires.*

18 S. F. Nadel, *A Black Byzantium: The Kingdom of the Nupe in Nigeria* (London, 1946), pp. 76–85.

19 J. Spencer Trimingham, *Islam in West Africa* (Oxford, 1959), p. 185.

20 Walter Cline, *Mining and Metallurgy in Negro Africa* (Menasha, Wis., 1937), pp. 11–17.

21 Stanley Diamond, "Dahomey: A Proto-State in West Africa," unpublished doctoral dissertation, Columbia University, 1951, p. 52.

22 Herskovits, *Economic Anthropology*, p. 118.

23 Melville J. Herskovits, *Dahomey, An Ancient West African Kingdom* (2 vols.; New York, 1938), I, 33 f.

24 Phillips, *American Negro Slavery*, pp. 6, 27; *Life and Labor*, pp. 188 ff.

25 Tillinghast, *The Negro*, pp. 25, 38; Dowd, *The Negro Races*, I, 91–99.

26 Herskovits, *Dahomey*, I, 82 f, 99, 102; II, 97.

27 Nadel, *Black Byzantium*, pp. 85, 196 ff.

28 R. S. Rattray, *Ashanti* (Oxford, 1923), pp. 223–27; and *The Tribes of the Ashanti Hinterland* (2 vols.; Oxford, 1932), I, 261–68; II, 348 f, 402 f, 564.

29 C. K. Meek, *Law and Authority in a Nigerian Tribe* (London, 1937), pp. 5–8, 102 f, 133 f, 204.

30   Daryll Forde, *The Yoruba-Speaking Peoples of South-Western Nigeria* (London, 1951), p. 4.

31   A. Norman Klein, "Some Structural Consequences of 'Slavery' and 'Pawnage' in Precolonial Ashanti Social and Economic Structure," unpublished draft of the first chapter of a forthcoming book on statemaking in West Africa. I am indebted to Mr. Klein for permission to quote and for allowing me to see his unfinished manuscript. When published, it will rank as our first analysis of precolonial slavery and a major contribution to the history of West Africa as well as to the problem of state formation in general.

32   H. J. Nieboer, *Slavery as an Industrial System: Ethnological Researches* (The Hague, 1900), p. 154. Phillips read and referred to this book.

33   *Ibid.*, pp. 145–49; [H. P. Smit], *The Native Tribes of South-West Africa* (Cape Town, 1928), pp. 33 f, 41; L. Marquard and T. L. Standing, *The Southern Bantu* (London, 1939), p. 50. For an introduction to the vast literature on Angola and the Congo see C. R. Boxer's chapter, "Angola—The Black Mother," in his superb *Salvador de Sá and the Struggle for Brazil and Angola, 1602–1686* (London, 1952).

34   Mamadou Dia, *Réflexions sur l'économie de l'Afrique noire* (nouv. ed.; Paris, 1960), p. 23.

35   "Slavery on the British West India Plantations in the Eighteenth Century," *JNH*, XI (Oct. 1926), p. 594.

36   *Myth of the Negro Past*, p. 161.

Four ■ Cotton, Slavery, and Soil Exhaustion

⚡ *Soil Exhaustion as a Historical Problem*

The South, considered as a civilization, found itself locked in an unequal, no-quarter struggle with the more modern and powerful capitalist civilization of the free states. The concentration of wealth in the hands of an aristocratic ruling class retarded the accumulation of capital and the evolution of a home market and thereby spelled defeat for the South's efforts at matching the North's industrial progress. Paradoxically, the agrarian South could not keep pace with the North in agricultural advancement, and the attempt to break the pattern of one-crop farming and colonial dependence on the export trade largely ended as a failure. The South's inability to combat soil exhaustion effectively proved one of the most serious economic features of its general crisis.

Although historians long held that soil exhaustion in the South resulted from slavery and the plantation system, revisionist scholars have raised doubts and offered alternative explanations. Fortunately, the study of other areas and other periods has occasioned similar disputes and helped clarify many relevant problems.

During the early part of the twentieth century, students of

85

European economic history engaged in a lively and illuminating, although not altogether conclusive, debate on the impact of soil exhaustion on social change. V. G. Simkhovitch opened the controversy with the assertion that the Roman Empire and late medieval English society decayed primarily because of a decline in the fertility of the soil.[1] He did not fully develop his ideas, but one of his talented students, Harriet Bradley, has contributed an able monograph on England.[2] Simkhovitch and Miss Bradley have tried to interpret whole epochs in this way, but their arguments, although attractive, have been subjected to withering criticism. Miss Bradley rejects the idea that the early enclosures and the growth of sheep raising were due to increased demand and higher wool prices. She argues that wool prices fell during the fifteenth century and failed to rise as rapidly as wheat prices during the sixteenth. The conversion of arable land to pasture, she notes, did not cease during the seventeenth century, when the profits from wool growing fell. She concludes that the fertility of the common fields had declined as a result of the strip system, which prevented individual initiative in such practices as crop rotation.

However plausible, her thesis contains serious flaws. First, the prevalent high agricultural wages might well have made sheep raising more profitable than wheat growing despite an unfavorable price differential. Second, her price data are based on the work of Thorold Rogers, who, as Miss Bradley acknowledges, had warned that the evidence for wool prices is scanty and inconclusive.[3]

Reginald Lennard has replied to Miss Bradley and Simkhovitch by citing the "facts of general economic history" and especially the growth of centers of cloth manufacture and other enterprises stimulating the demand for foodstuffs. He has also drawn attention to agronomical evidence indicating that plants grown year after year on the same land will continue to yield a minimum output.[4] A study of British wheat yields by

M. K. Bennett confirms Lennard's observations. Although his statistics are incomplete, Bennett finds that from 1200 to 1450 British wheat yields were eight or nine bushels per acre and that output had tended to rise slowly rather than fall.[5] A. P. Usher has added that so long as minerals are returned to earth absolute exhaustion is impossible, although depletion may become sufficiently serious to render "practical agriculture" unprofitable.[6] The question, then, is: What is practical agriculture?

The critiques of Lennard, Bennett, and Usher satisfactorily dispose of the thesis of an absolute and continuous deterioration of the soil, but we must still account for the role of soil exhaustion in the changes that took place on the English countryside after 1200. The minimal output of eight or nine bushels per acre could do little more than permit the peasantry to survive. The economic changes of the sixteenth century required more than the maintenance of this minimum output; they required a marked increase in productivity to sustain a growing urban population and the demands of a developing world market. So long as agriculture served local areas low productivity was permissible, but once production had to be adjusted to competitive national and international markets, ways had to be found to increase yields.[7]

The commercial exploitation required by capitalism made greater demands upon the soil. The medieval peasant understood quite well the need for manuring, but social conditions prevented him from applying his knowledge. The lord maintained the right to fold all sheep, and sometimes cattle, on his own land. A peasant could rarely afford to feed his stock through the winter and could not maintain enough animals to provide him with sufficient manure.[8] Under these circumstances the soil continued to yield enough to feed the peasantry but hardly enough to supply urban or foreign markets. A radical economic adjustment had to be made before the land could be made to yield greater returns.

The essence of soil exhaustion is not the total exhaustion of the land, nor merely "the progressive reduction of crop yields from cultivated lands,"[9] for the reduction may be arrested at a level high enough to meet local needs. An acceptable general theory of the social effects of soil exhaustion must be sufficiently flexible to account for the requirements of different historical epochs. The rise of capitalism requires a theory that includes the inability of the soil to recover sufficient productivity to maintain a competitive position. The main problem lies in the reaction of social institutions, rather than in the natural deterioration of the soil. The Old South, specifically, had to compete in economic development with the exploding capitalist power of the North, but its basic institution, slavery, rendered futile its attempts to fight the advance of soil exhaustion and economic decline.

⚝ The Role of Slavery

Although the land of the Black Belt ranked among the finest in the world and although cotton was not an especially exhausting crop, the depletion of Southern soil proceeded with a rapidity that frightened and stirred to action some of the best minds in the South. Many of the principles of soil science have only recently come to be understood, and many misleading ideas prevailed during the nineteenth century. Several important points had nevertheless been settled by the mid-1850s: that crops require phosphates and salts of alkalis; that nonleguminous crops require a supply of nitrogenous compounds; that artificial manures may maintain soil fertility for long periods; and that fallowing permits an increase in the available nitrogen compounds in the soil. Southern reformers, especially the talented Edmund Ruffin, had discovered these things for themselves and were particularly concerned with counteracting soil acidity.[10] Southern agricultural periodicals and state geological surveys repeatedly stressed the need for deep plowing, crop rotation, the use of legumes, manuring, and so forth.

Although the results of the agricultural reform movement were uneven at best and although John Taylor of Caroline, the South's first great agricultural reformer, had called slavery "a misfortune to agriculture incapable of palliation,"[11] later agronomists denied that slavery contributed to the deterioration of the soil. Ruffin, for example, attributed soil exhaustion to the normal evolution of agriculture in a frontier community and assumed that economic pressures would eventually force farmers and planters to adopt new ways.[12] Ruffin's attitude has been resurrected and supported by many historians, who have held that slavery did not prevent the adoption of better methods and that the Civil War interrupted a general agricultural reformation.[13] Lewis C. Gray accepts this idea but adds the important qualification that whereas the North overcame the effects of soil exhaustion by agricultural and industrial diversification, the South found it difficult to combat the effects of the one-crop system.[14]

Slavery contributed to soil exhaustion by preventing the South from dealing with the problem after the frontier conditions had disappeared. Bagley argues that "the slaveowner cannot because of slavery escape wearing out the soil,"[15] but the greater weakness lay in the slaveholders' inability to restore lands to competitive levels after they had become exhausted naturally in a country with a moving frontier. The one-crop system perpetuated by slavery prevented crop rotation; the dearth of liquid capital made the purchase of fertilizer difficult; the poor quality of the implements that planters could entrust to slaves interfered with the proper use of available manures; and the carelessness of slaves made all attempts at soil reclamation or improved tillage of doubtful outcome.[16]

✂ *The Use of Fertilizers*

The direct and indirect effects of slavery greatly restricted the use of fertilizers. For cotton and corn the application of fertilizers to hills or rows is far superior to spreading it broadcast, and considerable care must be taken if the labor is not to be wasted.[17] The planter had to guarantee maximum supervision to obtain minimum results. Planters did not have the equipment to bury fertilizers by deep plowing, and the large estates, which inevitably grew out of the slave economy, made fertilization almost a physical and economic impossibility. In certain parts of the Upper South planters solved the problem by selling some of their slaves and transforming them into liquid capital with which to buy commercial fertilizers. The smaller slave force made possible greater supervision and smaller units. This process depended upon the profitable sale of slaves to the Lower South and was therefore applicable only to a small part of the slave region. In the Southeast the use of fertilizers proceeded, as did reform in general, slowly and painfully. Despite the pleas of the reformers, the reports of state geologists, and the efforts of local or state agricultural societies, county after county reported to the federal Patent Office, which was then responsible for agricultural affairs, that little fertilization of any kind was taking place.[18]

Many planters used cottonseed, which was most effective in the cornfields, as fertilizer in the 1850s, but the cotton fields had to depend largely on barnyard manure. This dependence need not have been bad, for barnyard manure probably supplies plants with needed iron, but planters did not keep sufficient livestock and did not feed their animals well enough to do much good. To be of use barnyard manure requires considerable care in storage and application, and even today much of it is lost. In 1938 experts in the Department of Agriculture estimated that one-half was dropped on uncultivated land and that the valuable liquid portion of the remainder was often lost. Improper application rendered much of the rest useless, for manure mùst be applied at the right time according to soil conditions and climate.[19] This fertilizer requires all the time, care, supervision, and interest that farmers can provide and that slaves cannot or will not. Overseers or even planters themselves hardly had the desire to watch their laborers with the unrelenting vigilance that was needed.

The poor quality of the livestock and the careless way in which it was tended led Oscar M. Lieber, South Carolina state geologist, to remark in 1856 that "no manure worth mentioning is saved under the present system."[20] J. M. Gallant told the Agricultural Society of Amite County (Mississippi) in 1857 that the methods used to store that little manure which was accumulated resulted in a two-thirds depreciation of its value.[21]

Even in such livestock-raising states as Kentucky the accumulation of sufficient manure proved difficult. Stock raising was conducted largely as a separate industry, and tobacco and hemp growers often did not keep an adequate supply of animals. The increase in the number of animals sold out of the state intensified the difficulty. Barnyard manure cost about two dollars per ton in Kentucky in the 1850s, and the state geologist estimated that about four hundred tons were needed to restore an exhausted acre. Thus, the accumulation of manure by stock raisers did not necessarily benefit the planters and farmers of the state.[22] For good reason the state geologist of Mississippi scoffed at those who urged a great increase in cattle raising in order to produce more manure. He pointed out that it was ridiculous to think that animals could profitably be kept for manure alone. Half the slave force, he added, would be required to give the animals the necessary care.[23] While the slave states lacked urban development there was no possibility for creation of the markets necessary for profitable stock raising.

The difficulties in accumulating barnyard manure stirred a

growing interest in marl, which Ruffin recommended so highly as an agent capable of counteracting soil acidity and of "deepening the soil" by lowering the level of good earth.[24] In 1853 he claimed that properly marled land in Virginia had increased in value by 200 per cent.[25] Craven's study demonstrates that guano should be credited with much of the improvement in Virginia and Maryland and that marl was not always useful.[26] His judgment corresponds to the present opinion of the Department of Agriculture's experts on marl as a fertilizer.[27] Since guano was expensive and marl readily at hand Southern geologists concentrated on finding marl deposits and making recommendations for their exploitation.[28] The state geologist of Mississippi, L. Harper, even suggested that marl was superior to guano since its benefits lasted for several years whereas guano's were bestowed on a single crop. He admitted that few in Mississippi could afford guano anyway, and we may pardon his excessive praise for a fertilizer that his readers had some chance of obtaining. Yet by 1860 few in Mississippi used either guano or marl. Perhaps in time more of these fertilizers would have been used, but not many planters could possibly have borne the cost of transporting enough marl for their huge estates, much less the cost of buying and transporting enough guano. Planters and farmers in Alabama and Georgia used little marl before 1850, and there is no evidence of an appreciable improvement in the fifties.[29] When they did use marl, they generally had it applied so badly that Ruffin despaired of ever teaching them to do it properly. To make matters worse, errant planters only succeeded in convincing themselves that Ruffin was, after all, only a "book farmer."[30]

Peruvian guano emerged as the great hope of planters and farmers with exhausted lands. The desire for guano reached notable proportions during the 1840s and 1850s: whereas less than 1,000 tons were imported from Peru during 1847–1848, more than 163,000 tons were imported during 1853–1854.[31] In a single year the 17,000 white inhabitants of Kent County, Delaware, reportedly spent $175,000 for guano,[32] and the citizens of Maryland and Virginia reclaimed their worn-out lands largely with its aid. Guano proved particularly effective for wheat, and the planters of the tidewater had excellent results with it. Planters and farmers in the interior benefited much less, for they were concentrating on improving the quality of their tobacco crops, and guano made the tobacco coarser. Then too, they generally had small slave forces to begin with and could not so readily sell surplus slaves to pay large bills for commercial fertilizers.[33]

Guano, like other fertilizers, required considerable care in application; if not used intelligently, it could damage the land. The less expensive American guano required more attention than the Peruvian, especially since it contained hard lumps that had to be thoroughly pulverized.[34]

Two fine historians of Southern economic life, Rosser H. Taylor and Weymouth T. Jordan, claim that significant quantities of guano were used in the Lower South in the 1850s. Taylor asserts that the supply could not keep up with the demand in the Southeast but admits that in South Carolina, at least, application occurred largely in the coastal areas.[35] Jordan insists that guano was used widely in North Carolina, but his evidence, drawn from an article in an agricultural periodical, is limited and unsupported. He refers only to the "noticeable" trade in Charleston and Savannah and provides no figures for the imports through New Orleans and Mobile.[36] In view of the lack of corroboration, it seems fair to conclude that these usually careful historians have been misled into hasty generalization from special local conditions.

When guano did come into use in the Lower South indications are that wealthy coastal planters applied it to their badly exhausted fields.[37] True, some guano did reach the Cotton Belt through the efforts of Thomas Affleck and others, but the agricultural periodicals, which provided so much detail on innovations of all kinds, could not supply figures on sales.[38] Most of the counties of the Lower South polled by the Patent Office in the early fifties failed to respond to questions about fertilizers, and we may suspect that there was nothing to report. The counties and localities that did respond—Habersham and Harris in Georgia, Laurensville in South Carolina, Edwards in Mississippi, Jackson in Alabama, and others—generally reported no commercial fertilizers in use and little fertilization of any kind.[39]

According to the *Report on Agriculture* submitted by the Commissioner of Patents in 1854, about 300 pounds of Peruvian guano had to be applied to fertilize an acre of exhausted land, with a second dressing of 100 to 200 pounds recommended for land planted to Southern staples.[40] That is, cotton land required about 450 pounds of guano per acre.[41] Although the American Guano Company claimed that 200 to 350 pounds of its brand would do, the more objective De Bow's *Industrial Resources* insisted on 900 pounds of this inferior but adequate guano.[42] At forty dollars per ton a planter with 250 acres would have had to spend somewhere between $500 and $2,500 for this second-rate guano; and since its effects were not lasting he would have had to spend it regularly. Whatever the advantages of the relatively inexpensive American variety, it required more cash than all but a few planters had.

Some guanos, the Venezuelan for example, could be obtained for as little as thirty dollars per ton. Even that price was too high for most planters, and the product was of dubious value.[43] Peruvian guano sold for forty-five or fifty dollars per ton during the fifties, but the costs of transportation were such that planters in Mississippi had to pay sixty-five dollars and those in the Southeast about sixty dollars.[44]

Consider the experience of Captain A. H. Boykin of the Sumter District of South Carolina. He applied nine tons during one year of the 1850s and smaller amounts in other years. Those nine tons sufficed for from forty to sixty acres—the actual number of acres fertilized was not given—and could not have cost less than $450. Boykin owned 4,314 acres, so his expenditure benefited only a tiny portion of his estate.[45] In the interior of South Carolina the expense would have been $540 and in Mississippi at least $505. When one considers the size of the plantations of the Cotton Belt and the careless, wasteful way in which the slaves worked, planters cannot be blamed for ignoring the results of neat experiments conducted by a few unusual men like David Dickson of Georgia or Noah B. Cloud of Alabama. James S. Peacocke of Redwood, Louisiana, summed up some of the planters' problems:

> In respect to our worn out lands, it is almost useless for anyone to waste paper and ink to write the Southern planter telling him to manure. It is well enough for Northern farmers to talk; they can well afford to fertilize their little spots of ten or a dozen acres; but a Southern plantation of 500 or 600 acres in cultivation would require all the manure in the parish and all the force to do it justice . . . Again, we have no time to haul the large quantities of manure to the field, for it generally takes until January to get all our cotton, and we have to rush it then, to get time to make repairs before we go to plowing for our next crop.[46]

Peacocke was writing about barnyard manure, but all that he needed to add to account for other fertilizers was that few planters, and fewer farmers, could afford to buy them.[47]

❧ Crop Rotation

Rotation of staple crops with alfalfa, clover, and other legumes might have protected and restored Southern soils. Rotation helps counteract the effects of leaching and erosion, and green manure, although probably less useful than barnyard manure, increases the supply of nitrogen in the soil. Ebenezer Emmons, state geologist of North Carolina, pointed out that marl could be harmful if too much was applied and that proper crop rotation and plowing under of peas could offset the danger of excessive lime.[48]

The South is not the best grass country, although in recent years its share of the nation's grassland has risen remarkably. There was no natural obstacle to the production of more alfalfa, oats, rye, cowpeas, clover, hairy vetch, and other soil-improving crops. Although nitrogenous manuring for cereals tends to encourage the growth of straw relative to grain, the reverse is true for cotton and corn. Yet, the Lower South accounted for an insignificant portion of the modest grass and clover-seed output of the slave states. John Hebron Moore has shown that the production of cowpeas in Mississippi has been underestimated by historians, who have failed to realize that cowpeas were left in the field for livestock and therefore not harvested. He admittedly has had to build his statistical analysis on a great deal of supposition. Probably, he is quite right in insisting that far more cowpeas were produced than has been appreciated, but, as he acknowledges, the cotton-corn-cowpea sequence did not return enough elements to the soil to prevent a steady decline of fertility.[49]

Exceptions to the no-rotation rule appeared only here and there. Ruffin used a fine six-field system, and a fellow Virginian, Colonel Tulley, rotated his wheat with clover and got excellent results.[50] Most planters, especially in the Cotton Belt, were unwilling and more often economically unable to take land away from their cash crop. The ways in which slavery impeded the accumulation of adequate livestock—e.g., by restricting the growth of an urban market for foodstuffs and by preventing the accumulation of sufficient capital to buy good breeds—also made rotation difficult, for there was not much chance of turning hay into cash. The slaves, who worked best when concentrated in gangs in the cotton fields, simply did not provide the animals with that minimum care necessary.

Even so enlightened a planter as M. W. Philips generally ignored legumes and depended on a rotation of cotton and corn, with only a few acres put aside for oats and vegetables. Alexander McDonald of Eufala, Alabama, boasted of a system of rotation that assigned 267 acres to crops other than cotton. Of these, he planted 200 to corn. Of the 900 or so acres cultivated on the estate of George Noble Jones in Florida, only about 150 were given over to oats and none to clover.[51] In 1860, Eugene W. Hilgard, Mississippi state geologist, wrote that the only rotation practiced on a large scale was that of cotton and corn, and similar reports came from throughout the Lower South.[52]

✂ *The Exhaustion of the Soils of the Lower South*

Charles Sackett Sydnor, in calculating charges arising from the depreciation of the land in Mississippi in the 1850s, estimates a cost of 3 per cent of the value of the land per year.[53] Thomas P. Govan, in a critique that has gained wide acceptance, challenges this estimate with the assertion that there can be no justification for assuming a thirty-three-year life span for Mississippi's land. That land is still growing cotton, he argues, and the costs of manuring might have been offset by the increased yields produced by the improvements.[54] We have seen the kind of measures taken to restore the soil, and the facts concerning the rapid deterioration of Mississippi's soils contradict the suggestion of a significant increase in yields. Daniel Lee, editor of the *Southern Cultivator*, estimated in 1858 that 40 per cent of the South's cotton land was already exhausted, and he was given considerable support by other competent observers.[55] Mississippi hired several able geologists and agronomists to study the problem, and their reports should dispel any lingering doubts. Harper reported in 1857 that the state's nonalluvial areas, especially those with prairie soils, were rapidly being exhausted. "Mississippi is a new state," he wrote. "It dates its existence only from 1818; and notwithstanding all its fertility, a large part of the state is already exhausted; the state is full of old deserted fields."[56] Harper's successor, Hilgard, reported in 1860 that the state's land gave way after about thirty years of cultivation. Some parts of Mississippi reminded him of the descriptions of Europe after the Thirty Years' War.[57] As early as 1842 the *Southern Planter* had reported worn-out lands across the interior of Mississippi, and the soil deteriorated steadily thereafter.[58]

Similar accounts came from the older areas such as the Southeast, where few doubt that much of the land had been exhausted.[59] Even the western parts of the Upper South suffered greatly. In 1841, President Chitwood Allen told the Kentucky State Agricultural Society that the best districts in the state were deteriorating rapidly.[60] In 1854 the state geologist expressed similar fears about the rich soil of the bluegrass country.[61]

Govan's assertion that Mississippi still grows cotton is yet more puzzling than his doubts about the extent of exhaustion during the antebellum period. Certainly, Mississippi still grows cotton, but in 1930 the South (the ex-slave states except Missouri, Maryland, Delaware, and Texas), with only one-sixth of the nation's crop land, accounted for two-thirds of the fertilizer tonnage. Forty-one per cent of the cost of farm operations in the South went into fertilizers, whereas the cost in the rest of the country reached only 5 per cent. Fertilizers absorbed more than 7 per cent of the South's farm income, compared with 1 per cent for the rest of the country, although only fifteen bushels of corn were produced per acre, compared with forty-three bushels in New England and thirty-six in the Middle Atlantic states.[62] Parts of South Carolina in 1920 required about 1,000 pounds of fertilizer per acre of cotton land, and the general requirements of Mississippi ranged from 200 to 1,000 pounds.[63] The South still grows cotton only because of tremendous expenditures for the fertilizers with which to strengthen its exhausted soils.

Slavery and the plantation system led to agricultural methods that depleted the soil. In this respect the results did not differ much from those experienced on the Northern frontier, but slavery forced the South into continued dependence on exploitative methods after the frontier had passed. Worse, it prevented the reclamation of the greater part of the worn-out land. The planters had too much land under cultivation; they lacked the necessary livestock; they could practice crop rotation only with difficulty; and they had to rely on a labor force of poor quality. Under such circumstances, notwithstanding successes in some areas, the system could not reform itself. When reforms did come to Maryland, Virginia, and certain counties of the Lower South, it was either at the expense of slavery altogether or by a reduction in the size of slaveholdings and the transformation of the surplus slaves into liquid capital. The South faced a dilemma of which the problem of soil exhaustion formed only a part. On the one hand, it needed to develop its economy to keep pace with that of the free states, or the proud slaveholding class could no longer expect to retain its hegemony. On the other hand, successful reform meant the end of slavery and of the basis for the very power the planters were trying to preserve.

NOTES

1 "Rome's Fall Reconsidered," *PSQ*, XXXI (June 1916), 201–43; and his earlier "Hay and History," *PSQ*, XXVIII (Sept. 1913), 385–403.

2 *The Enclosures in England: An Economic Reconstruction* (New York, 1918).

3 For a fuller discussion of the weaknesses of Rogers' wool-price data see R. H. Tawney, *The Agrarian Problem in the Sixteenth Century* (London, 1912), p. 196.

4 "The Alleged Exhaustion of the Soil of Medieval England," *Economic Journal*, XXXII (March 1922), 12–27.

5 "British Wheat Yields per Acre for Seven Centuries," *Economic History*, III (Feb. 1935), 12–29, esp. p. 28.

6 "Soil Fertility, Soil Exhaustion, and Their Historical Significance," *QJE*, XXXVII (May 1923), 398.

7 Cf., Norman Scott Brien Gras, *A History of Agriculture in Europe and America* (2nd ed.; New York, 1940), p. 20; and Usher, *op. cit.*, p. 397.

8 H. S. Bennett, *Life on the English Manor* (Cambridge, Eng., 1937), pp. 77 ff.

9 As suggested by William Chandler Bagley, Jr., *Soil Exhaustion and the Civil War* (Washington, D.C., 1942), p. 2.

10 Cf. Ruffin, *An Essay on Calcareous Manures* (5th ed.; Richmond, Va., 1852; first ed., 1832); see also Avery O. Craven, *Edmund Ruffin, Southerner* (New York, 1932), pp. 56 ff.

11 *Arator; Being a Series of Agricultural Essays, Practical and Political* (2nd ed.; Georgetown, D.C., 1814), p. 57.

12 *Address on the Opposite Results of Exhausting and Fertilizing Systems of Agriculture* (Charleston, S.C., 1853), p. 6. Only occasionally after 1830 was a voice raised against

slavery as a major obstacle to reform. See, *e.g.*, Cassius Marcellus Clay, *Writings . . . Including Speeches and Addresses* (New York, 1848), p. 74.

13 *Cf.* Craven, *Soil Exhaustion;* Robert R. Russel, "The General Effects of Slavery Upon Southern Economic Progress," *JSH*, IV (Feb. 1938), 34–56; James C. Bonner, "The Genesis of Agricultural Reform in the Cotton Belt," *JSH*, IX (Nov. 1943), 475–500.

14 *History of Agriculture*, I, 445.

15 *Soil Exhaustion*, p. 84.

16 Simkhovitch cites as sound and sensible Columella's advice to Roman farmers to manure their lands but adds that whether or not the advice could be followed was "another question." *PSQ*, XXXI (June 1916), 211. Similarly, Tenney Frank opposes Simkhovitch by referring to the well-known skill of Roman farmers in the use of manures, legumes, crop rotation, etc., and Pitirim Sorokin adds that since Chinese farmers restored their soil he fails to understand why the Romans could not have done so. Simkhovitch's "another question" still remains. He missed the chance to pursue the matter and undermine the criticism, for Frank's Roman farmers and Sorokin's Chinese were not slaves working on latifundia. See Frank, "Recent Work on the Economic History of Ancient Rome," *JEBH*, I (Nov. 1928), 110; Sorokin, *Contemporary Sociological Theories* (New York, 1928), 591–94.

17 *Cf.* Robert M. Salter, "Methods of Applying Fertilizers," U.S. Department of Agriculture, *Yearbook of Agriculture, 1938: Soils & Men* (Washington, D.C., 1938) pp. 558 ff.

18 See, *e.g.*, U.S. Commissioner of Patents, *Report on Agriculture, 1847*, p. 387; *1849*, pp. 144, 170; *1851*, p. 329; *1854*, pp. 114 ff. The list could be expanded considerably.

19 Robert M. Salter and C. J. Schollenberger, "Farm Manure," in U.S. Department of Agriculture, *Soils & Men*, p. 445.

20 South Carolina Mineralogical, Geological, and Agricultural Survey, *Annual Report on the Survey of South Carolina, 1856*, by Oscar M. Lieber (Columbia, S.C., 1856), p. 128.

21 *The Mississippi Planter and Mechanic*, I (Dec. 1857), 286.
    Cf. Maryland, *Annual Report of the State Agricultural
    Chemist to the House of Delegates, 1850*, by J. Higgins
    (Annapolis, Md., 1850–1856), p. 16; *Report . . . 1851*,
    p. 25. Karl Kautsky suggests that as the Roman latifundia
    grew and cattle were entrusted to slaves, the amount of
    manure declined, and soil exhaustion proceeded with in-
    creasing rapidity. *Foundations of Christianity*, tr. Henry F.
    Mins (New York, 1953), p. 53.

22 Kentucky Geological Survey, *Annual Report of the State
    Geologist, 1857*, by David Dale Owen (Frankfort, Ky.,
    1857), pp. 25, 48.

23 Mississippi Geological Survey, *Report on the Geology and
    Agriculture of the State of Mississippi*, by Eugene W.
    Hilgard (Jackson, Miss., 1860), pp. 250–51.

24 *Calcareous Manures*, p. 169.

25 Virginia State Agricultural Society, *Journal of Transac-
    tions*, I (1853), 11.

26 *Soil Exhaustion*, pp. 148 ff.

27 Oswald Schreiner, Albert Merz, and B. E. Brown, "Fertil-
    izer Materials," in U.S. Department of Agriculture, *Soils &
    Men*, p. 517.

28 South Carolina Agricultural Survey, *Report on the Com-
    mencement and Progress of the Agricultural Survey of
    South Carolina for 1843*, by Edmund Ruffin (Columbia,
    S.C., 1843); Missouri Geological Survey, *Second Annual
    Report*, by G. C. Swallow (Jefferson City, Mo., 1855),
    pp. 146 ff; Kentucky Geological Survey, *Report for 1854*,
    p. 19; Delaware Geological Survey, *Memoir on the Geo-
    logical Survey of the State of Delaware, 1837–1838*, by
    James C. Booth (Dover, Del., 1841), p. viii; North Carolina
    Geological Survey, *Report of Professor Emmons* (Raleigh,
    N.C., 1852), p. 53; Tennessee Geological Survey, *Seventh
    Geological Report to the General Assembly, 1843*, by G.
    Troost (Nashville, Tenn., 1843), pp. 32 ff; J. H. Allen,
    "Some Facts Respecting the Geology of Tampa Bay,"
    American Journal of Science and Art, Series 2, I (Jan.
    1846), 41.

29 Mississippi Geological Survey, *Preliminary Report on the Geology and Agriculture of the State of Mississippi* (Jackson, Miss., 1857), pp. 17, 172; Alabama Geological Survey, *First Biennial Report on the Geology of Alabama*, by M. Tuomey (Tuscaloosa, Ala., 1850), pp. 165 ff; see also the remarks of Governor Crawford of Georgia in *Southern Cultivator*, V (Jan. 1847), 3.

30 See the report of Ruffin's experience in Alabama Geological Survey, *First Biennial Report, 1850*, p. 166.

31 U.S. Commissioner of Patents, *Report on Agriculture, 1854*, p. 93. In 1860, the *Southern Planter* published a special advertising supplement in which eight of twenty pages were devoted to advertisements for guano. See XX ("Advertising Sheet" no. 8).

32 Gouverneur Emerson, *Address Delivered before the Agricultural Society of Kent County, Delaware* (Philadelphia, 1857), p. 8.

33 *Cf. DBR*, XIII (Dec. 1852), 627–30; U.S. Commissioner of Patents, *Report on Agriculture, 1851*, p. 286.

34 Joseph Jones, *First Report to the Cotton Planters' Convention of Georgia on the Agricultural Resources of Georgia* (Augusta, Ga., 1860), pp. 64 ff; *HMM*, VIII (May 1843), 485; Frederick Law Olmsted, *Journey in the Seaboard Slave States* (New York, 1856), p. 303.

35 "The Sale and Application of Commercial Fertilizers in the South Atlantic States to 1900," *Agr. Hist.*, XXI (Jan. 1947), 46–52; and "Commercial Fertilizers in South Carolina," *SAQ*, XXIX (April 1930), 179–89.

36 "The Peruvian Guano Gospel in the Old South," *Agr. Hist.*, XXIV (Oct. 1950), 218 f.

37 *Cf.* the report in the diary of John Berkley Grimball, III, 95, in the University of North Carolina; Capell Diary, 1849–50, last page, in Louisiana State University.

38 *Cf. American Cotton Planter*, I (Feb. 1853), 51. I have been unable to find any indication that he was successful.

39 U.S. Commissioner of Patents, *Reports on Agriculture, 1851*, pp. 318, 322, 336; *1852*, pp. 73, 82, 89.

40 Pp. 100 f.

41 Local conditions made a great difference; in some cases experiments with only 200 pounds were successful. See, e.g., *American Cotton Planter*, I (Feb. 1853), 61.

42 American Guano Company, *Report of Experiments with American Guano* (New York, 1860), p. 9; De Bow, *Industrial Resources*, I, 66.

43 *HMM*, XXXIV (March 1856), 440. Often these inferior guanos were sold as Peruvian and sold at high prices. See Maryland, *Annual Reports of the State Agricultural Chemist, 1853*, pp. 36 f; *1855*, pp. 84 ff.

44 Mississippi Geological Survey, *Preliminary Report, 1857*, p. 24; Rosser H. Taylor, *Agr. Hist.*, XXI (Jan. 1947), 47.

45 Boykin Papers, expenditures for 1852–59, in University of North Carolina.

46 *American Agriculturalist*, V (Sept. 1846), 273.

47 Mississippians generally admitted that no plantation or large farm could afford the cost of guano. See Moore, *Agriculture in Ante-Bellum Mississippi*, pp. 194 ff.

48 North Carolina Geological Survey, *Report, 1852*, p. 45.

49 Moore, *Agriculture in Ante-Bellum Mississippi*, pp. 60, 176, 234.

50 Craven, *Ruffin*, p. 86; *Niles' Weekly Register*, LXIX (Oct. 11, 1845), 92.

51 *American Agriculturalist*, V (Jan. 1846), 22, for McDonald; for Philips see F. L. Riley, ed., "Diary of a Mississippi Planter: M. W. Philips, Jan. 1, 1840 to April, 1863," *Publications of the Mississippi Historical Society*, X (1909), 339, 445 f. For Jones see J. D. Glunt and Ulrich B. Phillips, eds., *Florida Plantation Records from the Papers of George Noble Jones* ("Publications of the Missouri Historical Society," St. Louis, Mo., 1927), records for 1855–56. See also Hopeton Plantation Record Book, 1820–28, in Library of Congress, for a similar procedure in an earlier period.

52 Mississippi Geological Survey, *Report, 1860*, p. 241; The St. John's Colleton Agricultural Society (S.C.), *Report of the Special Committee on Professor Shephard's Analysis of*

the Soils of Edisto Island (Charleston, S.C., 1840), pp. 9, 13; U.S. Commissioner of Patents, *Report on Agriculture, 1852*, p. 94; *Report, 1860*, pp. 224–38, esp. pp. 226 f. The War for Southern Independence did little to solve the problem. For a discussion of the difficulties of practicing rotation under the share and tenant systems see U.S. Department of Agriculture, *Soils & Men*, pp. 406–30, esp. p. 423.

53 *Slavery in Mississippi*, pp. 196 ff.

54 "Was Plantation Slavery Profitable?" *JSH*, VIII (Nov. 1942), 522.

55 *Southern Cultivator*, XVI (Aug. 1858), 233; speech of Garnett Andrews of Georgia in the Southern Central Agricultural Society, *Transactions, 1851* (Macon, Ga., 1852); De Bow, *Industrial Resources*, II, 111.

56 Mississippi Geological Survey, *Preliminary Report, 1857*, p. 171, also pp. 19, 25.

57 Mississippi Geological Survey, *Report, 1860*, pp. 238 f.

58 *Southern Planter* (Natchez, Miss.), I (Jan. 1842), 13.

59 See, *e.g.*, Jones, *First Report* . . . , Chap. XX.

60 *Presidential Report* (Lexington, Ky., 1841), pp. 3–8.

61 Kentucky Geological Survey, *Annual Report, 1854*, pp. 276 ff, 374. Even the hemp lands wore out under the one-crop system, although hemp is a relatively nonexhausting crop. See James F. Hopkins, *A History of the Hemp Industry in Kentucky* (Lexington, Ky., 1951), p. 23.

62 Howard W. Odum, *Southern Regions of the United States* (Chapel Hill, N.C., 1936), pp. 65–68; Rupert Vance, *Human Geography of the South* (Chapel Hill, N.C., 1932), p. 97.

63 Hugh Hammond Bennett, *Soils and Agriculture of the Southern States* (New York, 1921), pp. 38, 80.

Five ■ Livestock in the Slave Economy

An Excess of Animals and a Shortage of Meat

For those familiar with the economic condition of the slave South, one assertion appearing at several decisive junctures in the preceding pages may seem to be the product of a theoretical model having nothing to do with well-known facts. Did not the South have a thriving livestock industry? Historians of Southern agriculture, misled by the usually reliable Lewis C. Gray, have paid too much attention to the number of animals in the slave states and too little attention to their quality. Gray notes that the South had half the country's cattle, 60 per cent of its oxen, and 90 per cent of its mules and that totals for the Lower South compared favorably with those for the Upper South.[1] He might have added that the value of livestock in the Lower South in both 1850 and 1860 exceeded that in the Upper South and increased faster during the decade.[2]

The South was confronted by a paradox: an abundance of livestock and an inadequate supply of meat and work animals. Contemporary agricultural writers repeatedly called attention to this curiosity.[3] The United States Agricultural Society reported in 1853 that thousands of American milch cows could not pay their way and were instead a tax on their owners.[4] This statement applied with particular force to Southern livestock.

Frank L. Owsley, summarizing his own researches and those of his students, describes what he believes to have been a flourishing livestock industry in the Lower South. Although the region easily had enough animals to feed the plantations, he argues, livestock raisers preferred to send their meat products to New Orleans, Mobile, Savannah, and Charleston for export to the West Indies and the Northeast because the warm, damp winters caused meat to spoil easily.[5] These assertions support the statistical studies of the Owsley group on the class structure of Southern society. Since the thesis of these studies is that the Southern yeomen were a prosperous and expanding class, the economic basis of their prosperity must be accounted for. Owsley's statistical framework has been thoroughly discredited by Fabian Linden's brilliant critique.[6] As for his nonstatistical argument, he does not explain the preference to export rather than to sell on the hoof to nearby planters, who bought in large quantities from drovers from the Northwestern and border states.

Kentucky and Missouri sent great numbers of animals south throughout the antebellum period. The two states sold almost $1,700,000 worth of animals to South Carolina alone in 1835, and work animals, hogs, cattle, and sheep worth more than that passed by the Cumberland Ford in 1838.[7] In 1836 drovers of horses and hogs from Kentucky, Missouri, and neighboring states sold $2,000,000 worth of animals to South Carolina, and by 1839 Kentucky alone earned as much from its southern trade.[8] This overland trade eventually gave way to railroad shipments, especially of bulk pork, but during 1849–1850 a total of 185,000 hogs went south from Kentucky and Tennessee; tobacco and cotton planters and farmers in North Carolina and elsewhere continued to buy large numbers of animals on the hoof.[9]

Owsley produces no figures to justify his assertion of exports to the Northeast and the West Indies. None of the studies of the economic development of the Northeast mentions a significant trade in meat or meat products with the South; for example, the excellent studies by Robert G. Albion on the coastal trade reveal no evidence of noteworthy meat or livestock shipments from Southern ports. On the contrary, Albion's inability to uncover such evidence in the course of his painstaking research suggests that none exists.[10] To mention only two of the other outstanding works, neither Bidwell's *Rural Economy in New England at the Beginning of the Nineteenth Century*, which deals with the early period, nor Schmidt's article on "Internal Commerce and the Development of the National Economy before 1860," which deals with the antebellum period itself, even hints at such a trade.[11]

Owsley's contention appears all the more dubious in the light of our knowledge that rail shipments of Midwestern meat in refrigerated cars was undermining the livestock industry of New England in the 1850s. Even the thrifty farmers of Vermont, known for their excellent cattle and sheep, were being forced to shift to other types of production.[12] It is difficult to imagine that Southern butter and meat helped push out New England products or that they rivaled Western products in the cities of the Northeast. The available figures on foreign trade show that, exclusive of New Orleans, which handled the exports of the whole Mississippi Valley, the value of the combined exports of meat and animal products from Savannah, Mobile, and Charleston was an insignificant $25,000 for the year ending June 30, 1856—the first for which we have reliable statistics.[13]

If Owsley's contention were correct, surely the South would have had a modest meat-packing industry. The plantation market, although limited, was of adequate proportions to sustain such an industry, and livestock need not have been exported at all; but the supply of raw material was inadequate. During the war the eastern part of the Confederacy suffered from a persistent meat shortage and made efforts to increase the number of good animals. Lack of time and experience, feed shortages, and the problems of livestock raising that had long afflicted the South prevented significant progress.[14]

That the reports on number and value of livestock cannot be accepted at face value becomes clear when we confront the nonstatistical evidence. Consider the situation in Georgia and Texas, the leading livestock-producing states of the Lower South. Owsley attaches great importance to the large numbers of animals reported to have been in the pine barrens of Georgia, but according to De Bow's *Industrial Resources*, there was no beef-raising industry in that or any other part of the state.[15] Reports from Georgia during the 1840s and 1850s stressed that thousands of animals had to manage for themselves during the winter and described their condition as miserable. First-class hogs for the planters' tables had to be imported from the free states, as did much of the mess pork for the slaves. The milch cows and beef cattle were of deplorable quality, and despite increasing attention at least half the work animals had to be imported.[16] Workers in Georgia's gold mines had to be fed from purchases made from hog drovers from Tennessee.[17] When the Southern Central Agricultural Society (of Georgia) issued awards to stock raisers in 1851, few Georgians were among the winners, and in some categories none could be found to enter.[18]

The quality of the livestock emerges as the paramount issue. The animals in the numerically great livestock-raising state of Texas did not even measure up to Southern standards. In 1860, Texas cattle were largely semiwild and probably worth only half as much as animals in other Southern states. Transportation difficulties prevented all except a small proportion of these salable beef cattle from being sent to market.[19] Miss Mendenhall, in her study of agriculture in South Carolina, concludes that the census figures for cattle cannot be taken as evidence of genuine interest in cattle raising, for a large number grew up on the range virtually without care.[20] In our own day India claims half the world's cattle, but according to De Castro, "they are so badly fed that they produce hardly any milk."[21]

A climate supposedly suitable neither for grasses nor for livestock took most of the blame for the poor condition of Southern animals. Even Edmund Ruffin used this argument and urged Southerners to concentrate on reforms other than livestock improvement. Yet after initial difficulties, Ruffin managed to improve his own breeds sufficiently to supply the needs of his plantation.[22] In 1868, Lewis F. Allen, in his study of American cattle, said bluntly that the soil and climate of the South were fine for animals and that expressions to the contrary were little more than excuses by planters who preferred to raise cotton.[23] Allen certainly told the truth, and many Southerners must have known it. In the twentieth century Southerners have been able to grow feed crops and to increase greatly the quality and quantity of their livestock. Alabama had an alfalfa and livestock boom after World War I; South Carolina tripled its hay production in the 1930s, and every Southern state improved on its stock significantly.[24]

In raising hogs the mild Southern climate actually works to advantage, for low temperatures in the early spring may cause a loss of pigs in farrowing. With this exception weather conditions do not matter much in hog raising.[25] Losses always fall heaviest on farms poorly equipped for caring for young pigs, and the slave plantations were especially vulnerable in this respect. The major difficulty grew out of neither soil nor climate but out of the combination of careless treatment and the lack of accessible, geographically concentrated markets that might have encouraged animal husbandry on a large scale.

Virtually every competent traveler to the Old South expressed astonishment at the brutal and careless treatment that slaves accorded livestock. James Redpath, for example, after describing how a slave tried to get a horse to move on difficult terrain by throwing rocks at its legs, commented, "This is a fair specimen of the style in which slaves treat stock."[26] In many areas slaves too old or infirm to work in the fields cared for the animals, and where livestock raising received serious attention, slaves were considered next to useless.[27] In addition to carelessness and negligence, slaves fell under suspicion of deliberately sabotaging plantation meat supplies by stealing hogs and plundering smokehouses. Perhaps these thefts were motivated by hunger or perhaps by rebelliousness; whatever the reason, they apparently were common.[28]

Aware of these obstacles, advocates of agricultural reform returned to a single theme: the need for careful management and proper treatment.[29] Food for stock was repeatedly wasted, they said, because even the most trusted slaves would pay no attention to the management of rations. Planters let their animals run wild or entrusted them to incompetent slaves. What else could they have done? One writer had an answer: "Such attention as can only be given by those who are farmers and not planters."[30]

In addition to the direct damage done to stock by careless handling and by allowing the animals to run wild during much of the year, a good deal of harm occurred indirectly. Weakness and vulnerability to disease plagued the surviving animals. Animal diseases caused concern throughout the country, but the number of complaints of widespread deaths in the South suggests special problems, especially since so many of the complaints came from areas where livestock was known to be particularly ill-treated and underfed.[31] Dependence upon imported animals presented special difficulties. Horses and mules suffered from the long journey from Kentucky and Missouri to the plantation areas, and animals that started in good condition often arrived unhealthy at their destination.[32] Animals sent to the Lower South had to be acclimated; many did not take the change well, and others not at all.[33]

The effects of ill-treatment constituted only part of slavery's contribution to the weakening of Southern livestock. Improvement of cattle breeds, the development of adequate transportation facilities, and a pork-packing industry required heavy investments of capital, which the South lacked in consequence of its plantation and slave economy. The pork-packing industry of the Middle West started after 1818, when Eastern capital appeared in large quantities to take advantage of a growing market. Ironically, the early market arose primarily from the Southern plantations, although during the later period the urban centers of the North far outdistanced the South as a market for meat and animal products.[34] Transportation facilities in the South were designed chiefly to carry cotton to the coast, and the urban market within the South remained drastically limited.[35]

Wherever the large plantations dominated the economy they produced the same results for each important class of animals: the slaves abused and neglected the animals on the plantations, and the livestock industry as a whole received inadequate attention because of the lack of capital, poor transportation, and the absence of an urban market.

Work Animals

Slaves seem to have taken the greatest delight in abusing the horses, oxen, and mules that were so essential to the day-to-day work of the plantations. If the hogs were not attended to, pork could be purchased, but there was no substitute for work animals.

After 1830, the ox, for two centuries the conventional draft animal on American farms, gave way to the more efficient horse. The number of oxen in the country increased by only 32 per cent during the 1850s, compared with an increase of 100 per cent in the number of horses and mules, but this shift was not the same in the free states and the slave. Southerners generally began to use mules; Northerners, horses. During that decade the ratio of horses to total number of work animals rose from 73.3 to 75.5 per cent in the free states, but declined from 58.0 to 54.0 per cent in the slave; more significantly, in the principal plantation states of Alabama, Mississippi, and Louisiana the percentage fell from 48.0 to 36.0, whereas the ratio of mules to total work animals rose from 23.0 to 35.0.[36] Some historians have suggested that the Southern preference for mules rather than horses indicated agricultural progress.[37] The reason for using mules, as most contemporaries admitted, was not that they worked better than horses but that they withstood more readily the punishment inflicted by the slaves.[38] As the plantation system grew, the proportion of mules to horses grew with it, and wherever slaves worked, mules came into increasingly greater use. In the sample counties studied (see Graph 1) the same tendency appeared: the larger the slave force the greater the dependence upon mules and oxen relative to the faster, more efficient horses, presumably because horses cannot take as much abuse as mules and need more care and more skill in driving.

❊ Hogs

The figures for the number of animals have nowhere been more misleading than in the case of hogs, which provided the main source of meat in the South. Kentucky, Tennessee, and the Northwest sold an undetermined number of animals to the Lower South; thus, an increase in stock did not necessarily mean an increase in animals raised at home. More important, the quality of Southern hogs did not approach that of the better fed, better bred, better housed hogs in the Middle West. Southern hogs frequently ran wild in the woods to provide

GRAPH I

Percentage of Horses to Total Work Animals
in Selected Southern Counties, 1860

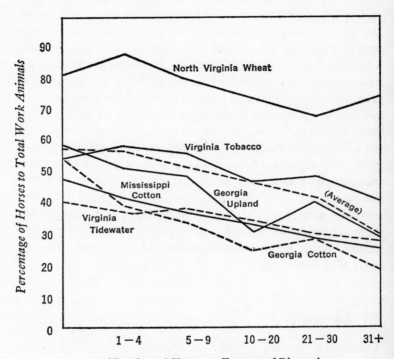

Number of Slaves on Farms and Plantations

SOURCE: computed from the manuscript census returns. The sample counties were selected on the basis of Lewis C. Gray's judgment. The counties are: Mississippi Cotton Belt (De Soto, Marshall); Georgia Cotton Belt (Dougherty, Thomas); N. Virginia wheat area (Fauquier, Prince William); Virginia tidewater (Charles City, Gloucester); Virginia tobacco area (Amelia, Buckingham); Georgia diversified farming area (Walker, Gordon). For a fuller discussion of the method of selection see Eugene D. Genovese, "The Limits of Agrarian Reform in the Slave South," unpublished doctoral dissertation, Columbia University, 1959, pp. 193 ff.

their own food throughout the winter as best they could; often, they received no grain at all during the year. Contemporary sources contain many reports of these practices. In one instance the hogs became so wild that no chance remained to fatten them even if they could be caught alive.[39] Mast-fed hogs sometimes got fat, but the meat was barely fit for the slaves. Usually, these animals weighed much less than hogs receiving at least a little corn. So poor was the treatment of stock that when, on occasion, superior animals were imported into the Lower South, their quality degenerated instead of effecting a general improvement in the herds.[40]

During the colonial period the hogs of New England weighed about 200 pounds. By 1860 the hogs in the Chicago market averaged 228 and those brought to Cincinnati about 200 or more.[41] According to twenty-four sets of plantation records that yield information on the weight of hogs slaughtered, the median weight of almost 4,000 hogs in eight states was only 140 pounds. These records were from the best plantations, and some of them came from the Upper South. The average weights were inflated by the inclusion of the heavier hogs bought from drovers to be slaughtered on the plantations. The small size of the hogs was a matter of indifference to some planters, who were interested only in hams;[42] in these cases the impracticability of raising enough pork for the slaves was conceded. In short, the actual average weight of Southern hogs undoubtedly fell well below the 140-pound figure. Thus, despite the reportedly large numbers of animals, the South had to import substantial quantities of hogs and pork.[43]

❧ Cattle

As with hogs, the importation of fine breeds of cattle resulted in a general improvement of stock in the North, but in a deterioration of fine breeds brought into the South. Beef for the planter's table frequently had to be bought from the out-side. The complaint of Confederate troops that the animals supplying them with beef had to be held upright for shooting[44] was more than a comment on wartime conditions. The shift from cotton to food production might well have offset the shortages and dislocation occasioned by the war, and there is no reason to believe that the prewar condition of the animals was any better. The cattle of central and western Virginia, for example, were plentiful but of mediocre to low quality.[45] How much did those wartime complaints differ from such prewar ones as that of the Reverend G. Lewis in 1845: Georgia cattle are "objects of pity, not to be fed upon but to be fed. Left to shift for themselves all winter, their bones look and stare at you."[46]

Milch cows fared little better. Of the states of the Lower South, only Louisiana produced more than 20 pounds of butter per cow, and South Carolina, Georgia, Texas, and Florida pro-duced 15 pounds or less. In the Upper South production ranged from 33 pounds in Tennessee to 43 pounds in Maryland, al-though Delaware—if we may consider it a slave state at all—produced 50 pounds. Of the free states, only four produced less than 50 pounds per cow, and Rhode Island, the poorest, pro-duced 34 pounds, while New York led with 85 pounds.[47]

Nor did the poor record of the slave states arise from a greater preference for milk rather than butter. There is ample evidence that planters wanted more butter and often imported it.[48] Although exact data are not available, Delaware, Maryland, and Virginia—easily the best producers among the slave states—are known to have consumed 25 per cent less milk (fluid and processed) than the free states.[49] Not all types of milch cows could have done well in the Southern climate and on Southern soils, but some adequate milkers could have, as recent experi-ence has proved. Here again we confront the interrelatedness of the various projects for agricultural reform, for an adequate cattle-raising industry would have required much greater progress in combatting soil exhaustion. Without soils adequate in phosphorus, or more precisely, adequate in phosphorus in a usable form, cattle raising is almost insurmountably difficult.[50]

✄ *A General View*

Southern attempts to increase nonstaple production and to improve livestock broke down in the face of enormous difficulties. The prevailing inefficient labor force and the backward business practices prevented all except a few unusual planters from accomplishing much; when they did succeed in raising their own food, they also succeeded in depriving local producers of markets. The stock raisers of the back country could not sell their produce in the North because of the prohibitive costs of transportation, and the planters saw no reason to vote for taxes to improve contacts with the back country, preferring to purchase supplies from Western drovers or through agents.

The planters had little surplus capital with which to buy improved breeds and could not guarantee the care necessary to make the investments worth while. Stock raisers did not have the capital either, and if they could get it, the investments would have been foolhardy without adequate urban markets.

Some planters, who did have the capital and might have solved the managerial problem, were prisoners of the plantation myth and scorned pursuits other than cotton growing. There were notable exceptions to these generalizations. Here and there moneyed planters with a businesslike attitude and exceptional managerial skill achieved brilliant successes. The retardative effects of slavery were not absolute; no individual planter was condemned by fate to defeat. Slavery did establish conditions such that maximum efforts by exceptional men were required for significant agricultural improvements in general and for significant improvement in livestock in particular.

N O T E S

1 *History of Agriculture*, II, 831 f, 1042.

2 Cathey, using a similar approach, concludes that North Carolina must have been self-sufficient in pork, for the state had an adequate number of swine. Curiously, he notes that cows were of poor quality but does not investigate the quality of swine. *Agricultural Developments*, pp. 175–78.

3 John Taylor, *Arator*, p. 165; *Southern Agriculturalist* (Charleston, S.C.), VIII (March 1835), 244; *Farmer and Planter*, IX (Jan. 1858), 5; *American Cotton Planter*, II (June 1854), 181; U.S. Commissioner of Patents, *Report on Agriculture, 1851*, p. 315. The same situation has persisted in large parts of the South well into this century, especially where tenantry has prevailed. James Westfall Thompson has even suggested that the great part of the South's livestock was bought from Kentucky and the free states. There is no way of proving this contention, and it does seem extreme. Yet his opinion is worth some attention, for it suggests how great the evidence is of animal buying. *A History of Livestock Raising in the United States, 1607–1860*, U.S. Department of Agriculture, Agricultural History Series No. 5 (Nov. 1942), p. 140.

4 *Journal of the United States Agricultural Society*, I, Nos. 3–4 (1853), 133.

5 Owsley, *Plain Folk*, pp. 34–50, 135 ff.

6 Linden, *JNH*, XXXI (April 1946), 140–89.

7 John Ashton, *A History of Hogs and Pork Production in Missouri*, The Missouri State Board of Agriculture, *Monthly Bulletin*, XXI, No. 1 (Jefferson City, Mo., Jan. 1923), p. 53; Mary Verhoeff, *The Kentucky Mountains*, Filson Club Publications, No. 25 (Louisville, Ky., 1911), p. 123.

8 Verhoeff, *Kentucky Mountains*, p. 99, note a; T. D. Clark, "Livestock Trade Between Kentucky and the South, 1840–1860," *Kentucky State Historical Society Register*, XXVII (May 1929), 570; J. S. Buckingham, *The Slave States of America* (2 vols.; London, 1842), II, 203 f; Elizabeth L. Parr, "Kentucky's Overland Trade with the Ante-Bellum South," *Filson Club History Quarterly*, II (Jan. 1928), 71–81.

9 U.S. Commissioner of Patents, *Report on Agriculture, 1850*, p. 563; *Report, 1853*, pp. 56 ff; Rosser H. Taylor, *Slaveholding in North Carolina: An Economic View* (Chapel Hill, N.C., 1926), pp. 36 f.

10 *Square-Riggers on Schedule* (Princeton, N.J., 1938), esp. p. 71; *The Rise of New York Port, 1815–1860* (New York, 1939), *passim*.

11 Percy Wells Bidwell, *Rural Economy in New England at the Beginning of the Nineteenth Century*, Transactions of the Connecticut Academy of Arts and Sciences, April 1916, pp. 352 f; Louis Bernard Schmidt, "Internal Commerce and the Development of the National Economy before 1860," *JPE*, XLVII (Dec. 1939), 80 ff.

12 T. D. Seymour Bassett, "A Case Study of Urban Impact on Rural Society: Vermont, 1840–1880," *Agr. Hist.*, XXX (Jan. 1956), 30.

13 U.S. Treasury Department, *Report of the Secretary of the Treasury Transmitting a Report of the Register of the Treasury of the Commerce and Navigation of the United States for the Year Ending June 30, 1856*, pp. 304–11.

14 Massey, *Ersatz in the Confederacy*, p. 61.

15 Owsley, *Plain Folk*, pp. 44 f; De Bow, *Industrial Resources*, I, 539.

16 *American Agriculturalist*, III (April 1844), 117; VI (June 1845), 176; U.S. Commissioner of Patents, *Report on Agriculture, 1849*, pp. 145 f; *Report, 1851*, p. 325; *Arator*, II (Oct. 1856), 577 ff.

17 Fletcher M. Green, "Georgia's Forgotten Industry: Gold Mining," *GHQ*, XIX (Sept. 1935), 211 f.

18 *Transactions, 1851*.

19 Lewis F. Allen, *American Cattle: Their History, Breeding and Management* (New York, 1868), p. 12; Edward Everett Dale, *Cow Country* (Norman, Okla., 1942), pp. 80 f; and *The Range Cattle Industry* (Norman, Okla., 1930), p. 24; J. Frank Dobie, "The First Cattle in Texas and the Southwest Progenitors of the Longhorns," *SHQ*, XLII (Jan. 1939), 184, 189; T. J. Cauley, "Early Meat Packing Plants in Texas," *Southwestern Political and Social Science Quarterly*, IX (March 1929), 466 f.

20 Marjorie Stratford Mendenhall, "A History of Agriculture in South Carolina, 1790 to 1860: An Economic and Social Study," unpublished doctoral dissertation, University of North Carolina, 1940, p. 298.

21 Josué de Castro, *Geography of Hunger*, pp. 174–75.

22 Edmund Ruffin, "Incidents of My Life," II, 15 f; III, 226 f (unpublished autobiography), Ruffin Papers in the University of North Carolina.

23 *American Cattle*, p. 23. Cf. *American Farmer*, XI (May 1830), 299; and the comments of De Bow in U.S. Commissioner of Patents, *Report on Agriculture, 1848*, p. 516.

24 Glenn N. Sisk, "Agricultural Diversification in the Alabama Black Belt," *Agr. Hist.*, XXVI (April 1952), 43. Cf. Odum, *Southern Regions*, 597.

25 On weather conditions and hog raising see G. C. Haas and Mordecai Ezekiel, *Factors Affecting the Price of Hogs*, U.S. Department of Agriculture, Department Bulletin No. 1440 (Nov. 1926), p. 25.

26 *The Roving Editor; Or, Talks with the Slaves in the Southern States* (New York, 1859), p. 241.

27 *Southern Agriculturalist,* VIII (Jan. 1835), 18. Charles William Ramsdell, "The Frontier and Secession," *Studies in Southern History and Politics Inscribed to William A. Dunning* (New York, 1915), p. 65.

28 See, *e.g.,* John Houston Bills Diary, 1843–1866, May 31, 1853, in the University of North Carolina; and Affleck's remarks in U.S. Commissioner of Patents, *Report on Agriculture, 1849,* p. 162.

29 *Farmer and Planter,* VI (Jan. 1855), 3; *Arator,* I (July 1855), 115; *Arator,* II (Dec. 1855), 267 f; *Farmer's Journal,* II (June 1853), 83; *American Cotton Planter,* II (June 1854), 181; and Dr. Walter Wade's Plantation Diary, Feb. 4, 1850, in the Mississippi State Department of History and Archives, Jackson.

30 *American Agriculturalist,* VI (June 1845), 253.

31 *American Cotton Planter,* XIII (Sept. 1859), 272; *Farmer and Planter,* IX (Aug. 1858), *passim;* Jewel Lynn De Grummond, "A Social History of St. Mary's Parish, 1845–1860," *LHQ,* XXXII (Jan. 1949), 49; Everard Green Baker Ms., II, 20, 39; Francis Terry Leak Diary, II, 109, 111, 274; Louis M. De Saussure Plantation Book, 1835–1864, pp. 8, 21, 35, in the University of North Carolina.

32 Edmund F. Noel in U.S. Commissioner of Patents, *Report on Agriculture, 1851,* p. 278.

33 *Farmer and Planter,* VI (Jan. 1855), 1; E. D. Fenner, *Southern Medical Reports* (2 vols.; New Orleans, 1849–50), I, 32 f.

34 Charles T. Leavitt, "Attempts to Improve Cattle Breeds in the United States, 1790–1860," *Agr. Hist.,* VII (April 1933), 51 ff, and "Transportation and the Livestock Industry of the Middle West to 1860," *Agr. Hist.,* VIII (Jan. 1934), 22.

35 *Cf.* Ulrich B. Phillips, *A History of Transportation in the Eastern Cotton Belt to 1860* (New York, 1908); U.S. Commissioner of Patents, *Report on Agriculture, 1852,*

p. 73; *Affleck's Rural Almanack, 1852*, p. 61; Cassius M. Clay, *Writings*, p. 179.

36 Computed from the census reports for 1850 and 1860; *cf. Eighth Census of the U.S., Agriculture*, p. cs.

37 Phillips, *American Negro Slavery*, p. 219; Francis Butler Simkins, *A History of the South* (New York, 1953), p. 121.

38 See, *e.g., American Cotton Planter*, XII (Aug. 1858), 238; *Farmer and Planter*, II (Nov. 1851), 151; (Dec. 1851), 164.

39 Theodora Britton Marshall and Gladys Crail Evans (eds.), "Plantation Report from the Papers of Levin R. Marshall, of 'Richmond,' Natchez, Mississippi," *JMH*, III (Jan. 1941), 51.

40 U.S. Commissioner of Patents, *Report on Agriculture, 1852*, pp. 74, 82.

41 Percy Wells Bidwell and John I. Falconer, *History of Agriculture in the Northern United States, 1620–1860* (New York, 1941), p. 44; Thomas Senior Berry, *Western Prices before 1861: A Study of the Cincinnati Market* (Cambridge, Mass., 1943), pp. 231 ff; De Bow, *Industrial Resources*, I, 378; St. Louis hogs averaged just under 200 pounds—see Ashton, *History of Hogs*, p. 56.

42 See the letter of Almira Coffin to Mrs. J. G. Osgood, May 19, 1851, in Katharine M. Jones, *The Plantation South* (Indianapolis, 1957), pp. 186–91.

43 Professor William N. Parker of Yale University has told me that my figures may be too low because of the method of weighing. The hogs probably lost some weight between the time they were prepared for slaughtering and the time they were weighed because of the manner in which they were handled. Hopefully, Professor Parker will in due time publish his own estimates of hog weights in several regions. Apparently, those estimates will not differ so greatly from my own preliminary estimates. At least there seems no reason to think that the main point made here will be shaken. I should caution, however, against relying on these estimates for close quantitative work.

Much more research will have to be done before we attain anything like precision.

44 Bell Irvin Wiley, *The Plain People of the Confederacy* (Chicago, 1963), p. 6.

45 Emmett B. Fields, "The Agricultural Population of Virginia, 1850–1860," unpublished doctoral dissertation, Vanderbilt University, 1953, pp. 64–65.

46 Quoted in Gates, *Farmer's Age*, p. 201.

47 *Journal of the United States Agricultural Society*, I (1853), 140 f. In general, what was true for butter production was also true for wool. See De Bow, *Industrial Resources*, I, 359; Jones, *Plantation South*, p. 190; Thomas L. Clingman, *Selections from the Speeches and Writings of* . . . (Raleigh, N.C., 1877), pp. 114 f.

48 *New Orleans Price-Current*, Oct. 17, 1849; Feb. 2, 1850; *Farmer and Planter*, VIII (Feb. 1857), 36; *Southern Planter* (Richmond, Va.), III (Aug. 1843), 177 f; Mrs. Hilliard's Diary, Jan. 19, 1850, in Tulane University; Duncan G. McCall Plantation Record and Diary, Vol. I, accounts for Oct.–Dec. 1851.

49 *HMM*, XLVII (Nov. 1862), 444. The states producing the largest amount of butter apparently used the most fluid milk. See *Farmer's Journal*, III (April 1854), 26 f.

50 De Castro, *Geography of Hunger*, p. 44.

Six ∎ The Limits
of Agricultural Reform

Since the appearance of Craven's pioneering study of soil exhaustion in Maryland and Virginia in 1926,[1] historians have generally believed that the War for Southern Independence interrupted the South's steady progress toward agricultural reform and economic diversification. In many cases this belief has been accompanied by the assumption that more rapid progress could and would have occurred if cotton prices had not been at such high levels in the 1850s. If so, it is stated, the South could have made adequate economic progress under the slave regime, and one important side of the sectional conflict would have resolved itself with time. Economic growth and balance might have replaced the South's dependence on a few staples with a moderately diversified and integrated economy, which might have removed many of the South's complaints and fears. In such an improved milieu peaceful discussions of outstanding political and social issues would have become a stronger possibility.

The assumptions on which this thesis of a self-reforming agriculture rests are subject to several objections. First, the overwhelming burden of evidence suggests that the reform movement, the presence of which historians have attested to in numerous books and articles for the past forty years, met noteworthy success below Virginia only in a few localities.

Second, the assumptions rest on a logical contradiction, for the sale of slaves, upon which, as will be demonstrated, steady progress depended, could not support more than a partial and geographically limited reform. Third, the reform process itself contained inherent contradictions and proceeded in such a way that each step forward forced a step backward.

The Agitation for Reform

Thoughtful Southerners, shaken by the terrible depression of the 1840s, did not permit the prosperity of the 1850s to make them overlook the grave weaknesses in their region's economy. Whatever boastful politicians might say and however complacent the average planter or farmer might be, Edmund Ruffin, M. W. Philips, Noah B. Cloud, Thomas Affleck, David Dickson, and many other less well known men carried forward the tradition of John Taylor of Caroline and tried to convince planters and farmers that wasteful frontier methods had to be abandoned if the South wished to place its progress and prosperity on safe ground. Although these men have rightly been honored by historians for their selfless efforts and genuine achievements, on the whole they failed. They assumed that the problem was one of normal evolution of better methods through the dissemination of information and that a thorough reformation could take place within the slave system.[2] In the prosperous 1850s some reformers virtually gave up their hopes of a diversified agriculture and emphasized measures to increase labor productivity in the cotton fields and to provide supplementary livestock. Even if this program had succeeded, it would not have done more than to make the South's dependence on industrial outsiders a bit more tolerable; it would not have removed the economic difficulties in the way of an understanding with the free states. At that, this more modest program, as we have seen, met insurmountable obstacles.[3]

The history of Southern commercial conventions during the 1830s and after is the story of frustration and failure: demands for direct trade with Europe, agitation for Southern manufactures, proposals for railway expansion, programs for the regulation of the sale or production of cotton, and some sentiment for reopening the slave trade. The proposals discussed at some of these meetings and at similar ones of cotton planters[4] revealed two main tendencies: an unwillingness to recognize that the South's problems had roots deep in the economic and social structure and could not be solved by quick and easy measures, and a preoccupation with political matters. As Phillips puts it, the conventions became absorbed primarily with political agitation and with giving the South a feeling of separate destiny.[5]

Ruffin, a practical man, usually concentrated on such modest and realizable projects as state aid for agricultural groups. He admitted that the political position of the South rested on a strict-construction interpretation of the national Constitution but argued that state governments should aid agricultural schools and societies. He bitterly criticized the prevalent *laissez-faire* attitude, which he regarded as the cause of Virginia's failure to assist agriculture.[6] The agitation for state aid had a long history in Virginia. In 1820 the Albemarle Agricultural Society, one of the oldest and best of such groups, demanded that an agricultural professorship be established in the University of Virginia and that steps be taken to assist planters and farmers.[7] In 1837 a Virginia agricultural convention petitioned the state legislature for grants-in-aid and an appropriation of $1,000 for an advisory board of agriculture. After years of campaigning, the reformers won a major victory in 1841 when a board was established; unfortunately, the legislators declined to appropriate any funds besides the inadequate traveling expenses of three dollars per member. Ruffin and the other members of the board tried to carry out their task of collecting and disseminating information, but when the legislators refused to grant additional money to meet their expenses, they ceased activity.[8] Virginia's experience paralleled that of other slave states, for funds simply were not available. During the prosperous 1850s some Southern states did better. In 1855, for example, the legislature of South Carolina appropriated $5,000 for the work of the state agricultural society, and in 1857 the legislature of Mississippi established a state agricultural bureau, which seems to have functioned primarily as a propaganda agency for secessionists.[9]

Although Southern agricultural reformers scored modest successes in their campaigns to organize state and local agricultural societies in the late 1840s and 1850s, the results were, on the whole, discouraging. Of the 912 agricultural, horticultural, and agricultural-mechanical societies in the country in 1858, only 197 were in the slave states; of those, only 76 were in the cotton states.[10] Fourteen state fairs were held during the same year, but only two were in the slave states.[11] It is easy to make much of those societies which did exist and to suggest that the South was becoming more and more conscious of the need for such groups, but small advances notwithstanding, there is little to indicate that Southern organizations had significant strength. In the 1830s, Ruffin ridiculed local societies and their programs. "The publication of their constitutions," he noted, "has so often been the prelude to [their] dissolution."[12] Ten years later a meeting was called in Richmond to organize a state agricultural society, but few attended besides politicians. The customary grandiose plans emerged, and Ruffin, who had refused to attend a meeting that he believed would lead to nothing, was elected president. He declined, and, as he predicted, the society proved worthless.[13]

When societies were organized, they too often repeated the

experience of the short-lived Anderson County (Tennessee) Agricultural and Mechanical Society: eighteen persons attended the organizational meeting, and eight were elected officers.[14] In Louisiana, De Bow reported that the only functioning society was poorly attended and accomplished little.[15] Agricultural societies revived during the 1850s in Mississippi and elsewhere, but too often they were little more than specialized secessionist clubs.[16] In general, Southern agricultural societies were dominated by planters who were more interested in social activities than practical affairs and who preferred raising race horses to raising work animals.

In 1858 the Patent Office polled the nation's agricultural societies to determine their size and effectiveness. About 35 per cent of those in the free states and territories (247 of 715) responded, whereas only 17 per cent of those in the cotton states (13 of 76) and 22 per cent of those in the Upper South (27 of 121) responded. Probably, those societies which failed to respond were relatively weak. The reporting free-state societies accounted for a membership of 91,480, compared with a membership of only 8,689 for the reporting slave-state societies. Of those in the South, only 2,474 were in the cotton states. Four free states (Illinois, New York, Ohio, and Pennsylvania) each boasted a larger membership than was reported for the entire South. Three other free states (Massachusetts, Michigan, and Indiana) each had a membership of more than 7,500.[17]

Some Southerners suggested that planters, living in isolation, could not be moved to participate in agricultural organizations,[18] and the participation of bankers, merchants, and other urban elements[19] does suggest upper-class associations devoted to discussion of broad social issues. A. G. Sumner of South Carolina wrote with noticeable exasperation in 1855: "Our old State Agricultural Society was ridden to death, in connexion with aspirations for office. . . . It was a gas society, which like all existences of allotted periods lived its time and was no more."[20] Planters, with a typically aristocratic preference, seem to have been far more interested in politics than in agriculture. In 1836, the *Southern Agriculturalist* estimated that nine-tenths of all Southerners who received a periodical chose a political one, and the *Southern Planter* made a similar observation twenty years later.[21] De Bow's famous *Industrial Resources of the Southern and Western States*, which concentrated especially on Southern agricultural and economic problems and was oriented principally toward a Southern audience, sold six times as many copies in the free states as in the slave, and its total circulation in the slave states was described as small.[22] To cite two individual cases: Henry Marston, a planter of East Feliciana, Louisiana, who was "an avid reader," subscribed to *Prices Current*, the Merchants Exchange *Reports*, *Scientific American*, four newspapers, and some religious and temperance journals, but did not subscribe to an agricultural journal; Judge Thomas Butler, a prominent planter of Louisiana, subscribed to at least nine publications including two commercial papers, but not to an agricultural journal.[23] Although Southern political journals did their best to publish information on agricultural affairs, they were no substitute for specialized journals.

The South published only nine of the country's forty-one agricultural periodicals in 1853, and whereas many of those in the free states appeared weekly or biweekly, only monthlies appeared in the slave states.[24] Many Southerners in fact preferred Northern publications. Ruffin partly blamed the demise of the *Farmer's Register* on Northern competition.[25] He noted that Northern journals had a much wider circulation and could be priced well below Southern. In 1852 the *Southern Star* expressed outrage because Southerners formed clubs to support Northern periodicals of their preference, but the authors of the complaint did not seriously inquire into the reasons for the preference. Southern agricultural journals were largely devoted to problems of plantation management and to crops and matters of interest to planters. Northern journals printed more information of use to Southern farmers than did Southern journals. In the words of Paul W. Gates: "The contents of Southern journals were designed for planters; rarely was there anything written particularly for the yeoman farmer. Not having the popular support enjoyed by such Northern journals as the *Country Gentleman* and the *American Agriculturalist*, they were generally one-man affairs and in consequence had to borrow heavily from other periodicals."[26]

There were reasons for the weakness of Southern societies deeper than the aristocratic attitudes of the planters and the weakness of the agricultural journals. In 1847 a planter wrote that if the societies were to give plows instead of cups for prizes the results might be better.[27] The planter had sensibly drawn attention to the lack of working funds that plagued the slave South in so many undertakings. In 1855 the Massachusetts Agricultural Society offered $1,000 for the best mower and, after making its selection, spent another $50,000 for the production and distribution of suitable implements.[28] The German farmers of Texas had a number of societies, one of which spent $12,000 during one year to introduce new trees and plants.[29] Even if the currently fashionable estimates of plantation profits withstand critical examination in future years, there would be nothing to indicate that the planters of the slave South could have raised such sums. Their consumption standards and aristocratic style of life, so typical of planter classes even today, precluded the rational use of funds generated by the economy.

The Southern reformers did their best and in some areas produced impressive results. The great agricultural revival in Virginia and Maryland during 1820–1860 has received considerable attention, and its general features are too well known to require review here.[30] In part, the experience of Virginia and Maryland was repeated in other sections of the South, and the 1850s have even been described as the "golden decade" of the State Agricultural Society of Alabama.[31] Yet, by 1858 there were only seven agricultural societies left in Alabama. The Alabama State Agricultural Society, organized in 1855, reported a life membership of 182 but did not give figures on annual memberships. The Lowndes County Agricultural Society, organized in 1858, reported a membership of only fifty; the other five did not respond to the Patent Office queries.[32] Throughout the South during the 1850s reports of reliance on the one-crop system and of little progress toward diversification continued to overshadow information to the contrary.[33]

The type of diversification that occurred below Virginia aimed at curbing the importation of foodstuffs, rather than at breaking the South's dependence on one or two cash crops. Cornelius O. Cathey's recent study, *Agricultural Developments in North Carolina,* provides a sober reappraisal of the reform movement. Although he refuses to link the state's backwardness to slavery and expresses a pardonable sympathy for the farmers and planters who wrestled with the problems of their day, he concludes that the tempo of change was painfully slow.[34] Similarly, John Hebron Moore reports that high cotton prices in the 1850s weakened the reform movement in Mississippi. Although individual planters continued to do commendable work, and although organized efforts, especially agricultural fairs, led to noteworthy if limited improvements, the organized impulse toward reform, which had appeared in the depressed 1840s, had waned.[35]

❧ *Problems of Diversification*

A glance at the results of the movement for diversification will illustrate the limited gains achieved. Per capita output of corn declined slightly in the slave states during 1850–1860; per capita output of wheat rose but just enough to return to the 1840 level; per capita output of rye rose but was still far below the 1840 level; and per capita output of oats fell sharply for the second consecutive decade.[36] In the Lower South there was a decline in per capita output of each of these crops except wheat, which was not produced in significant quantities.

Agricultural reformers urged that planters grow an adequate supply of food for plantation consumption regardless of the price of staples. In general, they succeeded only where the slave system declined sufficiently to permit the growth of an urban market for foodstuffs or where proximity to the free states permitted the sale of commodities to Northern towns and cities. Where the plantation system remained intact, the reformers had great difficulty in convincing planters to follow their recommendations.

Developments in Mississippi are particularly instructive since it has been claimed that significant advances in corn production occurred in the 1850s. According to Herbert Weaver, corn production in a selected cluster of counties rose by 38 per cent between 1850 and 1860.[37] If we turn instead to state totals and consider the increase in population, the results are quite different: per capita corn production held steady during the decade.[38] In view of the prevailing prosperity, Mississippians probably ate more than before and possibly fed their animals a bit more. Improved implements and machinery increased free-state corn yields substantially during 1850–1860. Despite these considerations, which might have led us to expect improved per capita production, no increase occurred. Weaver, relying on the statistics for improved acreage, claims that at least half the land of the big planters was given over to crops other than cotton, but Fabian Linden, in his critique, notes that census officials defined improved acreage to include land cleared for grass or grazing or lying fallow.[39] The quality of the land is of decisive importance, and the relevant data are unavailable. B. L. C. Wailes, the state geologist and agricultural surveyor, wrote in 1854 that if total corn output were distributed properly it might provide a "scant subsistence" for the farmers and planters of the state, but added that whole areas of the state, especially the northern cotton counties, had to depend on imports from Tennessee and Kentucky.[40]

The slave system made the augmentation of nonstaple production difficult, and the willingness or unwillingness of the planters to diversify was not the major problem. To take slaves away from a single money crop a manager would have had to divide his attention and supervise several operations simultaneously or to rely on drivers of questionable ability and usefulness. The slaves were quick to take advantage and to work even less energetically and skillfully than usual, and planters despaired of making diversification pay. In the words of John D. Ashmore, a cotton planter from the Sumter District of South Carolina:

> In planting corn it is impossible for the master or overseer to be present at the dropping or covering of every hill. I have found the best remedy against irregularity is to select a trusty woman (men are usually engaged at heavier work at this season) who covers, and is consequently present all the time, and hold her responsible not only for her own but for the work of both corn droppers and coverers—in other words to make an overseer of her for the time.[41]

Ashmore was a wise man, but just how could he tell whether or not the work was done properly and just what could "hold her responsible" mean under such circumstances?

Slaveholding wheat growers, especially in the Lower South, found it difficult to compete with Northern farmers, for poor handling and packing generally depreciated the value of the flour.[42] Jonathan N. Herndon, a planter of the Newberry District of South Carolina, indicated that he and other planters in the older areas managed to improve grain production by reducing acreage under cultivation by two-thirds and manuring and cultivating intensively.[43] This program required a small slave force and maximum supervision.

Recent studies show that manuring with nitrogen fertilizer will yield good crops if corn is planted close together and strict attention is paid to the manner of planting corn in rows forty-two inches apart, with seeds separated by eleven to fifteen inches.[44] Antebellum Americans had learned as much for themselves, and Northern farmers planted carefully in two- or three-foot squares. Most Southerners took fewer pains and planted corn in squares of from eight to fifteen or more feet. Carelessness or ignorance may have played a part, but the main reason is to be found in the poor quality of the land provided for crops other than cotton.[45]

Planters assigned their worst land to corn and other non-staple crops. C. G. Parsons saw many acres that produced only four bushels of corn, and in South Carolina eleven bushels was about average.[46] The advanced Capell plantation in Amite County, Mississippi, produced between thirteen and eighteen bushels per acre, and other planters and yeomen who kept records—and these were probably the best—recorded similar amounts or less.[47] In the greater part of Georgia fifteen to twenty bushels of corn per acre was maximum.[48] The cotton counties of Georgia averaged closer to twelve bushels, and the diversified farming counties about eighteen.[49]

Wheat production below Virginia was shifted to land that was even worse than that used for corn. In Georgia, the cotton counties yielded only eight bushels to the acre, and the diversified farming counties ten or twelve.[50] Similar results appeared in other states, although Southerners required enough wheat to arrange for heavy importations.[51] Land given over to hay production proved no better, and Olmsted estimated that Virginia, which was one of the better Southern states in this respect, produced less than one-eighth as much per acre as did New York or Massachusetts.[52]

Despite the problems arising from the inefficiency of the labor force and from the credit system, the plantations theoretically could have at least achieved self-sufficiency in food production. That they did not do so indicates the great strength of the one-crop tendency of the system.[53] The agricultural reformers complained in anguished tones that planters did not even raise enough food for their own use, but the more alert reformers also warned against the danger of producing more than could be consumed on the plantation, for there was usually no market for a surplus.[54] On the one hand, planters wanted to raise enough grain to feed the people on the plantations. On the other hand, they had to be careful not to raise a surplus, for it would go to waste and render the whole operation too costly.

To some extent, the border states took advantage of the Northern market. Tennessee, Kentucky, and Virginia produced large quantities of wheat. While the slave system dominated the South, the regional market remained limited and sufficient capital could not be found to bind the slave states to the free cities of the Northeast. Certain parts of the Upper South did raise corn and pork for the Cotton Belt, which had little to send in return. Increasingly, the border states looked to the widening market of the free states.

The pleas of the reformers for diversification consequently constituted little more than exhortations to pull the South away from the world market toward autarky. With a narrow regional market, progress in the production of foodstuffs necessarily lagged. With greater effort and support the reformers might have made the South self-sufficient in food, but the one-crop system, with its destructive effects upon the soil and the economy, would have been modified only slightly.

The program of the reformers could not have narrowed the growing gap between the economic strength of the free states and the slave states, nor resolved the dilemma of how to retain slavery and yet guarantee the preservation of Southern productive and political power. True diversification depended on new markets, and new markets depended on urbanization. Ironically, the reformers urged an increase in food production in order to strengthen the slave system by cutting down capital exports; but if deprived of their plantation market, the border states would have had to adjust their economy more thoroughly to that of the free states and, possibly, to finance the adjustment by selling their slaves south. The program to save slavery might have hastened its destruction in the Upper South and would have provided only temporary relief to the slaveholders of the Lower South.

🎇 The Labor Shortage in Virginia

The assumption that the reform movement would have proceeded smoothly in a course of natural evolution if the war had not intervened neglects the contradictions in the reform process.[55] The grave effects of slavery in retarding capital formation, providing inefficient labor, and preventing the rise of a home market made the task of the reformers virtually impossible.[56] Unless a conversion to free labor occurred, reform in one area only intensified the difficulties in another.

The success of the reform movement on a significant scale rested on the ability of the planters to fulfill two conditions: they had to accumulate the capital needed to finance reforms, and they had to guarantee closer supervision of the labor force than had occurred previously. The sale of surplus slaves provided the principal method of meeting both conditions simultaneously. These sales raised large amounts of cash and reduced the work force to that size which was best suited to local soil, crop, and managerial circumstances. Craven dates the agricultural revival in Virginia and Maryland from 1820;[57] the date is important, for the demand for slaves to work in the cotton fields of the Lower South rose steadily thereafter.

Slave sales constituted the one sure way to raise large sums quickly. Kentucky and Missouri sold their surplus regularly during the late antebellum period, and the Carolinas and Georgia followed Maryland and Virginia into regular slave exporting before 1830.[58] The sale of surplus slaves did not preclude an absolute rise in the slave population. James C. Bonner, for example, is not altogether correct when, in his excellent study of the reform movement in Hancock County, Georgia, he writes that the number of slaves increased during 1850–1860.[59] The number increased absolutely, not relatively. Although the slave population rose from 7,306 to 8,137 during the decade, it should have risen, if we consider the rate of natural increase, to 9,016; in other words, 879 slaves were sold or taken out of the county, compared with only 182 during 1840–1850. The export of slaves, after dropping from its high of 3,000 during 1830–1840, again began to gain momentum as prosperity returned.[60] These sales produced funds for fertilizer, improved implements, and better breeds of animals.

The writings of J. D. B. De Bow illustrate clearly the economic dilemma facing the slave South. For years he warned against the dangers of a surplus Negro population and stressed the need for sending excess slaves into factories. Yet, in the 1850s he vigorously championed the reopening of the African slave trade as a measure to increase the size of the Southern labor force and to provide the population to guarantee political parity with the free states.[61] De Bow's attempt to maintain both positions typified the efforts of Southern economists, who were unable to resolve the paradox of a simultaneous labor shortage and labor surplus.

In 1844, Nathaniel A. Ware wrote that one-third of the slaves engaged in food production in the Upper South could be removed from agriculture without diminishing total output.[62] Ware had approached the essence of the problem: the South was gripped by a perpetual and deepening case of disguised unemployment. On the one hand, the South suffered from a redundant population, for per capita returns were less than they would have been if the agricultural population had been smaller and better organized; on the other hand, it suffered from underpopulation, for its numbers did not grow fast enough to keep pace with the prerequisites of economic and political power.

Initially, slavery provided the South with an economic advantage, for the importation of cheap black labor compensated for the scarcity of white labor; under conditions of a plentiful and inexpensive labor supply the most effective method of production was the lavish use of labor. Low marginal productivity and disguised unemployment were inherent in this method, and although at first insignificant, they grew increasingly serious as labor became dearer. There was some truth in the observation of an unidentified Southerner who wrote in 1852 that the superiority of Northern agriculture arose not so much from its use of free labor as from prevailing conditions of labor scarcity, which led to the development of labor-saving methods.[63]

Elimination of disguised unemployment must precede industrialization or proceed along with it, although agricultural productivity cannot be raised much above its initial gains unless industry grows and helps improve agricultural technique. An agricultural reorganization that could have raised a prosperous yeomanry in the place of dependent laborers and marginal farmers with minimal purchasing power would have required, above all, the elimination of slavery. The United States was fortunate in having a remarkably favorable geographical position and virgin land with which to lure capital and skilled labor, but the South, once slavery took root, faced a powerful competitor within its national boundaries and found its land quickly absorbed by large slaveholdings. Thenceforth, the South needed more than modest and gradual reforms if it hoped to avoid falling further and further behind.

In 1856, A. L. Scott of Virginia drew attention to a growing labor shortage in his state and argued that if the slave trade were not reopened, agricultural reform would grind to a halt.[64] Others, most notably James H. Hammond, had argued less clearly along the same lines for years. Gray accepts much of this approach and suggests that the high price of slaves made continued agricultural reform difficult, that the substitution of free labor for slave would have been a long and costly process, and that great hardship and stagnation would have accompanied the transition.[65] The latter contention is doubtful, for such a transition was making steady advances in Maryland, where agriculture improved more rapidly than in Virginia. Wherever the reform movement took hold, free labor came into wider use, at least as a supplement to slave labor.[66]

In 1859, Ruffin pointed out that without slave sales to the Lower South the main source of capital accumulation would be shut off and reform would stop. At the same time he feared that continued sales would undermine the slave system in the Upper South.[67] Reform was being impeded by a labor shortage brought about by the depletion of the labor supply, whereas paradoxically, curtailment of the slave exports would have ended hopes for further progress.

This notion of a labor shortage needs clarification. The labor shortage in Virginia essentially consisted of a deficiency of workers with a level of productivity above that of the average slave. Since the economy could maintain only a certain number of small slaveholdings, there were limits, easily reached, beyond which the slave force could not be cut. Virginia needed skilled and semiskilled agricultural and industrial workers who could function in a growing and diversified economy. If the drain of slaves to the Lower South had stopped, the accumulation of capital for further reforms would also have stopped; the paring of the slave force for intensive reforms would have been reversed; and the tendency toward larger holdings would have reasserted itself. A marked concentration in slaveholding did take place in parts of Virginia during the 1850s. In Fauquier County planters (twenty or more slaves) increased their share of the total slave force from 67 to 75 per cent. A tendency toward larger landholdings developed across Virginia's coastal plain.[68]

Thus, the Virginians were damned with or without continued slave exports. The first contradiction in the reform process was manifesting itself: progress based on slavery was narrowly circumscribed; either the economy followed that of Maryland into a pronounced conversion to free labor, or the old difficulties and weaknesses of plantation slavery would reassert themselves with greater force than ever.

The activity and teaching of the Southern agricultural reformers stressed better methods of work as the way to save the slave system. In a sense the successes achieved in Maryland produced a defeat for them by undermining slavery. The force of economic development might have changed the thinking of the South's dominant strata, but given their deep commitment to slavery and everything connected with it, they probably would have refused to tolerate any reform program that spawned an agrarian revolution threatening the social structure of the South's heartland. Consider what surely must have been the reaction to methods such as those of C. C. Baldwin of Rockbridge, Virginia. Baldwin explained the prosperity of his modest sixty-acre farm by reference to his policy of "no domestic restraints" on his slaves, who ate as much as they pleased, had keys to everything, and lived as well as the farm could afford.[69] These slaves were half-free, and the slaveholders as a class could hardly have approved. If the fears of the reformers about the direction of Southern agricultural development approached realization and the South found itself in danger, solutions other than agricultural reform could be called upon. Specifically, the economic gains that ostensibly would accompany secession and political independence presented a constant temptation.

The second contradiction lay in the relationship between slave sales and the ideological exigencies of the slave system. Regardless of whether or not planters deliberately raised slaves for sale, the systematic reduction of the slave force corroded that pride in slaveholding which was so essential to the ideology of slavery. Slaveless and small slaveholding farmers, as well as others in the white middle and lower classes, upon whose loyalty to the slave system the hegemony of the planters depended, would no longer have before them the lure of prestige and power through slaveholding. A road to status and power could be opened by the accumulation of money for its own sake through rational production, as in the free states. The intrusion of bourgeois values so antithetical to plantation society might be fought off in the tradition-bound Virginia tidewater, but for the South as a whole it represented a grave threat to the foundations of slave society and the domination of the slaveholding class.[70]

✂ *An Analysis of Some Counties*

G. W. Featherstonhaugh wrote in the early 1840s that the annexation of Texas would convert the older slave states into a "disgusting nursery" for the production of slaves for sale.[71] Except for an occasional writer like Frederic Bancroft, historians did not treat this view kindly until recently. The appearance of the Conrad-Meyer study of the profitability of slavery[72] has helped to separate the economic question (to what extent did the economy of the older states rest on slave sales?) from the social question (to what extent was slave raising deliberate?). For our immediate purposes only the former question is relevant.

Conrad and Meyer do make some dubious assertions in their discussion: that smallholders who could not produce crops profitably could and did sell surplus slaves to produce regular income, and that only the natural increase in the slave force was being sold out of the border states. First, there is no evidence of such an economic balance between small and large slaveholders in the South; slave buying and selling essentially constituted an interregional business, as they themselves demonstrate. Second, the white population of Maryland rose by 77 per cent during 1830–1860, whereas the slave population declined by 15 per cent; the white population of Delaware rose by 57 per cent, whereas the slave population declined by 45 per cent. Only in Virginia, of the states of the relevant Upper Southeast, did the slave population rise slightly, by 4 per cent, but the white population rose by 51 per cent; clearly, the slave population was declining relative to the emergence rate of white family units.

Ideally, we should like to know the relationship between the net income from agricultural production in the improving counties of the Southeast and the income from slave sales. Unfortunately, no such statistical analysis can be made. First, we can measure the export of slaves from given counties by one of two methods, one of which was used by Bancroft, but we cannot separate the slaves sold from the slaves removed with their masters. Bancroft offered guesses about the ratios in different years, and he may well have been close enough for general purposes, but for quantitative analysis such guesswork is untenable and could convince no one. Second, attempts to measure net income would present all the difficulties encountered in the attempts to measure profitability in the Cotton

Belt, and many more. The economy of the older areas having been more complex, the problems attending such an attempt look—at least at our present state of work—insurmountable.

To get a more precise idea of the situation in the improved counties we shall have to eschew a frontal assault for something less direct. We can compute gross agricultural income for the census years 1850 and 1860, which offer reliable data.[73] Of the twenty-three improved counties under consideration (selected from Maryland, Virginia, and Georgia in accordance with their contemporary reputation and the judgment of historians of Southern agriculture), five showed a decrease in gross agricultural income from 1850 to 1860, eleven showed small to moderate increases, and only seven showed substantial gains.

Hints about the size of slaveholdings and its relationship to income may be gleaned from the figures for white and slave populations during 1830–1860, when the process of reformation was under way. By constructing a schedule of the percentage of slaves to the total population we uncover the following pattern: in Maryland, the percentage of slaves to total population declined in six of the nine counties and remained about the same in the other three (Calvert, Charles, and St. Mary's). In Virginia, the percentage declined in four counties (Fairfax, Hanover, James City, and Prince William), remained about the same in two (Amelia and Prince George). In Georgia, on the other hand, the percentage declined in only one county (Baldwin) and rose in all others. Significantly, of the five counties in which total gross agricultural income declined between 1850 and 1860, three (Clarke, Wilkes, and Oglethorpe—all in Georgia) were among those in which the percentage of slaves increased, whereas a fourth (Charles, Maryland) was one of those in which the percentage remained about the same.

From these data it appears that the areas in which the reform movement was oldest and most thorough had become less dependent on slave selling and more on crop production. Thus white emigration slowed down, and increasing numbers of whites settled down to a more productive agriculture. In the more recently or less thoroughly reformed areas of Georgia, slave selling was still increasing and white farmers were still being driven out in large numbers by low agricultural returns.

The great reform movement failed to produce a healthy agricultural economy based on slave labor. Rather, it seems only to have brought agriculture to the point where slave-holders could live moderately well, especially when aided by the supplementary income from periodic slave sales. Only in areas that had undergone transition for thirty years or so did agricultural production again become a profitable enterprise, and those areas showed a marked shift away from slave labor altogether. Unfortunately, we cannot analyze that shift as closely as we might like to, for there are not enough reliable statistics on such relevant developments as the spread of white tenantry and sharecropping. That such a spread was occurring is beyond doubt.[74]

We are thus confronted with the third and most important contradiction in the reform process: although continued progress rested on the retention of markets for surplus slaves, the advance of the reform movement destroyed those markets. So long as sufficient fertile land existed in the Southwest to permit continuation of the wasteful methods of gang-labor exploitation, the reform movement of the Upper South had room to expand southward. When the Lower South turned its attention to the reconstruction of its agriculture, the markets for slaves had to close, and the whole reform process had to break down. Since reform in one area depended on the maintenance and extension of old, wasteful methods in other areas, a general reformation of Southern agriculture could not take place while slavery was retained.

N O T E S

1 *Soil Exhaustion.* This little book is well known and respected, especially by economic historians, but I am not certain that its enormous influence has been fully appreciated. In several respects it marked a turning point for Southern economic and political history.

2 We may refer, for one of countless examples, to Charles W. Turner's study, "Virginia State Agricultural Societies, 1811–1860," *Agr. Hist.*, XXXVIII (July 1964), 164–77. He cites the president of the state society in 1852 as referring to three current needs: "(1) to encourage youth to practice scientific agriculture; (2) to preserve the institution of slavery; (3) to secure the concern of the General Assembly in order to get them to adopt a farm program" (p. 170).

3 See the preceding studies of productivity, soil exhaustion, and livestock for documentation. In this study I wish to focus on the general movement for reform and the specific movement for crop diversification.

4 Herbert Wender, *Southern Commercial Conventions, 1837–1859* (Baltimore, 1930), pp. 10 f, 15 f, 25, 35 ff; also, *DBR*, I (Jan. 1846), 7–21; XI (July 1851), 30 ff; De Bow, *Industrial Resources*, I, 132; *HMM*, XXXIV (March 1856), 392 f; Weymouth T. Jordan, "Cotton Planters' Conventions in the Old South," *JSH*, XIX (Aug. 1953), 321 ff.

5 Ulrich B. Phillips, "The Central Theme of Southern History," *AHR*, XXXIV (Oct. 1928), 35.

6 *Farmer's Register*, I, No. 11 (1834), 690 ff; V, No. 7, (1837), 429 f; VI, No. 11 (1838), 695–99.

7 Rodney H. True, "The Early Days of the Albemarle (Va.) Agricultural Society," and True (ed.), "The Minute Book of the Albemarle (Va.) Agricultural Society," both

in the *American Historical Association Report for 1918*, Vol. I.

8 Rodney H. True, "The Virginia Board of Agriculture, 1841–1843," *Agr. Hist.* XIV (July 1940), 97–103; *Farmer's Register*, IV, No. 1 (1837), 55–63; IX, No. 5 (1841), 239, 323; X (1842), 232, 241, 257, 298, 335, 383, 512; *Southern Planter* (Richmond, Va.), II (Jan. 1842), 39.

9 Mendenhall, "A History of Agriculture in South Carolina, 1790–1860," p. 305.

10 Computed from data in U.S. Commissioner of Patents, *Report on Agriculture, 1858*, p. 91.

11 *Kentucky Farmer*, I (July 1858), 8. One fair was in Kentucky, the other in Alabama.

12 *Farmer's Register*, III, No. 9, (1838), 575.

13 "Incidents of My Life," unpublished autobiography in Ruffin Papers, III, 223, in the University of North Carolina. Note the experience of James Mallory of Talladega, Ala., Diary, Aug. 5, 1850, papers in the same library.

14 Constitution and Minutes for 1856, pp. 7, 13, in David K. Young Papers in the University of North Carolina.

15 De Bow, *Industrial Resources*, I, 62 f.

16 An increasing number of historians have come to this conclusion in the course of their independent investigations. See the studies of Moore (Mississippi), Jordan (Alabama), and Smith (South Carolina), cited elsewhere.

17 Computed from data in the U.S. Commissioner of Patents, *Report on Agriculture, 1858*, pp. 91–220.

18 See, *e.g.*, the speech of the Rt. Rev. Stephen Elliott, Jr., to the Southern Central Agricultural Society, *Transactions, 1851; cf.* the perceptive remarks of W. J. Cash, *The Mind of the South* (Garden City, N.Y., 1954), p. 45. For similar problems in the slave colonies of the British West Indies see Joseph Lowell Ragatz, *The Fall of the Planter Class in the British Caribbean, 1763–1833* (New York, 1928), pp. 12, 68 ff.

19 See, *e.g.*, Chalmers S. Murray, *This Our Land: The Story of the Agricultural Society of South Carolina* (Charleston, S.C., 1949), pp. 70 f.

20 *DBR*, XIX (Aug. 1855), 223.

21 *Southern Agriculturalist*, IX (Aug. 1836), 411; *Southern Planter* (Richmond, Va.), XV (Jan. 1855), 81. *Cf.* the speech of Garnett Andrews to the Planters' Club of Hancock, Ga., in the *American Agriculturalist*, I (March 1843), 367; and Robert W. Williams, "Thomas Affleck: Missionary to the Planter, the Farmer, and the Gardener," *Agr. Hist.*, XXXI (July 1957), 45 ff.

22 *DBR*, XIV (June 1853), 532.

23 Jacob Edward Pulwers, "Henry Marston, Ante-Bellum Planter and Businessman of East Feliciana," unpublished M.A. thesis, Louisiana State University, 1955, p. 187; Emma Louise McLin Dawes, "Judge Thomas Butler, of Louisiana, A Biographical Study of an Ante-Bellum Jurist and Planter," unpublished M.A. thesis, Louisiana State University, 1953, pp. 77 f.

24 *Journal of the United States Agricultural Society*, I (1853), 263.

25 Ruffin, "Incidents of My Life," II, 47, in his Papers.

26 *Southern Star*, as quoted in *South-Western Monthly*, I (June 1852), 373; Gates, *Farmer's Age*, p. 347.

27 *Southern Cultivator*, V (Jan. 1847), 77.

28 D. M. Dunham, *The History of Agricultural Implements* ("Eighteenth Report to the Maine Board of Agriculture, 1873"), pp. 370 f.

29 Ella Lonn, *Foreigners in the Confederacy* (Chapel Hill, N.C., 1940), p. 17.

30 The most important study is Craven's *Soil Exhaustion*, but see also Kathleen Bruce, "Virginian Agricultural Decline to 1860: A Fallacy," *Agr. Hist.*, VI (Jan. 1932), 3–13; and Charles W. Turner, "Virginia Agricultural Reform, 1815–1860," *Agr. Hist.*, XXVI (July 1952), 80–89.

31 Weymouth T. Jordan, "Agricultural Societies in Ante-Bellum Alabama," *Alabama Review*, IV (Oct. 1951), 241; *cf.* Report of J. A. Whitten of Georgia in the U.S. Commissioner of Patents, *Report on Agriculture, 1847*, pp. 386 ff.

32 U.S. Commissioner of Patents, *Report on Agriculture, 1858*, p. 92.

33 *Cf., e.g.*, Thomas Affleck in *Affleck's Southern Rural Almanack, 1856*, p. 15; South Carolina Mineralogical and Geological Survey, *Report of 1857*, pp. 113 f.

34 *Passim.* This awareness of tempo alone renders doubtful the judgment of at least one reviewer, who said that there was nothing new in an otherwise competent book. On the contrary, Cathey's understanding of the pace at which the movement grew indicates an important break from the now traditional revisionist view. For an earlier, still useful appraisal with similar merit see W. H. Yarbrough, *Economic Aspects of Slavery in Relation to Southern and Southwestern Migration* (Nashville, Tenn., 1932), pp. 54 f.

35 Moore, *Agriculture in Ante-Bellum Mississippi*, p. 91.

36 Computed from the U.S. Census reports for 1840, 1850, and 1860.

37 *Mississippi Farmers* (Nashville, Tenn., 1945), pp. 100 ff.

38 Computed from *Statistical View of the United States, 1850: Compendium of the Seventh Census*, pp. 171 ff; *Eighth Census of the United States, 1860, Agriculture*, pp. 184 ff.

39 Weaver, *Mississippi Farmers*, p. 49; Linden, *JNH*, XXXI (April 1946), 169. Linden also found serious errors in Weaver's calculations.

40 Mississippi Agricultural and Geological Survey, *Report, 1854*, p. 186.

41 Plantation Journal, 1853–1857, p. 72. Typescript in University of North Carolina.

42 *South Carolina Agriculturalist*, I (Aug. 1856), 97. This complaint was rarely heard in Virginia or Maryland, where a smaller slave force made possible closer supervision. When

handled properly, Southern flour was rated high. See the report of Professor L. C. Beck of Rutgers University in the U.S. Commissioner of Patents, *Report on Agriculture, 1848,* pp. 267 f.

43 *Southern Agriculturalist* (Laurensville), I (Aug. 1853), 226.

44 E. John Russell, *Soil Conditions and Plant Growth,* p. 65.

45 *Arator,* I (Nov. 1855), 235; *Farmer and Planter,* II (March 1851), 30; Southern Central Agricultural Society, *Transactions,* p. 205; Moore, *Agriculture in Ante-Bellum Mississippi,* p. 116.

46 Parsons, *Inside View of Slavery,* p. 81; Hinton R. Helper, *The Impending Crisis of the South: How to Meet It* (New York, 1857), pp. 69 ff; *Carolina Planter,* I (Feb. 5, 1840), 25 f.

47 Capell Diary, p. 124 and Account Book, back of cover page; also John Houston Bills Diary, III (July 20 and Sept. 15, 1859) and Columbus Morrison Journal and Accounts, 1845–1862, Dec. 31, 1845, in the University of North Carolina.

48 See the report of Dr. J. A. Whitten of Hancock County, Ga., in the American Institute of the City of New York, *Annual Report, 1847.*

49 Data for the amount of corn produced per acre was found in Schedule IV ("Social Statistics") of the manuscript census returns. Why these data were not included in the Agricultural Schedules is not clear, and they seem to have been overlooked by historians. According to Gray, *History of Agriculture,* I, 531–35, the following counties were typical of the upland cotton area: Coweta, Hancock, Newton, Thomas, Dougherty, Houston, Monroe, and Sumter; the following were typical diversified farming counties: Gordon, Floyd, Chatooga.

50 See note 49 above. The cotton counties were Troup, Monroe, Hancock, Newton, Stewart; the farming counties were Gordon, Walker, Floyd, Chatooga, Cobb, and Hall.

51 U.S. Commissioner of Patents, *Report on Agriculture, 1852,* p. 73. Emerson David Fite estimates that the slave

states imported ten million bushels annually from the North. If so, the South annually spent more than eleven million dollars for wheat. See *Social and Industrial Conditions in the North During the Civil War* (New York, 1910), p. 18, n. 1.

52 Olmsted, *Journey in the Seaboard Slave States*, pp. 44, 166; Ashmore Plantation Journal, April 27, 1857; William Massie Papers, June 27, 1841, in Duke University; *Farmer and Planter*, II (Feb. 1841), 4.

53 *E.g.*, on Rome see Tenney Frank (ed.), *An Economic Survey of Ancient Rome* (5 vols.; Baltimore, 1933–40), I, 68 f, 162 f. On the British West Indies see Frank Wesley Pitman, *JNH*, XI (Oct. 1926), 585. The Jesuit colonies in Brazil and Paraguay would seem to have been an exception, but they were basically feudal rather than slave: see João Dornas Filho, *A Escravadão no Brasil*, pp. 28 f; Oreste Popescu, *El Sistema Económico en las Misiones Jesuíticas* (Bahia Blanca, 1952), pp. 11 f, 41, 57, 114.

54 See *infra.*, Chapter VII.

55 See the works previously cited of Craven, Jordan, Bruce, and Smith, and two important articles by James C. Bonner: "Advancing Trends in Southern Agriculture," *Agr. Hist.*, XXII (Oct. 1948), 248–59, and "Profile of a Late Ante-Bellum Community," *AHR*, XLIX (July 1944), 663–80.

For a criticism of the work of Cathey, Smith, Moore, and Jordan see Eugene D. Genovese, "Recent Contributions to the Economic Historiography of the Slave South," *Science & Society*, XXIV (Winter 1960), 53–66.

56 On the problem of markets see *infra.*, Chapter VII, and the critique by Alfred H. Conrad and John R. Meyer in their polemical postscript to *The Economics of Slavery*, pp. 223–36.

57 *Soil Exhaustion*, pp. 122 f.

58 Gray errs in assuming that South Carolina did not export slaves until 1850 (*History of Agriculture*, II, 651). Alfred Glaze Smith, Jr., indicates that there is evidence of large exports as early as 1830, and a statistical reconstruction based

on the method contained in the last chapter of Frederic Bancroft's *Slave Trading in the Old South* (New York, 1959) will bear him out. See Smith's *Economic Readjustment of an Old Cotton State: South Carolina, 1820–1860* (Columbia, S.C., 1958). For the upper Southwest see H. A. Trexler, *Slavery in Missouri, 1804–1865* (Baltimore, 1914), pp. 47 f, and Ivan F. McDougle, *Slavery in Kentucky, 1792–1865* (Lancaster, Ky., 1918), pp. 15–19.

59 *AHR*, XLIX (July 1944), 666.

60 For the method used in these computations see the last chapter of Bancroft's *Slave Trading*.

61 De Bow's shift is traced in Robert F. Durden, "J. D. B. De Bow: Convolutions of a Slavery Expansionist," *JSH*, XVII (Nov. 1951), 441–61, and Joseph Dorfman, *The Economic Mind in American Civilization* (London, 1947), II, 950. Neither explores the implications of the contradiction. *Cf.* De Bow, *Industrial Resources*, II, 314. The only biography of De Bow, Ottis C. Skipper's *J. D. B. De Bow: Magazinist of the Old South* (Athens, Ga., 1958), does not mention the problem.

62 *Notes on Political Economy as Applicable to the United States by a "Southern Planter"* (New York, 1844), p. 30. That Ware did not develop his insights concerning Southern weakness is perhaps explained by his "national view of economics." His analysis of labor intensity had a national rather than a state or regional focus. See William Diamond, "Nathaniel A. Ware, National Economist," *JSH*, V (Nov. 1939), 501–26, esp. 514–15.

63 In U.S. Commissioner of Patents, *Report on Agriculture, 1852*, p. 379.

64 *Proceedings of the Southern Convention Held in Savannah, Georgia, Dec. 1856*, Supplement to *De Bow's Review* (New Orleans, 1857), p. 211.

65 *History of Agriculture*, II, 691, 931 f.

66 *Cf.* Craven, *Soil Exhaustion*, p. 158; Bonner, *AHR*, XLIX (July 1944), 667 ff; Cornelius O. Cathey, "Sidney Weller:

Ante-Bellum Promoter of Agricultural Reform," *NCHR*, XXI (Jan. 1954), 1–17.

67 *DBR*, XXVI (June 1859), 650.

68 *Cf.* Fields, "The Agricultural Population of Virginia, 1850–1860," pp. 111 and *passim*.

69 *Southern Planter*, XII (Aug. 1852), 243.

70 These several last paragraphs imply a number of theses on the nature of antebellum slave society that cannot properly be defended here. For a preliminary statement see *infra*, Chapter I.

71 *Excursion Through the Slave States* (2 vols.; London, 1844), II, 189.

72 *Economics of Slavery*, pp. 43–92. Matthew B. Hammond, in *The Cotton Industry. An Essay in American Economic History* (New York, 1897), p. 634, wrote: "Slaves were seldom kept in Virginia and Maryland for the sake of raising crops, but crops were often cultivated for the sake of raising slaves." His statement has usually been treated as an absurd exaggeration, but with qualifications and in less sweeping form it is essentially accurate. Brazilian slaveholders were delightfully frank: "The most productive feature of slave property," said a slaveholders' manifesto, "is the generative belly." Quoted in Gilberto Freyre, *The Masters and the Slaves* (2nd English language ed., rev.; New York, 1956), p. 324.

73 The counties are as follows:

In Maryland: Dorchester, Queen Anne, Somerset, Worcester, Prince George, Anne Arundel, Calvert, Charles, and St. Mary's.

In Virginia: Fairfax, James City, Hanover, Prince George, Charles City, Amelia, Fauquier, and Prince William.

In Georgia: Baldwin, Clarke, Hancock, Oglethorpe, Putnam, and Wilkes.

These counties were well known as reforming counties. See Craven, *Soil Exhaustion*, pp. 143, 151 and *passim;* Bancroft, *Slave Trading*, p. 129; Paul Murray, "Agriculture in the Interior of Georgia, 1830–1860," *GHQ*, XIX (Dec. 1935), 295; U.S. Commissioner of Patents, *Report on Agriculture, 1851*, pp. 274 f. For the prices used to translate the amounts reported in the census returns into values, see my unpublished doctoral dissertation, "The Limits of Agrarian Reform in the Slave South," Columbia University, 1959, Appendix III.

74 Cf. Fields, "Agricultural Population," pp. 58 f, 181; Mendenhall, "History of Agriculture in South Carolina," pp. 224 ff; Bonner, *AHR*, XLIX (July 1944), *passim;* and Richard B. Morris, "The Measure of Bondage in the Slave States," *MVHR*, XLI (Sept. 1954), 219–40.

PART THREE ✖ THE SUBSERVIENCE OF TOWN TO COUNTRY

It must be considered that there is nothing more difficult to carry out, nor more doubtful of success, nor more dangerous to handle, than to initiate a new order of things. For the reformer has enemies in all those who profit by the old order, and only lukewarm defenders in all those who would profit by the new order, this lukewarmness arising partly from fear of their adversaries, who have the laws in their favor; and partly from the incredulity of mankind, who do not truly believe in anything new until they have had actual experience of it.

■ NICCOLÒ MACHIAVELLI, *The Prince*

Seven ■ The Significance of the Slave Plantation for Southern Economic Development

Historians are no longer sure that plantation slavery produced the economic woes of the Old South. The revisionists' doubts rest on two propositions of dubious relevance: that slave labor could have been applied successfully to pursuits other than the raising of plantation staples; and that slave agriculture possibly generated as high a rate of profit as alternative industries and cannot be held responsible for the unwillingness of Southerners to use their funds more wisely.[1] The first proposition confuses slave labor and its direct effects with the slave system and its total effects; the latter is at issue, with the versatility of slave labor a secondary consideration. The second rests on the assumption that the master-slave relationship was purely economic and not essentially different from an employer-worker relationship. Yet, when confronted with the issue direct, who could deny that slavery gave rise to a distinct politics, ideology, and pattern of social behavior and that these had immense economic consequences?

We need not examine at the moment the precise relationship

between slavery and the plantation. Certainly, plantation economies presuppose considerable compulsion, if only of the *de facto* type now prevalent in parts of Latin America. The historical fact of an antebellum plantation-based slave economy is our immediate concern, although, undoubtedly, postbellum developments preserved some of the retardative effects of slavery.

Those retardative effects were too many even to be summarized here. A low level of capital accumulation, the planters' high propensity to consume luxuries, a shortage of liquid capital aggravated by the steady drain of funds out of the region, the low productivity of slave labor, the need to concentrate on a few staples, the anti-industrial, anti-urban ideology of the dominant planters, the reduction of Southern banking, industry, and commerce to the position of auxiliaries of the plantation economy—all these are familiar and yet need restudy in the light of the important work being done on the economics of underdeveloped areas. For the present let us focus on another factor, which in itself provides an adequate explanation of the South's inability to industrialize: the retardation of the home market for both industrial and agricultural commodities.

Thirty years ago Elizabeth W. Gilboy complained that economic historians studying the process of industrialization concerned themselves too much with supply and not enough with demand.[2] Her complaint was justified despite brilliant work on the problem of markets by a few outstanding men from Karl Marx to R. H. Tawney and Paul Mantoux. Since then, demand has received much more attention, although possibly not so much as it deserves. Important essays by Maurice Dobb, Simon Kuznets, H. J. Habakkuk, and Gunnar Myrdal, among others, have helped to correct the imbalance,[3] as has new research on European industrialization and the economics of underdeveloped countries. If there is one lesson to be learned from the experience of both developed and underdeveloped countries, it is that industrialization is unthinkable without an agrarian revolution which shatters the old regime on the countryside. While the peasantry remains tied to the land, burdened with debt, and limited to minimal purchasing power, the labor recruitment and market preconditions for extensive manufacturing cannot emerge. "Land reform"—that is, an agrarian revolution—constitutes the essential first step in the creation of an urban working class, the reorganization of agriculture to feed growing cities, and the development of a home market.

Of the several ways in which agricultural reorganization can provide markets for manufactures, we may consider two. First, when the laborers are separated from the land, as during the English enclosures, they necessarily increase the demand for clothing and other essentials formerly produced at home. Paradoxically, this expansion of the market does not preclude a marked reduction in the laborers' standard of living. Second, the farmers left on the countryside to produce for growing urban markets provide an increased demand for textiles, agricultural equipment, and other commodities.

The North rose on the rapid expansion of the rural market, whereas the South remained dominated by slave plantations until a predatory foe interested in a new system of rural exploitation imposed a reorganization from without. An adequate home market could not grow in the antebellum South and has evolved slowly and painfully during the last century.

❊ *The Nature of the Market*

In 1860 about 75 per cent of the South's cotton crop went abroad; during no antebellum year did the grain exports of the United States exceed 5 per cent of the total crop. No doubt, cotton profits helped finance the economic growth of the

United States, but the question is, were the profits siphoned off to build up the Northern economy? The credit mechanisms alone, to a considerable extent, had such an effect. The South's dependence on the export trade, in contradistinction to the North's primary reliance on its home market, indicates not merely a social division of labor but the economic exploitation of the exporting South.

Robert G. Albion, in his excellent examination of the colonial bondage of the South to the North, concludes that the South's lack of direct trade with Europe constituted an irrational arrangement secured by the impudence of New York's aggressive entrepreneurs. We can agree that had the South imported from abroad as much as the North and West, there could have been no sensible reason to route through New York either the South's cotton or its share of European goods, but the assumption made by Albion, and by such contemporaries as George McDuffie and T. P. Kettell, of a rough equality of imports cannot be substantiated. The South's total market for manufactured goods did not match that of the free states; although the South depended upon Europe as well as the North for manufactured goods, its imports from Europe were smaller in value than imports into the North and West and smaller in bulk than the staples it exported. If the ships carrying cotton had sailed from Southern ports direct to Europe and back, they would have had to return in ballast.[4] New York's domination of the Southern market was therefore not accidental. If the South's share in American imports had been as Albion suggests, and if the coastal trade had been as large as he implies, the greater part of the goods sent from New Orleans to the plantation areas would have originated in Europe and been reshipped through New York rather than being, as we know to have been the case, of Western origin.[5]

Albion's acceptance of the assumption of nearly equal imports surprises all the more in view of the evidence of restricted

Southern demand. The Southern cotton, iron, paper, wool, and railroad industries—to mention a few—struggled with indifferent results against a low level of Southern patronage. Antislavery leaders like Henry Ruffner and Cassius M. Clay made slavery's effects on a home market a cardinal point in their indictment. Thoughtful proslavery Southerners also commented frequently on the market problem. The opinion of the editor of the *Southern Agriculturalist* in 1828 that the South lacked sufficient customers to sustain a high level of manufacturing echoed throughout the antebellum period. The speech of Colonel Andrew P. Calhoun to the Pendleton, South Carolina, Farmers' Society in 1855, for example, had a similar tone and content. On the other side, someone like Beverley Tucker would occasionally argue that Northerners would never risk a war "which, while it lasted, would shut them out from the best market in the world."[6] It is difficult to imagine that many, even those who adopted such arguments for political purposes, took seriously a proposition so palpably false.

Alfred Glaze Smith, Jr., and Douglass C. North have traced the low level of Southern demand, in part, to plantation self-sufficiency. This view is not borne out by the data in the manuscript census returns from the Cotton Belt, which reveal only trivial amounts of home manufactures on even the largest plantations and which bear out the judgments of Rolla M. Tryon and Mary Elizabeth Massey on the weakness of Southern household industry.[7] In De Soto and Marshall counties, Mississippi, the big planters (thirty-one or more slaves) averaged only $76 worth of home manufactures in 1860, and farmers and small planters averaged much less. In Dougherty and Thomas counties, Georgia, the small planters (twenty-one to thirty slaves) led other groups of slaveholders with $127, and the big planters produced only about half as much. Most of the planters in both clusters of counties recorded no home manufactures at all.[8] Sample studies from Virginia's tobacco area, wheat area, and tidewater reveal the same. Plantation manuscripts show surprisingly frequent and often large expenditures for artisans' services and suggest that plantations were much less self-sufficient and exhibited much less division of labor than is generally appreciated.[9] The root of the insufficient demand must be sought in the poverty of the rural majority composed of slaves, subsistence farmers, and poor whites.

The United States, both North and South, suffered from a deficiency of both capital and labor during the nineteenth century. Farmers, who provided a large market for goods and tools, spurred industrial development, and manufacturing rose on the foundation of this immense rural demand. Eastern manufacturers gradually awoke to their dependence on this rural market and by 1854 were supporting homestead legislation not only to gain support for higher tariffs and for purposes of speculation but to expand the market for their goods. Farmers in New England saw their futures linked with industrial development, and their hostility toward commercial middlemen was not usually transferred to the manufacturers.[10] The same was true in the West. As the shrewd Achille Murat noted in the 1830s, the manufacturing interest of the West "is not constituted by the manufactories which exist, but by those which they look forward to in prospective."[11] An agrarianism uncompromisingly hostile to industry and urbanization—to "manufacturing as a system"—existed only in the South and cannot be separated from the ideological leadership of the slaveholding planters. Even there, those seriously interested in economic progress saw the link between agricultural reform and industrialization and tried to work out proposals for increased manufactures that would be palatable to their fellow slaveholders.[12]

The West could import capital because Eastern manufacturers and European creditors had confidence in her growth and prosperity. Outside credits at that time had to be accumulated by the importation of commodities and the maintenance of an unfavorable trade balance. The immense internal market guaranteed the West an import surplus until 1850. Its insatiable demand for manufactured articles contributed to the unfavorable trade balance of the United States, but on the whole this problem was not a serious one for the country. American importers had enough strength to obtain long-term credits on relatively easy terms, and during the 1850s profits from shipping and other invisible gains largely restored the balance.[18] Thus, on the one hand, the national economy had the resources to overcome the worst effects of a trade deficit, and on the other hand, the agrarian West could obtain the credits required for industrial development. The South did not benefit from this arrangement. It provided an exportable surplus, which although of great help to the national economy in offsetting the large quantity of imports, fell prey to Northern capital. Those invisible gains so important to national growth were made partly at the expense of the South.

The population statistics for 1860 offer a clue to the structure of the market. If we exclude Maryland, in which slavery was declining, and Delaware, which was a slave state in name only, the median population per square mile in the slave states was 18, and Kentucky was high with 31. In comparison, Massachusetts had a population of 158 per square mile; Rhode Island, 138; Connecticut, 98; New York, 84; New Jersey, 81; and so forth. In the West, Ohio had 59; Indiana, 40; and Illinois, 31.

These figures do not tell the important part of the story. A country that is sparsely settled, in absolute terms, may have a high population density, in economic terms, if its systems of transportation and commodity production are well developed and integrated. The Northern states in 1860, for example, had a much higher population density—from an economic point of view—than the thickly populated countries of Asia. The superiority of Northern transportation and economic integration, relative to those of the South, meant that the difference in the magnitude of the market greatly exceeded that suggested by the population figures.

Historians, since the pioneering researches of Ulrich B. Phillips, have appreciated that the Southern transportation system tied the staple-producing areas to the ports and that this was the best possible arrangement for the planters. The planters controlled the state legislatures in an era in which state participation was proving decisive in railroad construction and generally refused to assume the tax burden necessary to open the back country and thereby encourage and strengthen politically suspect farmers. Without a fully developed railroad network tying the South into an economic unit, the absorption of nonstaple producers into the market economy, except in a peripheral way, was impossible. Poor transportation, for example, contributed toward the retardation of the Southern cotton textile industry.[14]

With good reason alert Southerners spoke of the connection between railroads, markets, diversified agriculture, and manufacturing. James Robb pointedly described improved transportation and greater industry as necessary ingredients in the process of unifying the South. Oscar M. Lieber noted that without an adequate transportation system South Carolina's farmers could not enter the market as corn producers. Senator John Bell of Tennessee warmly supported federal land grants to railroads to strengthen the bonds of commodity production.[15] Within the South these men could, at best, expect to be received with an impatient silence. Their message sometimes gained attention in the Upper South, as for example in what came to be West Virginia; the subsequent construction of road and railroad links to existing markets generally bound parts of the Upper South to the free states and helped remove them from the slaveholders' domain.

In the slave South the home market consisted primarily of the plantations, which bought foodstuffs from the West and manufactured goods from the East. The planters needed increased Southern manufacturing, but only for certain purposes. They needed cheap slave clothing, cotton gins and a few crude agricultural implements, rope for cotton bagging, and other such items. This narrow market could not compare with the tremendous Western demand for industrial commodities of all kinds, especially for agricultural implements and machinery on the more capital-intensive Western farms. The Northeast had the capital and skilled labor for fairly large-scale production and had established its control over existing markets in the North and West. Southern manufacturers could not hope to compete with Northern outside the South, and the same conditions that brought about Northern control of the Northern market made possible Northern penetration of the Southern market despite its costs of transportation.

The South found itself in a dilemma similar to that facing many underdeveloped countries today. On the one hand, it provided a market for outside industry. On the other hand, that very market was too small to sustain industry on a scale large enough to compete with outsiders who could draw upon wider markets. Only one-fifth of the manufacturing establishments of the United States operated in the South, and their average capitalization was well below that of the manufacturing establishments of the free states. Consider the situation in two industries of special importance to the South—cotton textiles and agricultural implements. New England had almost three times as many cotton factories as the entire South in 1860, and yet the average capitalization was almost twice as great. The concentration in this industry had proceeded so far by 1850 that of the more than one thousand cotton factories in the United States only forty-one had half the total capital investment. As for the agricultural implement and machinery industry, New York, Pennsylvania, Ohio, and Illinois each had a greater total capital investment than did the entire South, and in three of these the average capitalization was between two and two-and-a-half times as great as the average in the South.[16] This Northern advantage led Edmund Ruffin and Thomas L. Clingman, among others, to look forward to a Southern Confederacy protected by high tariffs against Northern goods.[17]

Data on the cotton textile industry almost invariably reveal that Southern producers concentrated upon the production of the cheapest and coarsest kind of cloth to be used in the making of slave clothing.[18] Even so, local industrialists had to compete for this market with Northerners who sometimes shipped direct and sometimes established Southern branches and who had facilities for the collection and processing of second-hand clothing.[19] Just as New England supplied most of the South's "Negro cloth," so did it supply much of the boots and shoes. For example, Batchellor Brothers of Brookfield, Massachusetts, produced cheap shoes especially for the Southern market and as early as 1837 opened a branch at Mobile to consolidate its Southern market.[20]

Producers of better cotton goods had little hope of making a living in the South. Occasionally, a William Gregg could penetrate Northern markets successfully, but Southern demand for such goods remained too small to have much effect on the industry generally. Northern firms like the Pepperell Manufacturing Company or the A. A. Lawrence Company did little business in the South. On the other hand, a rising demand for textiles in the agrarian West had greatly influenced the New England cotton industry since 1814.[21]

The Southern iron industry, hampered by restricted railroad development in the slave states, also had its troubles. American iron producers generally faced the handicap of large importations of railroad iron. The small scale of operations and resultant cost schedules, which hurt the industry nationally, hit the Southern manufacturers especially hard. Dependent upon a weak local market, Southern iron manufacturers had great difficulty holding their own even during the prosperous 1850s.

No wonder the Augusta, Georgia, Commercial Convention added to its demand that Southerners buy Southern goods the qualification, "unless you can get Northern cheaper." And no wonder the proposal was ridiculed as amounting to "Never kiss the maid if you can kiss the mistress, unless you like the maid better."[22]

✄ *The Size of the Rural Market*

We cannot measure precisely the extent of the Southern market nor even make a reliable, general, quantitative comparison between the Southern and Western rural markets, but we can glean from various sources some notion of the immense difference. For example, Phelps, Dodge & Co., a prominent cotton-shipping firm that also distributed metals, tools, machinery, clothing, and an assortment of other items, reported at the beginning of the Civil War that only 5 per cent of its sales went south and that those went primarily to the noncotton states. We do not know the extent of the firm's participation in the cotton export trade, but it was considerable. Phelps, Dodge & Co. was in an excellent position to exchange industrial goods for cotton, but the Southern demand for imported goods could not compare in bulk or value with the supply of cotton.

In the West, on the other hand, farmers and townsmen provided a growing and lucrative market, and the firm had more customers in Ohio than in any other state except New York.[23]

An examination of the manuscript census returns for 1860 and other primary sources pertaining to two representative cotton counties in Mississippi and to two in Georgia permits us to judge roughly the extent of the market in the Cotton Belt by estimating the expenditures made by planters and farmers in these counties. (See note 8, p. 175.) The estimates are the most generous possible and exaggerate the extent of the Southern rural market in relation to the Western in two ways: there were far more rural poor with little or no purchasing power in the Cotton Belt than in the West, and the concentration of landholdings in the South resulted in fewer landowners than could be found in a Western area of comparable size. Thus, even if the estimate of the expenditures made by these Southern planters and farmers had been larger than the expenditures of a similar group of individual proprietors in the West, the total purchased in each county would still have been much less than in a comparable Western area. Since Southern expenditures consisted, to a considerable extent, of food purchases, the market for industrial commodities was much smaller than might appear.

The concentration of landholding and slaveholding in the Mississippi counties meant that 6 per cent of the landowners commanded one-third of the gross income and probably a much higher percentage of the net. That is, the majority of landowners received a disproportionately small portion of the total income accruing to the cotton economy as a whole.

Only the largest planters—10 per cent of the landowners—spent more than one thousand dollars a year for food and supplies, and they rarely spent more. These expenditures include the total purchases for the slaves. The slaveholding farms and plantations in Mississippi annually spent about thirty or thirty-five dollars per person for food and supplies; nonslaveholders spent about twenty-five dollars per person. In Georgia, slave-holding farms and plantations spent about twenty-five dollars per person, and nonslaveholders were just about self-sufficient.[24] In contrast, Philip S. Foner reports that contemporary newspapers and other sources indicate that the small farmers who made up the great majority of the rural population of the West accumulated store bills of from one hundred to six hundred dollars.[25] Even if we allow for considerable exaggeration and assume that the accounts were generally closer to the lower estimate, these figures, which are exclusive of cash purchases, mail orders, payments to drummers, and so forth, are at least a clue to the impressive purchasing power of the Western countryside.

However imprecise the estimates for the South may be, they indicate the lack of purchasing power among the rural population of the Cotton Belt and demonstrate how greatly the situation differed there from that in the West. With such a home market the slave economy could not sustain more than the lowest level of commodity production apart from that of a few staples. The success of William Gregg as a textile manufacturer in South Carolina and the data produced by Professor John Hebron Moore showing that a cotton textile industry could and did exist in antebellum Mississippi seem to contradict this conclusion; but Gregg, who was aware of the modest proportions of the home market, warned Southerners against trying to produce for local needs and suggested that they focus on the wholesale market. His own company at Graniteville, South Carolina, produced fine cotton goods that sold much better in New York than in the South. Gregg's success in the Northern market could not easily be duplicated by others, and when he discussed the Southern market, he felt compelled, as did B. L. C. Wailes and other astute observers, to advocate production of cheap cotton goods for the plantations.[26] Moore's conclusion that his data prove the adaptability of manufacturing to the Lower South requires for substantiation more than evidence of particular successes, no matter how impressive;[27] it requires evidence that Southern producers had enough strength to drive out Northern competition and, more important, that the market was large enough to sustain more than a few firms.

The plantation system did have its small compensations for industry. The planters' taste for luxuries, for example, proved a boon to the Petersburg, Virginia, iron industry, which supplied plantations with cast-iron fences, lawn ornaments, balconies, fancy gates, and other decorative articles.[28] A silk industry emerged briefly but was destroyed by climatic conditions as well as by a shortage of capital.[29] The hemp industry, which supplied rope for cotton baling, depended heavily on the plantation market.

Some Southern industrialists, especially those in the border states, did good business in the North. Louisville tobacco and hemp manufacturers sold much of their output in Ohio. Botts and Burfoot of Richmond, Virginia, reported the sale of $1,000 worth of straw cutters in the North during a six-month period. The more successful Southern iron producers worked in the Upper South and sold outside the slave states. Smith and Perkins of Alexandria, Virginia, began production of locomotives and railroad cars in the 1850s and obtained a good many orders from the North. The company failed because shipping costs made consolidation of its Northern market difficult and because only a few orders came from the South to take up the slack. Similarly, the paper industry in South Carolina did well until the 1850s, when Northern orders dropped and no substantial Southern orders appeared.[30]

The political dangers of these links with the free states did not escape the slaveholders. The Virginia Commercial Convention reported that West Virginia was being cut off from the South in this way.[31] During the Civil War, William Henry Holcombe, a thoughtful doctor living in Natchez, listed in his diary various reasons for the adherence of the border states to the Union and placed close commercial ties high on the list.[32] There was more than hindsight here, for politically sophisticated Southerners sensed the danger well before 1861. But what could they have done about it?

❖ The Urban Market for Foodstuffs

The inability of the South to generate an adequate rural market inhibited industrialization and urbanization, which in turn limited the market for agricultural produce and undermined attempts at diversification. With the exception of New Orleans and Baltimore the slave states had no large cities, and few reached the size of 15,000. The urban population of the South could not compare with that of the Northeast, as is generally appreciated, but more to the point, it could not compare with that of the agrarian West either. The urban population of the Lower South in 1860 was only 7 per cent of the total population, and in the western part of the Lower South, embracing most of the Cotton Belt, there was a relative decline during the preceding twenty years. In New England the percentage was 37; in the Middle Atlantic states, including Ohio, 35; and perhaps most significantly, in Indiana, Illinois, Michigan, and Wisconsin, 14.[33]

Even these figures do not tell the full story of the underdevelopment of the South's urban market. If we except New Orleans, which was a special case, three cities of the Lower South had a population of 15,000 or more: Mobile, Charleston, and Savannah, with a combined population of 92,000. Of this number, 37 per cent were slaves and free Negroes, who may be assumed to have represented only minimal purchasing power. In the 1850s, American families certainly did not spend less than 40 per cent of their incomes on food, and the importance of a large urban market for foodstuffs may be judged accordingly.[34]

Southern authorities on agriculture pointed repeatedly to the pernicious effects of a limited home market. Eugene W. Hilgard, state geologist of Mississippi, explained his state's failure to develop a cattle industry largely by the absence of local markets. Oscar M. Lieber, state geologist of South Carolina, warned farmers in a state that was never comfortably self-sufficient in corn not to produce more corn than they could consume, for there was no place to market the surplus. Charles Yancey of Buckingham County, Virginia, wrote that planters and farmers would not grow oats because the only possibility of disposing of them lay in person-to-person barter.[35]

The weakness of the market for agricultural produce had many detrimental consequences for the South, of which we may mention only two. First, those sections of the border states which found markets in the Northern cities increasingly moved into the political-economic orbit of the free states at the moment when the slave states required maximum solidarity to preserve their system. Second, the weakness of the market doomed the hopes of the agricultural reformers and transformed their cry for diversification into a cry for a backward step toward natural economy.

When that great antislavery Kentuckian, Cassius M. Clay, finally receives from historians the honor and attention that he deserves, he will surely be recognized as one of the most penetrating commentators on the economics of slavery. Consider his remarks on the problem of markets, with which we are presently concerned:

Lawyers, merchants, mechanics, laborers, who are your consumers; Robert Wickliffe's two hundred slaves? How many clients do you find, how many goods do you sell, how many hats, coats, saddles, and trunks do you make for these two hundred slaves? Does Mr. Wickliffe lay out as much for himself and his two hundred slaves as two hundred freemen do? . . . All our towns dwindle, and our farmers lose, in consequence, all home markets. Every farmer bought out by the slave system sends off the consumers of the manufacturers of the town: when the consumers are gone, the mechanic must go also. . . . A home market cannot exist in a slave state.[36]

Plantation slavery so limited the purchasing power of the South that it could not sustain much industry. That industry which could be raised usually lacked a home market of sufficient scope to permit large-scale operation; the resultant cost of production often became too high for success in competition with Northern firms drawing on much wider markets. Without sufficient industry to support urbanization, a general and extensive diversification of agriculture was unthinkable. Whatever other factors need to be considered in a complete analysis, the low level of demand in this plantation-based slave society was sufficient to retard the economic development of the South.

NOTES

1 *Cf.*, *e.g.*, Robert R. Russel, *JSH*, IV (Feb. 1938), 34–54, or the more recent statement by Conrad and Meyer, *JPE*, LXVI (April 1958), 95–130. Curiously, Russel was one of

the first to challenge the assumption of men like T. P. Kettell that the South imported as much as the North. His *Economic Aspects of Southern Sectionalism, 1840–1861* (New York, 1960; first published, 1924), contains much valuable material and many excellent insights on the weaknesses of the South's home market.

2 "Demand as a Factor in the Industrial Revolution," in *Facts and Factors in Economic History: Articles by the Former Students of Edwin F. Gay* (Cambridge, Mass., 1932), pp. 620–39.

3 Dobb, *Studies*, pp. 6 ff, 87 ff, 98 ff, 290–96; Kuznets, "Toward a Theory of Economic Growth," in Robert Lekachman (ed.), *National Policy for Economic Welfare at Home and Abroad* (New York, 1955), pp. 12–77; Habakkuk in Dupriez (ed.), *Economic Progress*, pp. 149–69; Myrdal, *Rich Lands and Poor*, esp. pp. 23–38.

4 Albion, *Rise of New York Port* and *Square-Riggers on Schedule*. For similar arguments by contemporaries see De Bow, *Industrial Resources*, I, 125, 365, and *DBR*, IV (1847), 208–25, 339, 351. For a perceptive Northern reply see [Daniel Lord], *The Effects of Secession upon the Commercial Relations Between the North and South and upon Each Section* (New York, 1861), p. 15. For the weakness of the Southern import trade see George Rogers Taylor, *The Transportation Revolution, 1815–1860* (New York, 1951), p. 198; Philip S. Foner, *Business & Slavery* (Chapel Hill, N.C., 1941), pp. 6–7; and Samuel Eliot Morison, *The Maritime History of Massachusetts, 1783–1860* (Boston, 1921), pp. 298–99. Many of the lines carrying cotton from Northern ports were deeply involved in bringing immigrants to the United States. These immigrants, too, helped guarantee that ships returning from Europe could escape being in ballast. John G. B. Hutchins, *The American Maritime Industries and Public Policy, 1789–1914* (Cambridge, Mass., 1941), pp. 262–63.

5 Emory R. Johnson *et al.*, *History of the Domestic and Foreign Commerce of the United States* (2 vols.; Washington, D.C., 1915), I, 242; R. B. Way, "The Commerce

of the Lower Mississippi in the Period 1830–1860," Mississippi Valley Historical Association, *Proceedings*, X (1918–1919), 62; Louis Bernard Schmidt, "The Internal Grain Trade of the United States, 1850–1860," *Iowa Journal of History and Politics*, XVIII (Jan. 1920), 110–11.

6 *Southern Agriculturalist* (Charleston, S.C.), I (Sept. 1828), 404; *Farmer and Planter*, VI (Dec. 1855), 270–71; *SQR*, XVIII (Sept. 1850), 218.

7 Smith, *Economic Readjustment*, p. 134; North, *The Economic Growth of the United States, 1790–1860* (Englewood Cliffs, N.J., 1961), pp. 132–33; Tryon, *Household Manufactures in the United States*; Massey, *Ersatz in the Confederacy*, pp. 80, 98.

8 From five Mississippi and five Georgia Cotton Belt counties regarded as typical by Gray in his *History of Agriculture* (I, 334–35, and II, 918–21), I have analyzed for each state the two that come closest to the mode in the only variable for which there is clear evidence—the size of slaveholdings. A review of the economic and natural conditions of the South reveals nothing to suggest that the four counties so chosen were not roughly typical of the Cotton Belt. I have used the four counties primarily for an investigation of purchasing power—to gain clues to the general structure of the market—and the insignificant expenditures recorded indicate that even with due allowance for the possibility of a wide, say 50%, deviation in other counties and for incorrect reporting in the census returns, the results could not conceivably be substantially different.

As a random sample, I selected the first ten names on each page of U.S. Census, 1860, Georgia, Schedule 4, Productions of Agriculture, Dougherty and Thomas counties (Library, Duke University, Durham, N.C.) and U.S. Census, 1860, Mississippi, Schedule 4, De Soto and Marshall counties (Mississippi State Archives, Jackson). From the U.S. Census, 1860, Georgia, Schedule 2, Slave Inhabitants, Dougherty and Marshall counties (National Archives, Washington), I determined the number of slaves held by each agriculturalist in my sample. Where Schedule 4 gave the amount of produce but not the monetary value, I used a specially prepared price schedule in order to translate the amounts into dollar values. For methodological details, see my unpublished doctoral dissertation, "The Limits of Agrarian Reform in the Slave South," Columbia University, 1959, appendices.

9 *Supra*, Chapter II.

10 Roy M. Robbins, *Our Landed Heritage* (New York, 1950), p. 177; Joseph Brennan, *Social Conditions in Industrial Rhode Island, 1820–1860* (Washington, D.C., 1940), p. 18; Samuel Rezneck, "The Rise and Early Development of Industrial Consciousness in the United States, 1760–1830," *JEBH*, IV (Aug. 1932), Supplement, 784–811; Isaac Lippincott, *History of Manufactures in the Ohio Valley to the Year 1860* (New York, 1914), pp. 63–65; Grace Pierpont Fuller, *An Introduction to the History of Connecticut as a Manufacturing State* (Northampton, Mass., 1915), p. 45; James Neal Primm, *Economic Policy in the Development of a Western State: Missouri, 1820–1860* (Cambridge, Mass., 1954), pp. 56–59; Frank W. Taussig, *The Tariff History of the United States* (7th ed.; Cambridge, Mass., 1923), pp. 68–108; and Bray Hammond, *Banks and Politics in America* (Princeton, N.J., 1957).

11 *America and the Americans*, p. 19.

12 For examples see the remarks of M. W. Philips and John J. Williams, *Mississippi Planter and Mechanic*, II (May, 1858), 157–58; of Thomas J. Lemay, *Arator*, I (Nov. 1855), 237; and of Andrew Johnson, *Congressional Globe*, XXIII, 312.

13 See Simon Kuznets, *Economic Change* (New York, 1953), pp. 307 ff; and Charles F. Dunbar, *Economic Essays* (New York, 1904), p. 268.

14 See Milton S. Heath, *Constructive Liberalism: The Role of the State in Economic Development in Georgia to 1860* (Cambridge, Mass., 1954), pp. 290–91; and Seth Hammond, "Location Theory and the Cotton Industry," *JEH*, II (1942, Supplement), 101–17. The opposition of entrenched landowning classes to the extension of transportation has been general in colonial and underdeveloped

countries. See George Wythe, *Industry in Latin America* (New York, 1945), p. 4.

15 De Bow, *Industrial Resources*, II, 154; Oscar M. Lieber, *Report on the Survey of South Carolina . . . 1857* (Columbia, S.C., 1858), p. 106; *Congressional Globe*, XXI, Pt. 1, 867–68.

16 U.S. Census Office, *Manufactures of the United States in 1860 . . .* (Washington, D.C., 1865), pp. xxi, ccxvii, lxxiii, 729–30; Evelyn H. Knowlton, *Pepperell's Progress: History of a Cotton Textile Company, 1844–1945* (Cambridge, Mass., 1948), p. 32. The average capitalization of manufacturing establishments in 1850 was more than 25% higher in the free states and territories than in the slave states, and the gap widened in the 1850s, when the increase in average capital investment was 68% in the free states and territories and only 51% in the slave states. The Lower South (including North Carolina but excluding Tennessee) fell even further behind. The average capitalization here, 38% less than in the free states in 1850, was 47% less by 1860. Furthermore, the rate of increase in the number of establishments during this decade was appreciably greater in the North than in the South.

17 Ruffin, "Incidents of My Life," pp. 19–20, Ruffin Papers; Clingman, *Speeches*, pp. 233–54, esp. p. 250.

18 U.S. Commissioner of Patents, *Report on Agriculture, 1857*, pp. 308–9, 318; and Richard H. Shryock, "The Early Industrial Revolution in the Empire State," *GHQ*, XI (June 1927), 128.

19 Jesse Eliphalet Pope, *The Clothing Industry in New York* (New York, 1905), pp. 6–7.

20 Hazard, *Boot and Shoe Industry*, pp. 57–58.

21 Knowlton, *Pepperell's Progress*, pp. 83–84; Caroline F. Ware, *The Early New England Cotton Manufacture* (Boston, 1931), pp. 48, 55.

22 Wender, *Southern Commercial Conventions*, p. 25.

23 Richard Lowitt, *A Merchant Prince of the Nineteenth*

Century: William E. Dodge (New York, 1954), pp. 31 ff, 37.

24 In Mississippi a sample of 584 units with 7,289 slaves and an estimated 2,480 whites spent about $316,500; in Georgia a sample of 100 units with 2,354 slaves and an estimated 710 whites spent about $73,300.

25 *Business & Slavery*, p, 143. Since the Western figures are for family units they fall below the lower limit for the cotton area, but they are of course partial. Therefore, they do suggest an immense spread between the two sections even if they do not allow us to calculate closely. I am indebted to Robert W. Fogel for pointing out the need for this qualification; apparently, some misunderstandings arose from the way in which I phrased the matter in the original article.

26 Gregg, *Essays on Domestic Industry*, p. 4; Wailes, *Address Delivered before the Agricultural, Horticultural and Botanical Society of Jefferson College* (Natchez, Miss., 1841), pp. 22–23; *DBR*, XXIX (Oct. 1860), 496-97; Broadus Mitchell, *William Gregg, Factory Master of the Old South* (Chapel Hill, N.C., 1928), p. 106.

27 John Hebron Moore, "Mississippi's Ante-Bellum Textile Industry," *JMH*, XVI (April 1954), 81.

28 Edward A. Wyatt IV, "Rise of Industry in Ante-Bellum Petersburg," *William and Mary College Quarterly*, XVII (Jan. 1937), 32.

29 Southerners were very much interested in silk cultivation and manufacture and saw fine market possibilities. See Parsons, *Inside View*, pp. 71 ff; Cathey, *NCHR*, XXI (Jan. 1954), 6; Spalding Trafton, "Silk Culture in Henderson County, Kentucky," *Filson Club History Quarterly*, IV (Oct. 1930), 184-89.

30 Lippincott, *Manufactures in the Ohio Valley*, p. 64; *Southern Planter*, III (April 1843), advertisement on back cover; Lester J. Cappon, "Trend of the Southern Iron Industry under the Plantation Regime," *JEBH*, II (Feb. 1930), 361, 371, 376; Quenzel, *VMHB*, LXII (April 1954), 182 ff; Lander, *NCHR*, XXIX (April 1952), 225 ff.

31 De Bow, *Industrial Resources*, III, 465.

32 Holcombe Diary, entry for Sept. 6, 1855, but obviously written in 1861.

33 Urban areas defined as incorporated places of 2,500 or more. See U.S. Bureau of the Census, *Urban Population in the U.S. from the First Census (1790) to the Fifteenth Census* (1930).

34 This estimate is from Edgar W. Martin, *The Standard of Living in 1860* (Chicago, 1942), pp. 11–12, and may greatly underestimate the situation in urban households. According to Richard O. Cummings, laborers in Massachusetts probably spent about three-fourths of their weekly wages on food in 1860. *The American and His Food* (Chicago, 1941), p. 266.

35 Hilgard, *Report on the Geology and Agriculture of the State of Mississippi*, pp. 250–51; Lieber, *Report*, p. 106; See also U.S. Commissioner of Patents, *Report on Agriculture, 1849*, p. 137.

36 Clay, *Writings*, pp. 179, 227. Since this essay was written David L. Smiley has published a fine biography: *Lion of White Hall: The Life of Cassius M. Clay* (Madison, Wis., 1962).

Eight ∎ The Industrialists Under the Slave Regime

✂ *Pro and Contra*

The urban capitalists of the slave South, after having been ignored by generations of historians, are coming into their own. Unfortunately, neglect is too often giving way to exaggeration of their economic accomplishment, political influence, and moral virtue. No amount of the much-needed research into the urban classes is likely to upset the sound traditional view of Southern society as dominated by plantation slavery. Charles Grier Sellers, for example, did well to draw attention to the urban dimension of Southern Whiggery, but his view of the party as having been controlled by urban interests rests on the false assumption that the economic, political, and social relationship of town to country favored the former.[1] An analysis of the industrial capitalists, who stand out as having been bolder and more independent than the merchants and bankers, shows the reverse to have been true.

The significance of planter domination of industry extends far beyond the social basis of the Whig party, for the Southern industrialists were doing much less to subvert the slaveholders' regime than is generally thought. Specifically, however strange the question may seem, we need to ask whether or not the industrialists were making a strong contribution to Southern industrialism.

With the greater part of Southern capital tied up in slaves, with a home market greatly restricted by slavery's stifling effects on rural purchasing power, and with other such impediments to industrialization, the cause of Southern industrialism demanded, above all, the destruction of the slave regime. The individual interests of the functioning Southern industrialists, on the other hand, usually produced acquiescence in that very regime, for the planters were their best customers and investors and controlled the political mechanism on which they depended for protection. This conflict between class and personal interests reflected one of slavery's many paradoxes: the dominant rural slaveholders required some industrial expansion to support their plantation economy and political power but could not sustain economically or tolerate politically a general industrialization. Those industrialists permitted to operate in the South had to accept the prevailing social system despite the restrictions it imposed on the expansion of their wealth and power as a class.

Between the early 1840s and the outbreak of the war many Southerners gave up their opposition to industrial expansion but generally retained their hostility to "manufactures as a system."[2] Even during the war, after a brief period of enthusiasm for new factories, public opinion turned against the manufacturers with startling fury.[3] What were the slaveholders afraid of? An urban bourgeoisie with its own interests and the money to defend them; an urban proletariat of unpredictable tendencies; a semifree slave force subversive of labor discipline on the countryside—they feared these and more. Whether as warnings that manufactures generated ideas unassimilable to Southern life or as an insistence that the countryside stood against the passions and turbulence of parasitic urban classes, the opposition to industrialization displayed harsh persistence.[4] Yet, the need for increased manufactures intruded itself into the thinking of the most fearful critics and gave a peculiar cast to the opposition. Samuel

Walker, a wealthy Louisiana sugar planter, splendidly expressed this attitude of tempered hostility when he wrote in his diary in 1856:

> Slavery is from its very nature eminently patriarchial and altogether agricultural. It does not thrive with master or slave when transplanted to cities, where is assembled large crowds of indigent and many unprincipled whites, especially where there are many foreigners to earn or steal subsistence who do not consider the negro his inferior and whom in most instances the negro regards as beneath him with all the sleek and well fed insolence of a spoilt menial. . . .
>
> I do not care for the general introduction of manufacturing into the South as a system. The assemblage of negroes and whites, or even negroes alone in large bodies, in sedentary pursuits deteriorates the animal and unfits them for labor in the field and is to a less extent objectionable for the same reasons, regarding cities, manufacturing being usually pursued in villages or towns.
>
> Manufacturing to the extent of the wants and requirements of the planter himself and those of smaller means about him could be beneficially introduced to a larger extent than practiced.[5]

Those who spoke out in favor of manufactures usually differed only in degree from their opponents: they emphasized the need for industrial expansion instead of the limits to be imposed on that expansion. As for those few who defended manufacturing *per se*, the slaveholders usually regarded them as damned fools. And, after all, were their detractors wrong? Even today historians who admire and praise the advocates of manufacturing do so because they believe that industrial expansion would have undermined the slave regime. Why, then, should we not respect the sophistication of those slaveholders who saw the danger to their system and insisted on caution and carefully controlled changes?

The character and significance of the more enthusiastic

promanufacturing sentiment require attention especially since Professor Russel has convincingly demonstrated that its roots lay in the nullification and Bluffton movements in South Carolina.[6] In 1844 the State Agricultural Society of South Carolina, a stronghold of political extremism, advocated local manufactures, and the state government instructed its official geologist to report on possibilities.[7]

During the 1850s the campaign took on a distinct political and often secessionist tone across the South.[8] The economic support of manufacturing, like the political, arose out of the requirements of the rural slaveholders. As the cotton kingdom spread, they needed grist, flour, and saw mills, coarse cotton cloth factories, and the like, to render them less dependent on outside goods. Those restricted plantation requirements imposed narrow limits on the proposed industrial advance.[9]

The intention of the politically powerful supporters of manufacturing and the economic limits imposed by slavery on industrialization preclude consideration of antebellum Southern economic progress as a natural prelude to postbellum and twentieth-century developments.[10] Those intentions and economic limits account for the leveling off of industrial sentiment and performance in the 1850s despite rising pressure for economic independence. High cotton prices had their effect, but had they been the sole or even leading factor, we could hardly account for the deep ambivalence displayed during the war.

Beneath the demand for increasing manufacturing lay two estimates, offered most clearly by James H. Hammond: first, that the manufacturing interest would never be permitted to dominate the agricultural; and second, that some industrialization would bolster, rather than weaken, the slave regime on the countryside.[11] Gregg and Pratt, the most thoroughly bourgeois of the industrial spokesmen of the Lower South, bowed to the slaveholders and accepted their terms. Gregg assured South Carolina that he too neither desired nor expected a general industrialization.[12]

The slaveholders and their state governments gave manufacturing little support. Only projects like railroad building met a positive response, for they helped consolidate the hegemony of the Black Belt over the South. Instead of taxing the countryside to support manufacturing, the states taxed commerce and manufactures to support the staple-producing areas of the countryside. Since the South was falling behind the North in scale of enterprise, entrepreneurship, and the accumulation of industrial capital, it would have had to do much more to support manufacturing in order to catch up; instead, it did much less. Whereas, from the beginning of the century, community effort, state support, and private banks bolstered the industrial sector of the free states, in the slave states they supported only those ventures linked to the plantation system.

William Gregg, who might have been expected to ask for government aid to the struggling industrialists, expressed justifiable skepticism about state intervention in the economy. The readiness of slave-state governments to use penitentiaries as factories and to build railroads designed to strengthen the plantation, rather than the industrial sector, converted men like Gregg to *laissez-faire*.[13] Fear of offending free-trade sensibilities also led Gregg, unlike John Bell and Hamilton Smith, to repudiate the tariff until his change of mind in the 1850s, but he had always admitted that the manufacturers had benefited considerably from protection.

Gregg's suspicions burst into bitter denunciation during the war, when he accused the Confederate government of discouraging manufactures.[14] Manufacturers found themselves hemmed in by the Exemption Act and other measures and branded as unpatriotic profiteers by politicians and citizens outraged by deceptive reports of paper profits under conditions of inflation and increasing obsolescence. Except for steps deemed urgent and indispensable, the Confederate Congress refused to move in the direction of encouragement to industry.[15] In 1864, Gregg charged that public hostility was causing manufacturers to fear mob attacks on their property.[16]

In the end, the manufacturers received before and during the war only so much encouragement and support as could be made palatable to the planters. Since many of the more outspoken industrialists had achieved personal success already or were directly tied to the planter interest or feared to oppose prevailing sentiments, they often did not even get that much.

⚑ *The Economic Dependence of the Manufacturers on the Planters*

Southern manufacturers relied on the planters for their best, and often only, markets. The manufacturers needed the planters, but the planters, who could and all too often did patronize outsiders, did not have to depend on local manufacturers.[17] The pride of Daniel Pratt's various industrial enterprises rested in his famous cotton gins, which, with the exception of some sales to Europe, South America, and French Africa, went to the Cotton Belt.[18] The dependence of the Southern agricultural implement, hemp rope, and much of the iron industry, on the plantation needs no comment. The textile manufacturers found themselves in a similar position. Gregg, superb entrepreneur that he was, successfully invaded the Northern market with fine cloth, but even Pratt, like most others, produced mostly cheap cloth for slaves.[19]

The inability of the slave South to raise and sustain great cities hemmed in urban purchasing power. Since resident planters or merchants bound to the plantations dominated almost all the cities and towns of the Lower South, the substantial markets therein also bound the manufacturers to the regime.[20] Even New Orleans sustained little local manu-facture, so great was the hostility of the planter-merchant stratum and so narrow was the base of lower- and middle-class purchasing power.[21]

William Gregg could say all he wished about Southern in-dustrialists having to become bolder and strike out for the Northern and world markets. His little lectures on managerial efficiency presented no threat to the social system. The great barrier to industrialism was slavery's impediments to the ex-pansion of the home market, to capital accumulation and entre-preneurship, and to the political influence of the manufacturers. If Gregg had faced the market problem courageously, he could not have ignored the essential elements in its solution: the breakup of the plantations, the raising of a yeomanry with substantial purchasing power, and the consequent provision of a genuine basis for urbanization. Without such a solution the South would have room for some industrialists but not for a broadly based industrialization.

Gregg's talk of striking out for the non-Southern markets presented no threat because, given the strength of Northern industry, it was out of the question for all but a few. In other circumstances it might have represented a potential threat. In the border states, where proximity to free-state cities offered genuine opportunities, manufacturers grew strong outside the limits of the plantation slave regime and developed close ties with Northern business.[22]

Gregg argued that manufactures would generate purchasing power for the newly employed whites, who would, in turn, widen the home market for manufactures.[23] His program, in a rough way, looked forward to multiplier-acceleration effects that could guarantee the needed markets. His analysis was no better than that offered by the planter and agricultural re-former M. W. Philips in 1858, in which agricultural processing industries were expected to provide employment to local whites who would then expand the market for foodstuffs.[24] Without a prior expansion of rural purchasing power, which necessarily had to follow fundamental structural changes on the countryside, any such industrial expansion would either prove abortive or, under the best of circumstances, have room to operate only within narrow limits.

The extent to which planters and rural slaveholders owned the South's industrial enterprises cannot as yet be measured accurately, but it was clearly considerable.[25] For individual planters, however, investments in industry usually formed a minor interest, rarely large enough to influence significantly their social outlook. W. F. Leak of North Carolina, for example, wrote Thomas Ruffin in 1867 voicing concern for his industrial holdings, which, he said, he could have lost in ante-bellum days without much notice.[26] M. W. Philips figured prominently in the Southern Implement Company of Jackson, Mississippi. Edward McGehee, who owned seven plantations, 1,000 slaves, and 23,000 acres in 1860, promoted the big Wood-ville Manufacturing Company of Mississippi.[27] In Alabama rich planters like Ralph McGehee and Richard Walker invested heavily in iron; others, like Robert Jemison and C. M. Foster, spread their investments across several industries.[28] These men remained primarily planters, but some less wealthy planters, like John Hannah, developed a greater stake in industry.[29]

John G. Winter of Georgia illustrates another way in which businessmen were tied to the planter interest. After accumulating wealth as a merchant and banker in Georgia, the New York–born Winter, at the age of forty-three, bought a plantation to supplement his iron, timber, paper-milling, and flour-milling interests and presumably to improve his social status.[30] Other industrialists in Georgia were, like Joseph A. Turner, who manufactured hats, and like Charles J. McDonald, who manufactured cotton textiles, planters to begin with.[31]

The roster of planter-industrialists in South Carolina contains the names of the biggest plantation families. In addition to Governors Williams, McDuffie, Aiken, Allston, Bennett, and Hammond, it includes Daniel Heyward, Samuel N. Morgan, Vardry McBee, Daniel McCullough, John Ewing Colhoun, Robert W. Gibbes, Wade Hampton, the De Saussures, the Guignards, the Hugers, and many others.[32] If we were to include mining ventures and railroads, another long list would have to be drawn up, headed by the name of John C. Calhoun.[33] In South Carolina, especially, these investments supplemented the main business of the investors, which was planting.

Even in North Carolina planters played a prominent role in industry: many of the state's leading industrialists were planters, among them Patrick Henry Winston, Henry K. and T. P. Burgwynn, Paul Barringer, W. F. and John W. Leak, William C. Means, Stephen A. Norfleet, and Jonathan and John Milton Worth.[34]

The strongest voices of Southern industrialism, with those of Gregg and Pratt in the lead, pleaded with planters to invest in industry. Governor Henry Watkins Collier of Alabama, himself a prominent textile manufacturer, called on planters to co-operate in building enough mills to absorb 20 per cent of the state's slaves, as well as some poor whites.[35] Gregg pointed to New England to prove that aristocracy and manufactures could mix. To do so he had to gloss over the enormous differences in class position, economic strength, social status, and political power between the socially declining New England textile manufacturers and the powerful Southern planters; and, more significantly, he had to acknowledge, however inadvertently, every pretension of the planters to hegemony in Southern society.[36] Gregg's associate, James H. Taylor, went a step further and cried out to the planter to "grasp the hand of his brother, the manufacturer."[37] In his speech to the South Carolina Institute in 1851, Gregg virtually groveled before the big planters. "Persons who have any knowledge of the energetic character of our cotton and rice planters," he said, "must be aware that they are not surpassed in activity and management by any class of capitalists in our country. A portion of our capital directed with similar energy would be made to yield profit in any pursuit."[38] The best that may be said for Gregg's flattery is that it was patently untrue. One wonders, among other things, how many South Carolina planters Gregg knew who would have styled themselves "capitalists."

Pratt's views suggest the dilemma of the industrialists. Investments in manufacturing, he argued, would bring a more permanent form of wealth to Alabama than those in agriculture. Plantations yield to soil exhaustion, but factories and industrial equipment are permanent. Planters would therefore be wise to invest their surplus capital in manufacturing. "I regard capital invested in manufacturing as almost the only permanent capital!"[39] He quickly added, "I consider agriculturalists the bone and sinew of our country. . . . The principal object I have in view is to induce planters to invest in manufacturing." He explained that only such investments could root the planters firmly to their state. If Pratt's statements contain any logic at all, it suggests that planters would have to become primarily industrialists, for no amount of investments in industry would prevent the exhaustion of their plantations; but Pratt insisted that such was not his aim. It was all superbly Machiavellian. Unfortunately, the planters were quite as clever as Daniel Pratt and limited their participation in industry to a secondary level.

The ideological barriers to substantial planter investments remained formidable, for investments in land and slaves brought high status, whereas investments in industry did not, and those requiring the sale of surplus slaves might even bring social disapproval.[40] James Robb of New Orleans observed in 1852 that, however well disposed toward urban ventures planters might be, they could not be expected to incur indebtedness to buy stocks and bonds, as they did to buy land and slaves.[41]

Practical considerations operated together with the sentimental. Amos A. Lawrence, criticizing the sanguine calculations and expectations of C. T. James, said quite sensibly, "Though there are many rich men in the large cotton-growing States, the number of moneyed men is very small, and they are not usually the projectors of new enterprises. The planters are generally in debt, more or less . . ."[42] He warned Southerners to expect low profits from cotton manufacturing and offered little encouragement.[43]

Lawrence may have had ulterior motives, as James charged; even John Bell may have been suspect when he told the Senate that Tennessee and Kentucky needed federal aid to build railroads because, despite the presence of rich planters, they lacked capital for investment.[44] No one could suspect William Gregg. Commenting on Lawrence's pessimism, Gregg expressed doubts about his gloomy presentation but added that Southerners ought not to expect more than modest returns.[45] Gregg realized that he had a problem: How could planters be expected to overcome their hesitations if he honestly could not promise big and immediate dividends? He answered that the planters would, by such investments, provide employment to those presently living a marginal existence and lay the basis for a general advance in the regional economy. "In the face of low dividends," he wrote, "these illustrations will show the great advantages which may be derived from the introduction of manufactures, and it also explains satisfactorily how the Eastern people have grown rich from a pursuit which has paid capitalists a moderate interest on their money."[46] In short, the planters were to act out of social conscience and a sense of responsibility. This view, with its fallacious appraisal of previous Northern development, again implicitly recognized the patriarchal pretensions of the planters and their claims to hegemony. When Gregg rested his case on these social grounds, he unwittingly took a long step toward acceptance of that economic rationale for secession which was then becoming the fashion.

The industrialists found themselves caught in a vise. On the one side was the willingness of the planters to invest in industry for quick gains and to secure necessary agricultural processing as an adjunct to their plantation interests. On the other side was the unwillingness of the planters to assume full industrial responsibilities[47] or to extend their vision to include a general industrialization. When the Pratts and Greggs accepted the limited space offered by this vise as the best they could get, they also accepted the principle of limited industrialization and the perpetual hegemony of the rural slaveholders.

Many industrialists who were not planters, or at least not primarily so, had strong ties to the planters and their regime beyond those arising from markets and sources of capital. Marriages tied industrialist and planter families together. John Motley Morehead, for example, apparently committed most of his own slaves to industry and the household, but he married his daughters, Letitia and Ann Eliza, to planters.[48] Samuel Finley Patterson, whose son, Rufus, left agriculture for industry, himself preferred politics and planting to industry in his later years.[49] Allison Francis Page, who left agriculture for the lumber and other businesses and rose to prominence in postbellum days, was the son of a solid if not wealthy planter.[50]

Some men who must be classified primarily as manufacturers nevertheless owned plantations or substantial farms and maintained relationships of interest and affection with their rural neighbors. James Turner Morehead, Robert F. Hoke, Edwin M. Holt, and Daniel Pratt are a few prominent examples.[51] Holt, moreover, had received important financial assistance from his friend Thomas Ruffin, and was much in his debt.[52]

Industrial ventures linked industrialists to planters in several ways, among which the co-operation of John Ewing Colhoun, a planter and cousin of John C. Calhoun, or of C. C. Hickabee, an Alabama planter, with cotton and iron industrialists, respectively, may be considered typical. Colhoun and Hickabee provided money and slaves, whereas their partners provided the technical knowledge and machinery. Planters sometimes supplied slave labor in return for shares of stock, especially in railroad building. The case of Colhoun indicates some of the difficulties plaguing even the firmer of such arrangements, for he had to quit his successful venture because it was taking too much time away from more important activities.[53]

✖ The Politics of the Industrialists

The manufacturers of the South, Hammond said in 1850, could not muster enough strength to elect a single Congressman and perhaps not a single state legislator.[54] Hammond took great liberties, for he had surely heard of John Bell of Tennessee and surely knew of a long list of state governors with industrial holdings, among them John Motley Morehead of North Carolina, Henry Watkins Collier of Alabama, and Charles J. McDonald of Georgia. Hammond's South Carolina boasted as long a list as any, on which could be found the names of governors David Rogerson Williams, pioneer in the manufacture of cottonseed oil and investor in textile mills; George McDuffie in textiles and iron; Whitemarsh B. Seabrook and Hammond himself in textiles; and Pierce Butler in iron. Governors Thomas Bennett, R. F. W. Allston, and William Aiken headed the list of outstanding stockholders in the West Point Mills Company, a big rice-milling enterprise. We may assume, too, that Hammond knew of the industrial connections of Congressmen Abraham Rencher, D. S. Huger, Augustin S. Clayton, Mark Anthony Cooper, William Nesbitt, John

McQueen, Franklin H. Elmore, and many others. He could not help knowing about his friend Ker Boyce, who sat in the South Carolina legislature. Every slave-state legislature had such men.

Hammond may have been willing to exaggerate, but how much did he? Most of those men were also, and often primarily, planters. All, except one or two, had little desire or opportunity to represent the industrial cause against the plantation system. Jonathan Worth and Francis Fries, for example, spoke out for public schools and modest tax reforms in the North Carolina legislature but could make only the barest contribution to the promotion of manufacturing.[55] The significance of industrialists holding such high offices cannot be found in any particular influence wielded by the forces of industrialism, for the most independent and committed of these men rarely dared to oppose the regime. Their political prominence, if anything, suggests the power of those whose commitment was to modest industrial expansion within the context of planter control.

When the industrialists did take part in politics, their activities often placed them in the vanguard of the proslavery extremists. We have long taken for granted the political moderation and unionism of the majority of Southern industrialists but have neglected the opposing views of a large minority. Historians have noticed a few like Ross Winans, the big railroad machine-shop operator in Baltimore, who ardently championed the cause of Southern independence,[56] but there were many others. Augustin S. Clayton, part owner of Georgia's first cotton mill, spoke out for nullification while in Congress during the Jackson administration. Mark Anthony Cooper, with interests in banking, cotton manufacturing, iron production, and the other enterprises, was an early states-rights Whig Congressman who went over to Calhoun. Their fellow Georgian and textile manufacturer, Governor Charles J. McDonald, joined the prosecession faction at the Nashville convention.[57] Duff Green, the devoted friend of Calhoun and Southern nationalism, was no less devoted to Southern industrial development and had investments spread across several industries.[58] Henry Watkins Collier, one of Alabama's leading textile manufacturers, ranked as a conservative Democrat while governor during 1849–1853, but seems to have been extremist enough to be tolerated by the Yancey forces. Robert Looney Caruthers, pioneer textile manufacturer of Tennessee, who had been a staunch Whig and unionist when in Congress, went over to the secessionists in time to be chosen Confederate governor.[59]

In South Carolina many nullifiers and secessionists had important industrial interests, although often as supplements to planting. Dr. Thomas Cooper, a great forerunner of states-rights extremism, had set the pattern by his investments in South Carolina's biggest iron-manufacturing company.[60] To take a single example from late antebellum times, James Jones, who had invested in several textile firms including the Graniteville enterprise of his brother-in-law, William Gregg, became an ultra and apparently commanded South Carolina's Minute Men on the eve of secession.[61]

North Carolina, where extremism lacked the strength it had further south, offers several examples of ultras with significant industrial interests. Governor John W. Ellis, who had had investments in the Salisbury Manufacturing Company, led North Carolina into the Confederacy. Representative Abraham Rencher, who had holdings in the Cane Creek Cotton Factory, warned the North as early as the 1830s that the South would resist forcibly any tampering with slavery; in 1850 he insisted that the South ought to secede if the Fugitive Slave Law was not properly enforced. State Senator Andrew Joyner, with investments in the Weldon Manufacturing Company, voiced similar sentiments in 1850 and said bluntly that unbearable oppression would justify the overthrow of the government.

Henry K. Burgwynn, a powerful planter and cotton manufacturer, generally considered a moderate, became increasingly shrill in the 1850s. After a trip to New York and Massachusetts in 1859, he concluded that attempts to compromise were useless. The Barringer family broke ranks one at a time: D. M. Barringer joined the Democrats in 1850 and became an intimate associate of secessionist leader John W. Ellis, whereas his brother, Rufus Barringer, hesitated until the last minute before joining the secessionists. The Duncan Murchison family, well-known merchants and cotton manufacturers, were strong in their devotion to the cause of secession.[62]

Other industrialists, of whom David Worth may be taken as an example, were ostentatiously apolitical during the most trying days.[63] The leading spokesmen for Southern industrialization, William Gregg and Daniel Pratt, may to some extent have contributed to this apolitical strain in their class. Gregg joined his critique of Southern agrarianism with slighting references to politics and politicians. "It would indeed be well for us," he wrote, "if we were not so refined in politics—if the talent, which has been, for years past, and is now engaged in embittering our indolent people against their industrious neighbors of the North, had been with the same zeal engaged in promoting domestic industry . . ."[64] Pratt, as we shall see, spoke in similar accents during the critical years preceding secession. An apolitical stance and a condescending attitude toward politicians proved a poor substitute for political opposition to harmful practices and a retrogressive regime. Every industrialist who followed this strain in the thought of Gregg and Pratt—a strain that they themselves repudiated in practice—inadvertently bolstered the slaveholders' power.

Many industrialists and planter-industrialists did not eschew politics and did oppose secession but, like Jonathan Worth of North Carolina, Robert Jemison of Alabama, and John Bell of

Tennessee, could not offer substantial resistance when the time came.[65]

Gregg's political career provides a good basis for evaluating the politics of the industrialists. He went to the South Carolina legislature, with Hammond's blessings, in 1856, where he voted against a resolution to reopen the slave trade and argued for a program of internal development as an alternative to impractical railroad schemes aimed at securing Western trade. His hostility toward the banks and railroads, based on a correct appraisal of their subservience to the plantation interests, might have been the springboard for a comprehensive critique of the slaveholders' regime, but Broadus Mitchell tells us, "Gregg was an inveterate realist" and therefore kept his criticism within safe limits.[66] Like so many alleged realists, then and now, he spent his energies firing at the periphery, and eventually played into the hands of the secessionists.

James Martin, one of Alabama's foremost manufacturers, showed the same unwillingness to draw proper conclusions from his skillful arguments. Suppose, he began a remarkable article, the Northern states had to buy four million laborers at prices current for Negro slaves: "It would withdraw from their commerce and manufactures $2,800,000,000, leaving those branches quite in as low a condition as ours." He then shifted ground, maintained that slaves were overpriced by 25 per cent, and called on planters to drive slave prices down so that they could pour ten million dollars a year into manufactures without reducing slave purchases.[67] This incredible non-sequitur permitted Martin to evade the implications of his opening critical remarks.

Gregg's cleverness, too, repeatedly undercut his position. Was it, after all, necessary for him to bow to the gods of the regime and praise Calhoun as "our greatest oracle—a statesman whose purity of character we all revere—whose elevation to the highest office in the gift of the people of the United States would enlist the undivided vote of South Carolina"?[68] When he turned his attention to the extremists, his antisecessionist views revealed dangerously opportunistic tendencies, which ultimately defeated him. After a sarcastic attack on McDuffie, he added: "Those who are disposed to agitate the State and prepare the minds of the people for resisting the laws of Congress, and particularly those who look for so direful a calamity as the dissolution of our Union, should above all others, be most anxious so to diversify the industrial pursuits of South Carolina, as to render her independent of all other countries . . ."[69] Gregg apparently did not notice that his words actually represented a contribution to secessionist ideology. McDuffie did not need Gregg's advice. When, for example, he rose in the Senate on January 19, 1844, he declared that the South would answer the tariff by an industrial expansion aimed at securing its economic independence.[70] Pratt, among others, increasingly spoke out for more manufactures as a necessary prelude to a secession he supposedly did not want.[71]

Gregg's wavering took many forms. In his *Essays on Domestic Industry* he scoffed at the anti-Yankeeism of the extremists and called for an emulation of Northern industry and thrift. In a letter to Amos A. Lawrence, written in 1850, he insisted that Southern manufactures would complement Northern and that bitter competition between the two was unlikely.[72] A year later he brushed aside charges of pauperism and vice hurled against England and New England and maintained that these were merely the growing pains of a vigorous industrial society.[73] Yet, even as early as the *Essays on Domestic Industry* he could not resist appealing to those very anti-Yankee sentiments to call Northern clothing "trash" and to demand that the South be made independent of "foreign" products.[74] (It was only one short step from such language to that of Fitzhugh's *Sociology for the South*.) In his Address to the South Carolina Institute in 1851, Gregg again attacked Northern products and added: "It would be just as easy for a planter to have some three, four, or a half-dozen negroes employed in making brogans."[75] These words and others like them show how easy Gregg found the transition from an appeal for Southern industrialization to an appeal for autarky based on the existing plantation structure. He never recognized, or admitted, that the latter precluded the former.

We thus return to the fundamental commitment of the industrialists to the defense of slavery. Without being willing to follow the Cassius Clays into a repudiation of slavery and slaveholder hegemony, the Greggs and Pratts found themselves, step by step, led ideologically into the camp of their enemies. "With us," Gregg wrote to Amos A. Lawrence, "slaves are property, and it amounts to Many Millions, the protection and use of which is guaranteed to us by the Constitution, without that protection the Union is of no use to us."[76] A decade later, with the war clouds gathering, he emphatically defined slavery as "rooted in nature, and sanctioned by the Bible."[77] Pratt went even further in his proslavery statements, as did his fellow Alabama industrialist James Martin.[78]

What these men might have permitted themselves to say, or rather to think, if the power of the slaveholders had been less formidable will remain useless speculation. John Bell, feeling less pressure than Gregg, could speak of slavery even in the 1850s as an "accidental and enforced blemish."[79] In North Carolina, Paul Barringer, wealthy planter-industrialist, and John Motley Morehead, the distinguished ex-governor, considered slavery a curse and an impediment to economic progress.[80] Their private views and cautious public utterances disturbed few. Bell, in 1858, asserted, as he had for years, that secession would be a legitimate remedy if slavery and the rights of the slaveholders became jeopardized.[81] When Governor Ellis of North Carolina, himself an investor in manufactures, attacked the Republican party in 1860, saying, "The abolition of slavery here at home is the design of our opponents," he effectively reduced the viewpoint of the Moreheads to a mere quibbling over tactics and timing.[82]

Broadus Mitchell maintains that Gregg "might have led opposing sentiment" had the manufacturing interest been stronger, but that, as it was, he had to accommodate himself to a regime of planters and of merchants and bankers tied to planters.[83] We cannot profitably concern ourselves with such might-have-beens, although neither are we obliged to pass judgment on William Gregg. The Greggs and Pratts, and especially the planter-industrialists, could not and would not follow the example of the Cassius Clays and Hinton Helpers and risk their fortunes and safety to tell the nonslaveholding farmers that slavery prevented industrialization and the development of new markets.[84] Gregg and Pratt knew from their own experience how thoroughly the interests of agricultural reorganization and industrial advance were bound up, but they would never draw the appropriate conclusions.

Gregg's relationship to James H. Hammond helps explain the limits he allowed to be placed on his actions. Ker Boyce, the wealthy and influential Charleston merchant, seems to have been a central figure in the legislative and political, as well as financial, arrangements to found Graniteville. With the assistance of Boyce and Hammond, Gregg got a fourteen-year charter, which adequately demonstrated to all concerned that Gregg had better remain on good behavior if he expected to be allowed to remain active in South Carolina.[85] Such control over manufacturing corporations by legislatures dominated by rural slaveholders shows the limitations under which the manufacturers labored. Gregg grew closer to Hammond, ideologically and generally, as the years went by.

When Gregg told the South Carolina Institute in 1851 that slavery gave capital a "positive control over labor," he was speaking in Hammond's terms. "In all other countries," he continued, "and particularly manufacturing states, labor and capital are assuming an antagonistical position. Here it cannot be the case; capital will always be able to control labor, even in manufactures with whites, for blacks can always be resorted to in case of need."[86] If Hammond had been speaking, nothing of substance would have been added except perhaps a blunt comment that increased manufacturing would not jeopardize rural domination. Hammond occasionally went to great lengths to reassure his fellow planters, as when he expressed regret that the suffrage had not been restricted to landowners.[87]

By the beginning of 1860, if not earlier, Gregg had joined the secessionists. "We have been forced to the conclusion," he declared, "that the time has come when the Southern people should begin in earnest to prepare for self-defense and self-reliance. Abolition of Southern slavery was, but a few years ago, nothing more than an insignificant sectional political hobby. It has now become a religious sentiment."[88] On the next page of the article in De Bow's Review in which these words appear, the extremity of his viewpoint and the harshness of his tone toward the North approached those of a Rhett editorial.

What did Gregg see as the justification for secession? "We have been waging a political war against the Northern people for thirty-five years; first on account of the tariff, then negro slavery expansion."[89] His talk of a thirty-five-year war against the Northern people and of Southern resistance to the tariff must have sounded strange to those who knew that Gregg had always derided sectional agitation and had, a few years earlier, become a convert to protectionism.[90]

Finally, Gregg sang the praises of the slave regime in accents foreshadowing Stephens' Cornerstone Speech:

> Should an independent government be established by the Southern states, an era will be inaugurated, the like of which the world has not before seen. In its institutions will be blended a series of harmonious principles, the effect of which will be to create a nation, in which every element of moral and political success may be found. . . . Prominently in view stand two peculiar: the one a pure religion; the other a perfect labor system.[91]

Mitchell maintains that the Gregg-Hammond relationship provided a mutual influence,[92] but, in fact, Hammond had imprisoned Gregg within a limited industrialization program committed to the maintenance of planter hegemony. When Gregg congratulated Hammond for his controversial "mudsill" speech in 1858, he completed his capitulation.

However moderate and pro-Union the industrialists may have been, several of them, including such outstanding men as Gregg, Rufus L. Patterson, Simpson Bobo, and Robert Jemison, signed their states' ordinances of secession and thereby lent their names and reputations to the extremists' ultimate project.

⬛ *The Industrialists in the War*

Narrow opportunism, expressing itself in the quest for war profits, had already tempered the unionism of some by 1860. It was to be expected that a Mark Anthony Cooper should urge Howell Cobb in 1848 to press for the establishment of a national foundry in Georgia: state pride, secessionist hopes, and personal interest blended perfectly. Virtue received its reward when Governor Brown awarded Cooper an arms contract in 1860.[94] It was no less to be expected that Whig unionists like planter-industrialist William C. Means of North Carolina should calculate the short-run gains. His Concord Cotton Factory made little money during the twenty years preceding the war but produced good returns on the strength of the wartime demand.[95] Many found themselves in a similar position. Richard W. Griffin has shown, for example, that the big increase in the demand for cotton textiles occasioned by the outbreak of hostilities pulled North Carolina manufacturers out of a deepening slump.[96]

Industrialist opposition to secession had grown out of several attitudes, among which a principled objection to the slaveholding regime seems to have been virtually absent. One of the most important of these attitudes was fear of defeat and ruin for the South generally and themselves in particular. As men of enterprise they, much more than the planters or swaggering politicians, appreciated the census statistics on the material strength of contending parties and scoffed at the illusions pervading the dominant class. The industrialists felt gloomy about the chances of a Southern victory but were cautious about how they said so. Generally, they kept quiet, confiding their fears to intimates. When Representative James Turner Morehead of North Carolina, an old-line Whig industrialist like his famous brother, John Motley Morehead, paced the floor, weeping, during the bitter nights of the secession crisis of 1861, various quite different things flashed through his mind. On the one hand, he genuinely loved the old Union and the hopes for which it stood; on the other hand, he could not shake off the vision of catastrophic defeat.[97] Rufus L. Patterson, of the powerful industrialist Patterson family of North Carolina, signed the Ordinance of Secession with deep misgivings, for he saw inevitable defeat at the hands of a stronger foe, and what was worse, the specter of "civil war at home."[98]

Daniel Pratt typifies the attitudes of much of his class during the unfolding secession crisis. In 1851 he wrote to the *Montgomery Journal* urging that the South protect itself against Northern aggression but insisting that a boycott of Northern goods and the building of Southern factories, rather than political agitation, held out the best hopes of success. "When this shall take place . . ." he continued, "then we shall be in a much better condition to secede. Then the abolition chord [*sic*] will be loosened."[99] In 1859 he wrote to the *Cotton Planter* along the same lines:

I profess to be a Southern rights man, and strongly contend that the South ought to maintain her rights at all hazards. I would, however, pursue a somewhat different course from that of our politicians. I would not make any flaming, fiery speeches and threats, but on the other hand, I would go quietly and peaceably to work, and make ourselves less dependent on those who abuse and would gladly ruin us.[100]

Since Pratt had frequently pointed out that the value of the Union lay in its being an economic whole,[101] we may assume that he sincerely hoped that secession would be obviated by the industrialization of the South. When secession seemed imminent, he opposed it, as a colleague said, "fearing ability to sustain the same."[102]

A review of Pratt's course reveals that he had no viable alternative to the firebrands. Admitting their contention that the South was under attack, defending slavery as a proper social system, accepting secession as a legal and proper remedy, Pratt could only suggest different tactics. His impotence in the face of Yancey's onslaught was easily predictable.

Many industrialists joined the Confederate armed forces, generally serving as officers. Rufus Barringer of the planter-industrialist North Carolina Barringers, and Robert F. Hoke, with big holdings in cotton mills, iron, linseed oil, paper manufacturing, and other enterprises, became generals of distinction.[103] Kenneth M. Murchison, son of prosecessionist merchant and manufacturer Duncan Murchison, became a colonel.[104] The Bell-Yeatman families of Tennessee became staunchly Confederate: John Bell, his heavy heart notwithstanding, saw all his sons, stepsons, and sons-in-law in the Confederate service.[105]

Henry P. Hammett, a member of the South Carolina textile firm of William Bates & Company, served until the close of the war. John Milton Odell, a stockholder and salesman for the Cedar Falls Manufacturing Company of North Carolina, left his business interests to become a captain. John W. Leak, who had a plantation in South Carolina and interests in a cotton textile firm in North Carolina, served as a lieutenant colonel.

John Milton Worth, North Carolina planter and manufacturer, and numerous others served as officers.[106]

Others like Joseph R. Anderson of the famous Tredegar Iron Works in Richmond, Virginia, Mark Morgan, and Dexter E. Converse, among others, rushed to volunteer but were told that the war effort required their attendance at their factories.[107]

Samuel A. Ashe, in his massive *Biographical History of North Carolina*, writes: "It is a reflection that must be gratifying to every patriotic North Carolinian that, great as has been the development of the industrial interests of our people, many of the leaders and most successful men in these new enterprises . . . in their earlier days were among the brave and gallant followers of Lee and Jackson."[108] Respect for the bravery of these men or a charitable view of the motives impelling them cannot obscure their having fought so earnestly and willingly for a cause that, whatever else may be said of it, corresponded neither to their class interests nor to their vision of an industrial future for the South.

Prominent industrialists served in the Confederate government, adding their prestige and skill to the secessionist cause. Robert Jemison replaced Yancey in the Senate in 1863, where he "continued in quieter fashion Yancey's policies."[109] The records do not indicate that he made any effort in behalf of the manufacturing interest,[110] but with his background as a Whig unionist, he proved invaluable in quelling anti-Confederate agitation in northern Alabama.[111] Senator Wright of Georgia represented his iron interests to the extent of asking apologetically for the exemption of iron workers from military service.[112] Otherwise he, like Congressman John McQueen, a cotton manufacturer from South Carolina, could not be distinguished from the rural representatives in the Confederate Congress. John Motley Morehead added his splendid reputation to the cause by cheerfully serving in the Provisional Congress, where his main task seems to have been to introduce

North Carolina's resolution of confidence in the Confederate cause and war effort.[113]

Other industrialists added their names and talent to government service. Jonathan Worth, at considerable financial loss, acted as State Treasurer of Confederate North Carolina and helped block the efforts of William W. Holden to arrange separate state peace negotiations.[14] Daniel Pratt and Samuel Finley Patterson served in their respective state legislatures, where, if they did anything unusual, it has escaped notice.[115]

The most important contribution that industrialists could make to the secessionist cause arose from their entrepreneurial, not military or political, talents. Without the small band of able men to marshal Southern resources and run the factories would a war for secession have been possible? The efforts of Gregg and Pratt need no comment, although we may note that Pratt extended himself to organize the Red Mountain Iron and Coal Company to provide the war machine with arms.[116] Consider a few less prominent examples. David Worth, who had been in business with his father, Jonathan, removed to Wilmington, North Carolina, in 1861, where he served as superintendent of the Confederate salt works.[117] His brother, Jonathan Addison Worth, Fayetteville's most important businessman during the war, "carried much on his shoulders."[118] William C. Means, whose son became a Confederate officer, joined many others in making generous financial contributions to the war effort.[119] Duff Green successfully ran the Confederate Iron Works, supplying Bragg and Longstreet in East Tennessee.[120] The *Atlanta Intelligencer* happily reported a "handsome donation" of textiles from the Roswell Manufacturing Company to the war effort and added that it reflected "great credit upon the company, and [is] worthy of emulation by others in our State whom the war, thus far, has only pecuniarly [sic] benefitted."[121]

What else could the industrialists have done? We at least have before us the example of a few unionists whose allegiance was unencumbered by qualifications negating it in major crises. Judge David K. Young of Anderson County, Tennessee, advocate of agricultural reform and industrial development, stood firm and suffered arrest by Confederate troops.[122] More cautiously, Judge George W. Brooks of North Carolina, an outspoken critic of slavery, remained quietly loyal to the Union throughout the war and restricted his participation in the Confederate war effort to acts of kindness toward suffering individuals.[123]

What, we may ask, would have happened to the Confederate war effort had the industrialists decided that it was not their war? We need not consider the possibilities presented by active opposition; they merely had to withhold their talents. Since many of them doubted that the South could win, they clearly were not primarily motivated by the desire for private gain. In the long run, they stood to gain by taking a long vacation and claiming loyalty to the winning side. Their actions demonstrate their "patriotism" to the South and their ultimate ideological commitment to its slaveholding civilization.

❧ The Southern Industrialists: A Political Evaluation

The Southern industrialists, by their social and political subservience to slavery, negated the contribution they made to industrialism by their diligent and, in its own way, heroic day-to-day entrepreneurial effort. Gregg's biographer, telling us that he planned a social reorganization, calls him "the South's first great bourgeois, the forerunner of a new era."[124] The commitment of the Greggs and Pratts to slavery forced them to adjust their vision of an industrialized South to one dominated by a broadened slaveholders' regime. As such, it offered gloomy prospects for the South and the nation, for it necessarily meant a Prussian road to industrial capitalism, paved with authoritarianism, benevolent despotism, and aristocratic pretension. Withal, the Southern planters showed little interest. Major political and military disasters had to befall the old regimes of countries like Prussia and Japan before their ruling classes co-operated in a program of industrialization. The antebellum and Confederate experiences suggest that only hard blows could have brought the slaveholders around.

The continuity between the industrialist stratum of antebellum and postbellum days does not prove that the war had little effect;[125] on the contrary, it suggests that the war, or rather the defeat of the South, created some of the preconditions for the liberation of the industrialists and of industrialism. Yet, the South suffered terribly, some antebellum gains had to be sacrificed, and postbellum industrial interests had to contend with a Northern capitalism bent more on political and economic exploitation than on regional reconstruction. The Greggs and Pratts had supported the institutions of the old regime as the only realistic and sensible thing to do. Was professed realism ever so bitterly repaid? If the South were to have been led into the industrial era these men dreamed of, without another hundred years of outside domination, the impediments to industrialization had to be removed by Southerners, not by Northern crusaders with *Uncle Tom's Cabin* in one hand and a schedule of dividend payments in the other. When the Southern industrialists prostrated themselves before slavery, they betrayed their own class interests, but much more important, they betrayed the South they loved so much. The patriotism of those who declared, with appropriate posturing, that they stood with their states and local institutions was a patriotism of the easy kind. It is not necessary to like everything about the Cassius Clays and Hinton Helpers to realize that their Southern patriotism was made of tougher stuff. Cassius Clay, for all his occasional clownishness, not William

Gregg, carried the banner of Southern industrialism and of a better day.

If there is no reason to glorify the Greggs and Pratts or to see in them the builders of a new South, there is even less reason to follow those historians who credit them with greater wisdom or moral fiber than the rural slaveholders. The slaveholders, after all, stood true to their class interests, which they identified as the quintessence of Southern civilization, when they chose secession and risked war. The industrialists, whatever the extenuating circumstances, repudiated their class interests, which they too identified with Southern civilization, when they joined, however reluctantly, in a crusade on behalf of a social system they had every reason to abhor.

NOTES

1 "Who Were the Southern Whigs?" *AHR*, LIX (Jan. 1954), 335–46.

2 *Cf.* Chauncey Samuel Boucher, *The Ante-Bellum Attitude of South Carolina Towards Manufacturing and Agriculture,* "Washington University Studies," Part II: Humanistic Series III (April 1916), p. 256 and *passim;* Heath, *Constructive Liberalism,* p. 358 and *passim;* Alfred Glaze Smith, Jr., *Economic Readjustment,* Chap. IV.

3 *Cf.* E. Merton Coulter, *The Confederate States of America, 1861–1865* (Baton Rouge, La., 1950), pp. 218, 223, 229–30, 239.

4 *Southern Agriculturalist,* I (Aug. 1928), 357; *Farmer and Planter,* VI (Dec. 1855), 270–71; *DBR,* XXVI (March 1859), 314, quoting *Lynchburg Virginian;* Address of William C. Daniell to the Agricultural Association of the Slaveholding States, in *American Cotton Planter,* II (March

1854), 66; speech of Rep. Howell Cobb of Georgia, *Congressional-Globe*, XIII, 1st Session, 28th Congress, Appendix, pp. 594–98; Fabian Linden, "Repercussions of Manufacturing in the Ante-Bellum South," *NCHR*, XVII (Oct. 1940), 324–26.

5 Samuel Walker of Elia Plantation, Louisiana, Diary, 1856–1878, pp. 28–29, typescript of Ms. in Tulane University.

6 Robert R. Russel, *Economic Aspects*, Chap. II, esp. p. 37; Richard W. Griffin, "Poor White Laborers in Southern Cotton Factories," *SCHGM*, LXI (Jan. 1960), 26–40. The Whig party associated itself with the demand for industrial expansion as a prerequisite to regional independence in or out of the Union. See Arthur C. Cole, *The Whig Party in the South* (Washington, D.C., 1913), pp. 206–11.

7 *Niles' Register*, LXVII (Oct. 26, 1844), 116; South Carolina Geological and Agricultural Survey, *Report on the Geology of South Carolina*, by M[ichael] Tuomey (Columbia, S.C., 1848), pp. 20 ff.

8 The propaganda had its comic aspects. In 1859, for example, the *New Orleans Bulletin* announced the opening of a new machine-oil factory and commented: "Now we can with safety congratulate the entire South in the acquisition of another powerful weapon of defence against the aggression of the North." Quoted in *DBR*, XXVI (March 1859), 17.

9 See, *e.g.*, Thomas J. Lemay, *Arator*, I (Nov. 1855), 237; J. H. Lumpkin of Georgia in *DBR*, XII (Jan. 1852), 48; De Bow, *Industrial Resources*, II, 314. For an excellent discussion of the industrial sentiment and performance in Alabama, which reaches some conclusions different from those presented here, see Weymouth T. Jordan, *Ante-Bellum Alabama: Town and Country* (Tallahassee, Fla., 1957), Chap. VII, esp. pp. 140–44.

10 *Cf.* Harriet L. Herring, "Early Industrial Development in the South," *Annals of the American Academy of Political and Social Science*, CLIII (Jan. 1931), 9; Constantine G. Belissary, "Industry and Industrial Philosophy in Tennessee, 1850–1860," *Publications of the East Tennessee Historical Society*, No. 23 (1951), 54 ff; Richard W. Griffin and Diffie W. Standard, "The Cotton Textile Industry in Ante-Bellum

North Carolina—Part II: An Era of Boom and Consolidation, 1830–1860," *NCHR*, XXXIV (April 1957), 142–43; Herbert Collins, "The Idea of a Cotton Textile Industry in the South, 1870–1900," *NCHR*, XXXIV (July 1957), 372 f; in his "The Southern Industrial Gospel before 1860," *JSH*, XII (Aug. 1946), 386–408, Collins has a different, and I think less defensible, emphasis.

11 James H. Hammond, *An Address Delivered before the South Carolina Institute at Its First Annual Fair, on the 20th November, 1849* (Charleston, S.C., 1849), pp. 6, 38.

12 *DBR*, XI (Aug. 1851), 130. As for Pratt, Jordan has said it all: "Here was a man after the heart of the Southern nationalists." *Ante-Bellum Alabama*, p. 153.

13 On penitentiary factories see Moore, *JMH*, XVI (April 1954), 93–94; Clement Eaton, *A History of the Southern Confederacy* (New York, 1961), 241–42; Allen D. Candler (ed.), *Confederate Records of the State of Georgia* (6 vols.; Atlanta, Ga., 1909–11), II, 395; on the railroads see the excellent study by Phillips, *Transportation in the Eastern Cotton Belt*.

14 Mitchell, *William Gregg*, p. 221.

15 Wilfred Buck Yearns, *The Confederate Congress* (Athens, Ga., 1960), p. 127; *Journal of the Congress of the Confederate States, 1861–1865* (7 vols.: Vols. 25–31, 58th Congress, 2nd Session, Senate Doc. 234; Washington, D.C., 1903–1904), V, 162, 192; Charles W. Ramsdell (ed.), *Laws and Joint Resolutions of the Last Session of the Confederate Congress (November 7, 1864–March 18, 1865), Together with the Secret Acts of Previous Congresses* (Durham, N.C., 1941), p. 45; cf. Charles W. Ramsdell, "The Control of Manufacturing by the Confederate Government," *MVHR*, VIII (Dec. 1921), 231–49.

16 Mitchell, *William Gregg*, p. 209.

17 See *supra*, Chapter VII, and the view of Conrad and Meyer, cited *infra*, page 286, note 1.

18 Mrs. G. F. H. Tarrant (ed.), *Hon. Daniel Pratt, A Biography* (Richmond, Va., 1904), p. 16; Jordan, *Ante-Bellum Alabama*, p. 155.

19 *DBR*, XXIX (June 1860), 496–97; De Bow, *Industrial Resources*, II, 183–84; Jordan, *Ante-Bellum Alabama*, p. 152; Smith, *Economic Readjustment*, pp. 131–33; Shryock, *GHQ*, XI (June 1927), 127.

20 See, *e.g.*, Clanton W. Williams, "Early Ante-Bellum Montgomery: A Black Belt Constituency," *JSH*, VII (Nov. 1941), 495–525; Martha Boman, "A City of the Old South: Jackson, Mississippi, 1850–1860," *JMH*, XV (April 1953), 1–32; and the perceptive remarks of Edd Winfield Parks, *Segments of Southern Thought* (Athens, Ga., 1938), Chap. VII.

21 Norman Walker, "Manufacturing," Chap. XXI of *Standard History of New Orleans, Louisiana*, ed. Henry Rightor (Chicago, 1900). I have also relied heavily on Robert C. Reinders, "Ante-Bellum New Orleans: A Yankee Outpost," paper read to the Southern Historical Association meetings, Nov. 1961. I am indebted to Professor Reinders for allowing me to see his paper, which will hopefully be published soon, and for his unusual kindness in placing at my disposal his valuable notes on industry in New Orleans.

22 Some Northern businessmen, following Henry C. Carey, took steps to build up manufacturing in the border states with a view to undermining slavery there. See George Winston Smith, "Ante-Bellum Attempts of Northern Business Interests to 'Redeem' the Upper South," *JSH*, XI (May 1945), 177–213. See also the useful discussion of some of the economic problems of iron manufacturers in the Lower South and the border states in Cappon, *JEBH*, II (Feb. 1930), 360–61, 371, 376.

23 Gregg, *Essays on Domestic Industry*, p. 34.

24 *Mississippi Planter and Mechanic*, II (May 1858), 157–58.

25 Ernest M. Lander, Jr., "Ante-Bellum Milling in South Carolina," *SCHGM*, LII (July 1951), 131–32; and "The Iron Industry in Ante-Bellum South Carolina," *JSH*, XX (Aug. 1954), 343. The researches of Jordan, Moore, Griffin, and others reveal the same pattern.

26 Leak to Ruffin, April 1867, in J. G. de Roulhac Hamilton (ed.), *The Papers of Thomas Ruffin* (4 vols.; "Publications

of the North Carolina Commission"; Raleigh, N.C., 1918–20), IV, 177–78.

27 Moore, *Agriculture in Ante-Bellum Mississippi*, p. 185; John H. Napier III, "Judge Edward McGehee: Cotton Planter, Manufacturer, and Philanthropist," *THR*, I (Jan. 1960), 27.

28 Ethel Armes, *The Story of Coal and Iron in Alabama* (Birmingham, Ala., 1910), pp. 61, 70; Matthew William Clinton, *Tuscaloosa, Alabama: Its Early Days, 1816–1865* (Tuscaloosa, 1958), pp. 95, 102–4, 134.

29 Workers of the Writers' Program of the Works Projects Administration in the State of Alabama, *Alabama: A Guide to the Deep South* (New York, 1941), p. 63.

30 *DBR*, X (May 1851), 582.

31 Coulter, *Confederate States*, p. 230; Richard W. Griffin, "The Origins of the Industrial Revolution in Georgia: Cotton Textiles, 1810–1865," *GHQ*, XLII (Dec. 1958), 367; Richard H. Shryock, *Georgia and the Union in 1850* (Philadelphia, 1926), p. 111.

32 Richard W. Griffin (ed.), "List of North Carolina Cotton Manufacturers to 1880," *THR*, III (Oct. 1962), 222–31; I have repeatedly returned to this list and its counterpart for South Carolina to identify manufacturers: "A List of South Carolina Cotton Manufacturers, 1790–1860," *THR*, I (July 1960), 143–46. Also, Lander, *SCHGM*, LII (July 1951), 130–31; Lander, "The Development of Textiles in the South Carolina Piedmont before 1860," *THR*, I (July 1960), 92–94; Harvey Toliver Cook, *The Life and Legacy of David Rogerson Williams* (New York, 1916); Edwin L. Green, *George McDuffie* (Columbia, S.C., 1936); Arney R. Childs (ed.), *Planters and Business Men: The Guignard Family of South Carolina, 1795–1930* (Columbia, S.C., 1958), 41; Charles Edward Cauthen (ed.), *Family Letters of the Three Wade Hamptons, 1782–1901* (Columbia, S.C., 1953), 54, 83–84.

33 E. Merton Coulter, *Auraria: The Story of a Georgia Gold-Mining Town* (Athens, Ga., 1956), p. 55. Most of the

capital in Southern mining seems to have been Northern and English: *Niles' Register*, XL, 206; Foner, *Business & Slavery*, p. 3 and n. 15; Fletcher M. Green, *GHQ*, XIX (Sept. 1935), 223; Green, "Gold Mining in Ante-Bellum Virginia," *VMBH*, XLV (Oct. 1937), 357, 365; Green, "Gold Mining: A Forgotten Industry of Ante-Bellum North Carolina," *NCHR*, XIV (Jan. 1937), 13.

34 Samuel A. Ashe and others, *Biographical History of North Carolina* (8 vols.; Greensboro, N.C., 1905), I, 95–99, 111, 365; II, *passim;* III, 435–60; Hamilton (ed.), *Ruffin Papers*, IV, 177–78; J. Carlyle Sitterson, *The Secession Movement in North Carolina* (Chapel Hill, N.C., 1939), pp. 124–25; Cathey, *Agricultural Developments*, pp. 49, n. 8, 50, 62; D. A. Tompkins, *Cotton Mills, Commercial Features* (Charlotte, N.C., 1899), p. 186.

35 Richard W. Griffin, "Cotton Manufacture in Alabama to 1860," *AHQ*, XVIII (Fall 1956), 300–301; Aaron V. Brown, *Speeches, Congressional and Political, and Other Writings* (Nashville, Tenn., 1854), p. 547.

36 Aside from the fundamental difference of command of wage labor versus command of slave labor, consider a few others: the New England merchants and manufacturers were urban bourgeois despite their aristocratic affectations and genuine culture; they controlled a declining sector of the rapidly growing Northern economy; they did not determine the course of Northern life any longer. They were an object lesson for the planters, but in a sense radically different from Gregg's.

37 *DBR*, VIII (Jan. 1850), 25.

38 *DBR*, XI (Aug. 1851), 127.

39 Quoted by Jordan, *Ante-Bellum Alabama*, p. 157. See Chap. VII for an excellent account of Pratt; *cf.* E. Steadman, *A Brief Treatise on Manufacturing in the South*, pamphlet first published in 1851 and republished in *THR*, II (April 1962), 103–18. See p. 118 of the latter, which shall be cited hereafter.

40 As Shryock points out: *GHQ*, XI (June 1927), 123. During the Civil War, "Jefferson Davis complained bitterly

that many millions of dollars in private capital had been invested in blockade running, but very little money had been devoted to manufacturing." Eaton, *Confederacy*, p. 241.

41 *DBR*, XII (May 1852), 547.

42 *HMM*, XXI (Dec. 1849), 628. *Cf.* Robert C. Black III, *The Railroads of the Confederacy* (Chapel Hill, N.C., 1952), pp. 40–41.

43 *HMM*, XXI (Dec. 1849), 628–33; XXII (Jan. 1850), 26–35.

44 *Congressional Globe*, XIX, 1st Session, 31st Congress, pp. 867–68; also, XXII, 2nd Session, 32nd Congress, pp. 318–19; XXVII, 2nd Session, 35th Congress, pp. 107–8.

45 *HMM*, XXII (Jan. 1850), 107. Gregg's estimates appear sound, if not a bit optimistic: *cf. DBR*, X (March 1851), 343; XVIII (March 1855), 393–94; *HMM*, XXIV (1850), 262, and the writings cited elsewhere of Robert R. Russel and Ernest M. Lander on the cotton textile and other industries.

46 *HMM*, XXII (Jan. 1850), 108. No wonder Gregg was deeply disturbed when the will of Ker Boyce revealed that he had heavy investments in the free states; another stockholder in Graniteville moved permanently to New York. Mitchell, *William Gregg*, pp. 111, 295, n. 41.

47 *Cf.* Lander, *JSH*, XX (Aug. 1954), 343, on the problems of the big Nesbitt Iron Manufacturing Company, to which many outstanding planters subscribed but never paid in.

48 John Kerr in *Hon. John Motley Morehead: In Memoriam* (Raleigh, N.C., 1868), p. 35; John Motley Morehead III, *The Morehead Family of North Carolina and Virginia* (New York, 1921), p. 59.

49 Ashe, *Biographical History*, II, 328–33, on Samuel; and II, 334–43, on Rufus.

50 *Ibid.*, III, 308–14.

51 Morehead III, *Morehead Family*, p. 52; Ashe, *Biographical History*, I, 309–21; Tompkins, *Cotton Mills, Commercial*

Features, p. 185; *Dictionary of American Biography*, XV, 170 (on Pratt).

52 Hamilton (ed.), *Ruffin Papers, passim;* Griffin and Standard, *NCHR*, XXXIV (April 1957), 131–64.

53 Lander, *THR*, I (July 1960), 92; Joseph H. Woodward II, "Alabama Iron Manufacturing, 1860–1865," *Alabama Review*, VII (July 1954), 204; R. S. Cotterill, "Southern Railroads and Western Trade," *MVHR*, III (March 1917), 436.

54 *DBR*, VIII (June 1850), 509.

55 J. G. de Roulhac Hamilton (ed.), *The Correspondence of Jonathan Worth* (2 vols.; Raleigh, N.C., 1909), I, viii–ix and *passim;* Tompkins, *Cotton Mills, Commercial Features*, p. 184; Ashe, *Biographical Dictionary*, I, 309–21, on Michael Hoke.

56 Clement Eaton, *The Growth of Southern Civilization, 1790–1860* (New York, 1961), p. 246.

57 I am indebted to Professor Robin Brooks of Rochester Polytechnic Institute for permitting me to read his unpublished paper on the Whig party in Georgia, which has excellent material on the congressional careers of Clayton and Cooper; *cf.* Paul Murray, *The Whig Party in Georgia, 1825–1853*, (Chapel Hill, N.C., 1948), pp. 10–12; on McDonald see Griffin, *GHQ*, XLII (Dec. 1958), 367, and for his politics see Shryock, *Georgia and the Union*, p. 353.

58 Fletcher M. Green, "Duff Green: Industrial Promoter," *JSH*, II (Feb. 1936), 29–30.

59 Cole, *Whig Party*, pp. 188–89; Edward C. Williamson, "Robert Looney Caruthers, Tennessee Textile Pioneer, 1800–22," *THR*, I (July 1960), 126–27.

60 Lander, *JSH*, XX (Aug. 1954), 343; Dumas Malone, *The Public Life of Thomas Cooper, 1783–1839* (New Haven, Conn., 1926). Cf. Childs (ed.), *Planters and Business Men*, p. 37, for pronullification sentiment among the Guignard family.

61 Charles Edward Cauthen, *South Carolina Goes to War, 1860–1865* (Chapel Hill, N.C., 1950), p. 47 and n. 50;

August Kohn, *Cotton Mills of South Carolina* (Charleston, S.C., 1907), p. 18; John A. Chapman, *History of Edgefield County from the Earliest Settlements to 1897* (Newberry, S.C., 1897), pp. 382–84. Consider that so ardent an advocate of manufacturing had no trouble being an equally ardent advocate of secession.

62 Ashe, *Biographical History*, I, 104, 392–402; Sitterson, *Secession Movement*, pp. 35, 76, 79, 133, 160, 190, 232.

63 Ashe, *Biographical History*, III, 474–77.

64 Gregg, *Essays on Domestic Industry*, p. 12.

65 Cf. Ashe, *Biographical History*, III, 435–53; Hamilton (ed.), *Correspondence of Jonathan Worth*, I, v–xi, *passim;* Clarence Phillips Denman, *The Secession Movement in Alabama* (Montgomery, Ala., 1933), pp. 129–30; Clinton, *Tuscaloosa*, pp. 132–33; Joseph H. Parks, *John Bell of Tennessee* (Baton Rouge, La., 1950).

66 Mitchell, *William Gregg*, p. 181.

67 *DBR*, XXIV (May 1858), 385.

68 Gregg, *Essays on Domestic Industry*, p. 42.

69 *Ibid.*, p. 29n.

70 *Congressional Globe*, XIII, 1st Session, 28th Congress, Appendix, p. 108; *cf. HMM*, X (May 1844), p. 406, for a full account of the debate.

71 Cf. De Bow, *Industrial Resources*, II, 127, 154.

72 Gregg to Lawrence, Sept. 2, 1850, in Thomas P. Martin (ed.), "The Advent of William Gregg and the Graniteville Company," *JSH*, XI (Aug. 1945), p. 422. Martin has made an excellent selection of letters and provided a useful introduction.

73 *DBR*, XI (Aug. 1851), 127–28.

74 Gregg, *Essays on Domestic Industry*, pp. 21–22.

75 *DBR*, XI (Aug. 1851), 138.

76 Sept. 2, 1850, in *JSH*, XI (Aug. 1945), 422.

77 *DBR*, XXX (Jan. 1861), 103.

78 *American Cotton Planter* (Montgomery, Ala.), XIII (April 1859), 114–15 (Pratt); *DBR*, XXIV (May 1858), 385–86 (Martin).

79 *The Life, Speeches, and Public Services of John Bell* (New York, 1860), speech of July 2, 1856; *cf.* Parks, *John Bell*, p. 217.

80 Ashe, *Biographical History*, I, 95–99; Burton Alva Konkle, *John Motley Morehead and the Development of North Carolina, 1799–1866* (Philadelphia, 1922), p. 195.

81 *Life, Speeches, and Public Services of John Bell*, p. 86.

82 Quoted by Sitterson, *Secession Movement*, p. 161.

83 Mitchell, *William Gregg*, p. 203.

84 See, *e.g.*, David L. Smiley's able biography, *Lion of White Hall*, esp. pp. 107, 166.

85 *JSH*, XI (Aug. 1945), p. 394 of Martin's introduction; *cf.* David D. Wallace, "The Founding of Graniteville," *THR*, I (Jan. 1960), 21.

86 *DBR*, XI (Aug. 1851), 130.

87 Elizabeth Merritt, *James Henry Hammond, 1807–1864* (Baltimore, 1923), p. 87, n. 40; *DBR*, III, 36–37.

88 *DBR*, XXIX (July 1860), 77.

89 *DBR*, XXIX (Aug. 1860), 232.

90 *DBR*, XXIX (July 1860), 78.

91 *DBR*, XXIX (July 1860), 84.

92 Mitchell, *William Gregg*, pp. 132–33, 146–47; for the Gregg-Hammond Correspondence see *JSH*, XI (Aug. 1945), 404–8, 410–12.

93 *DBR*, XXX (March 1861), 358; Ashe, *Biographical History*, II, 334–43; Denman, *Secession*, p. 147; Clinton, *Tuscaloosa*, pp. 132–33.

94 Cooper to Cobb, Nov. 20, 1848, in Ulrich B. Phillips (ed.), *The Correspondence of Robert Toombs, Alexander H. Stephens, and Howell Cobb* ("Annual Report of the American Historical Association," 1911, Vol. II; Washington,

D.C., 1913), p. 137; Message of Gov. Brown to House of Representatives, Nov. 17, 1860, in Candler (ed.), *Confederate Records of Georgia*, II, 3.

95 Ashe, *Biographical History*, I, 365.

96 Richard W. Griffin, "The Civil War and Cotton Manufactures in North Carolina," *THR*, II (July 1961), 152. Some industrialists, like the Milner-Wood-Wrenn woolens group, sent word to their state governors months before secession advertising their ability to produce war supplies. *Cf.* Bernarr Cresap, "The Cowpen Factory," *THR*, I (April 1960), 61.

97 *Cf.* Morehead III, *Morehead Family*, p. 52.

98 Ashe, *Biographical History*, II, 334–43.

99 *DBR*, X (Feb. 1851), 227.

100 Reprinted in Tarrant (ed.), *Daniel Pratt*, pp. 75–76.

101 See, *e.g.*, Pratt's letter to the citizens of Temple, N.H., his home town, Sept. 8, 1858, in *ibid.*, pp. 80–81.

102 S. Mims in *ibid.*, p. 57.

103 Ashe, *Biographical History*, I, 116–24; 309–21.

104 *Ibid.*, I, 398–404.

105 Parks, *John Bell*, p. 405.

106 Kohn, *Cotton Mills*, biographical sketches of Hammett and Leak; Ashe, *Biographical History*, II, 315–19, III, 454–60.

107 T. C. De Leon, *Four Years in Rebel Capitals* (Mobile, Ala., 1892), p. 91; Ashe, *Biographical History*, II, 282–92; J. B. O. Landrum, *History of Spartanburg County* (Atlanta, Ga., 1900), p. 66; *Cyclopedia of Eminent and Representative Men of the Carolinas of the Nineteenth Century* (Madison, Wis., 1892), pp. 465–66.

108 *Biographical History*, II, 315.

109 Yearns, *Confederate Congress*, p. 56.

110 *Cf. e.g., Journal of the Congress of the Confederate States*, Vol. IV.

111 Paul Avery Meigs, *The Life of Senator Robert Jemison, Junior* (University, Ala., 1928), pp. 53–54.

112 *Proceedings of the Confederate Congress* ("Southern Historical Society Papers," XLIV–L, ed. Douglas Southall Freeman *et al.*, 1923–1953), XLIV, 192.

113 *Morehead: In Memoriam*, p. 32; *Journal of the Congress of the Confederate States*, I, 565.

114 Ashe, *Biographical History*, III, 435–53; Coulter, *Confederate States*, p. 235; Hamilton (ed.), *Correspondence of Jonathan Worth*, introduction.

115 Merrill E. Pratt, "Daniel Pratt, Alabama's First Industrialist," *THR*, II (Jan. 1961), 19–29; Ashe, *Biographical History*, II, 328–33.

116 *Ibid.*, pp. 24–25.

117 Ashe, *Biographical History*, III, 474; Ella Lonn, *Salt as a Factor in the Confederacy* (New York, 1933), p. 98.

118 Ashe, *Biographical History*, III, 462.

119 *Ibid.*, I, 365.

120 Fletcher M. Green, *JSH*, II (Feb. 1936), 38.

121 Quoted by the Augusta, Ga., *Daily Chronicle and Sentinel;* for a reprint see *THR*, II (Jan. 1961), 40.

122 David K. Young Books, Vol. I: Constitution and Minutes of the Anderson County Agricultural and Mechanical Society, 1856, of which Young was secretary; Oliver P. Temple, *Notable Men of Tennessee from 1833 to 1875* (New York, 1912).

123 Ashe, *Biographical History*, II, 20–26.

124 Mitchell, *William Gregg*, p. ix. Pratt, too, has been called, "The first 'industrialist' of the South." Merrill E. Pratt, *THR*, II (Jan. 1961), p. 19. With greater restraint, D. A. Tompkins writes of J. M. Morehead: "It was only by such men—strong and broad—that manufacturing was kept alive in the Old South, throughout the ascendancy of the

regime of slavery with its attendant agricultural aristocracy." *Cotton Mills, Commercial Features*, p. 188.

125 *Cf.* J. Carlyle Sitterson, "Business Leaders in Post-Civil War North Carolina, 1865–1900," in Sitterson (ed.), *Studies in Southern History* (Chapel Hill, N.C., 1957), pp. 111–21.

Nine ■ Slave Labor or Free in the Southern Factories: A Political Analysis of an Economic Debate

The excited and sometimes bitter debate between those who wished to use slaves in Southern factories and those who wished to use free white laborers quickly passed beyond discussion of the economic advantages of one or the other. Experience could be relied upon to settle the strictly economic question in particular industries and districts. Experience could not be relied upon to settle the social and political questions. A miscalculation of labor costs might produce ruin for a few investors but could make wiser entrepreneurs of their successors; a miscalculation of the effects of raising a class of urban factory slaves or white proletarians could prove fatal to the Southern social system. This debate over a seemingly economic question cannot be understood unless studied in its political context, the main feature of which was the intention of the rural slaveholders to maintain their hegemony at all cost.

The case for Negro labor, which always meant slave labor

since no one proposed using free Negroes, took several forms, basically social or political. Negroes were sometimes held to be as efficient as whites, all things being equal, but were rarely held to be more efficient. The proponents of Negro labor argued that all things were not equal and that, even if less efficient on a day-to-day basis, Negroes were more so on a season-to-season basis since they could not readily leave their jobs.

The Natchez *Ariel*, referring to the hemp factories of Kentucky, commented in 1827: "Why are slaves employed? Simply because experiment has proved that they are more *docile*, more constant, and cheaper than freemen, who are often refractory and dissipated; who waste much time by frequenting public places, attending musters, elections, etc., which the operative slave is not permitted to frequent."[1] This theme recurred throughout the antebellum period. In 1845, the Pensacola *Gazette* noted the use of slaves by the Arcadia Manufacturing Company and added: "It is determined to incur this last expense at once, in order to avoid the possible inconvenience of white operatives becoming disatisfied and leaving their work" [*sic*].[2] Samuel D. Morgan, the big Tennessee iron producer, said simply in 1852 that slaves did not strike and could not demand wage increases as their skill and productivity improved.[3]

William Gregg set the case in a more elaborate theoretical framework when he wrote that whereas labor and capital were becoming antagonistic in industrial countries, slavery united the interests of labor and capital in the person of the slave and thereby avoided the class struggle. Besides, he added, manufacturers "are not under the necessity of educating [slaves] and have, therefore, their uninterrupted services from the age of eight years."[4] Gregg admitted that the question of which kind of labor was the cheaper remained unsettled, and he soon made himself famous by his work at Graniteville, which relied on whites.

Slave labor had hidden virtues. Manufacturers found it difficult to induce planters to invest liquid capital in factories but easier to induce them to lease slaves in exchange for shares of stock. Under conditions of capital shortage and less than optimum cotton prices slave labor took on a special attractiveness, whatever the manufacturers' judgment of its relative efficiency.

The other side of the same appeal offered slaveholders a chance to improve their economic position by deflecting surplus slaves into industry. As Governor Aaron V. Brown of Tennessee wrote to the New Orleans Railroad Convention:

> You will never adjourn, I hope, without making the strongest appeals to our capitalists, and especially our planters, to engage in [industry]. The latter can build the houses necessary with their own hands. Two or three or half a dozen can unite in one establishment. They can select from their own stock of slaves, the most active and intelligent ones for operatives, without the necessary advances in money to white laborers. . . . I earnestly desire to see one-fourth of southern slave labor diverted from the *production* to the *manufacture* of cotton. One-fourth of such labor abstracted, would give a steadiness and elevation of prices to the raw material, which would better justify its cultivation.[5]

As Southern hopes for territorial expansion dimmed, manufacturing became, for some, a guarantee against a labor surplus.[6] In its more extreme political form this argument emerged as an appeal to "bring slave labor directly into competition with Northern labor."[7] E. Steadman, using an argument similar to Brown's, added, "And this is not all. These laborers from producers are turned into consumers. They convert a considerable portion of the cotton produced by those who remain in the field, and thus still further enhance the value of the crop."[8]

Tobacco factories buttressed the plantation regime on the

countryside in two ways: they provided a ready market for the crops and hired those slaves who were not needed in the fields.[9] The cotton textile industry, on the other hand, shifted to white labor as the years went by, although numerous slaves worked in factories in Alabama and elsewhere.[10] The iron industry in both the Lower and Upper South absorbed large numbers of slaves, as did the railroads, despite complaints, such as that of Confederate Senator Wright of Georgia, who described Negro colliers as irresponsible and worthless.[11] Slaves, sometimes purchased, more often rented, were generally recruited locally and provided a strong bond of interest between the planters and manufacturers.

Dependence on slave labor had its drawbacks, for rising slave prices might at any time dry up the sources of supply. In Charleston, South Carolina, for example, the industrial progress of the 1840s received a severe jolt from the return of high cotton prices in the 1850s, which generated a derived demand for slaves. Estimates placed the number of slaves sold out of Charleston during the 1850s at ten thousand.[12] "It was," writes Griffin, "the fervent hope of all the factory owners that immigration would bring sufficient white people back into the [industrial region of Georgia] so they could dispense with hiring slaves."[13]

If manufacturers had mixed experiences and unsettled thoughts on slave labor, planters found their own reasons for uneasiness. On the one hand, they had an economic stake in slave hiring and a deep suspicion of white labor; on the other hand, they looked askance at the social consequences of industrial urban slavery. On balance, Russel may be right when he observes, "It is hard to escape the conclusion that many Southerners were interested in manufactures only so long as it appeared possible to conduct them with slave labor; when experience finally demonstrated the superiority of white labor, their interest declined."[14]

That demonstrated superiority of white labor grew out of

superior incentives and training and was therefore not universal, for slaves often obtained both. Unfortunately, the more incentives and training they got, the more the rural slaveholders looked on with dismay. How were planters to react upon learning, for example, that slaves in the tobacco-manufacturing towns selected their own employer, received money with which to obtain food and lodgings as they pleased, and expected bonuses for extra work?[15] What were planters to think when they learned that so long as the slaves at Tredegar did their job they were, in the words of Kathleen Bruce, "pretty much on the basis of free labor"?[16] The story was the same in the hemp factories of Kentucky, the gold mines of Virginia, the railroads of Tennessee, and generally.[17] It could not be other, for the secret of making the slave into a good industrial worker lay precisely in giving him incentives well beyond those available to field hands. That this tendency could not be permitted to go far enough to undermine plantation discipline was lost on no reasonably alert planter.

"Whenever a slave is made a mechanic," James H. Hammond told the South Carolina Institute in 1849, "he is more than half freed, and soon becomes, as we too well know, and all history attests, with rare exceptions, the most corrupt and turbulent of his class."[18] The South Carolina legislative Committee on Negro Population considered several memorials asking for laws to prohibit slaves from hiring their own time and working in the mechanic arts. J. Harlston Read, Jr., the committee's chairman, agreed with the memorialists that the practices were "evil" and denounced the practice of allowing slaves "to conduct themselves as if they were not slaves." The practices were so deeply rooted in custom and interest, he explained, that nothing could or should be done.[19] In short, the antipathy of the slaveholders as a class had to be weighed against the established rights and interests of individual slaveholders.

The behavior of the urban Negroes gave planters reason

for concern. The attitude of New Orleans slaves toward whites shocked the sensibilities of all who knew of it. According to Tregle: "It was not unusual for slaves to gather on street corners at night, for example, where they challenged whites to attempt to pass, hurled taunts at white women, and kept whole neighborhoods disturbed by shouts and curses. Nor was it safe to accost them, as many went armed with knives and pistols in flagrant defiance of all the precautions of the Black Code."[20] The early experience of the Charleston District left a permanent impression. At the end of the eighteenth century "trustworthy slaves were practically in a state of industrial freedom," but the Denmark Vesey conspiracy of 1822 frightened the slaveholders into an intense reaction.[21]

An elite stratum of urban slaves offered advantages to the regime by giving the more talented and intellectually vigorous Negroes privileges to protect by good behavior, but it offered more serious disadvantages by tempting them into disorders, giving them opportunities to become literate, providing them with access to political news, and arousing their hopes for freedom. When Nathaniel A. Ware, a prominent banker, planter, and nationalistic economist, wrote an anonymous article for Cassius Clay's *True American* in which he drew logical conclusions from the practices associated with urbanizing Negroes and advocated gradual emancipation for slaves and political rights for free Negroes, the reaction was swift: it was this article which led to the famous mob assault against the crusading, antislavery newspaper.[22]

The use of whites did not guarantee a better work force than did the use of Negroes, for the South lacked an adequate pool of disciplined free workers. S. Mims, a close friend of Daniel Pratt, wrote in his eulogistic "History of Prattville": "Hands had to be trained. These were brought up from the piney woods, many of them with no sort of training to any kind of labor; in fact, they had to learn everything, and in learning many mistakes and blunders were made fatal to success."[23] At Graniteville, the South's other industrial show-case, the same story was told by Gregg's associate, James H. Taylor. Southern white labor was not disciplined to sustained labor, he admitted, but only time was needed to bring it up to Northern standards.[24] A prominent Negro politician of reconstruction days told of having had to keep accounts and write letters, while still a slave, for white workers in the Alabama salt works during the war.[25]

In many industries the problem remained unsolved. Southern timber, for example, had to be sent to Northern yards instead of supplying a Southern shipbuilding industry, primarily be-cause labor costs, with a shortage of skills, were prohibitive.[26] Since laborers ranked far down in the social scale, progress had to be slow. Factory workers did not command as much respect as the poorest farmers or even the landless agricultural workers.[27] As James Martin, the Florence, Alabama, indus-trialist, wrote in 1858: "We have not yet a sufficient amount of trained labor to enable companies to do well. . . . The strange notion that our young men have, in believing the train-ing of the mind and hand to any kind of handicraft causes them to lose caste in society" [*sic*].[28] In spite of the difficulties, sufficient progress did occur to enable Richard W. Griffin to write that the cotton textile industry came out of the war battered but with its most valuable resource intact—"the skilled labor and experienced supervisors."[29]

In view of the backwardness of the employable whites the main disadvantage of slave labor lay in the sacrifice of flexi-bility and the tying up of capital occasioned by purchase or renting. This disadvantage would have lost its significance if the whites had proved militant in the defense of their interests, but many Southern spokesmen expressed confidence in their steadi-ness and docility. As the debate proceeded, the main argument of the advocates of white labor became the social one: society's responsibility to do something for the poor. William Gregg, abandoning his earlier concern for slave labor, led the appeal on behalf of the poor whites. Industry would absorb the thousands of landless poor, he argued, and would simultaneously uplift society's downtrodden, widen the home market, and help raise the economic and cultural level of society as a whole.[30]

Most participants in the debate went further than Gregg in the social argument and warned that the absorption of the poor whites by industry was essential to the maintenance of the slaveholders' regime. Increasingly, the appeal for industrial expansion based on white labor took this form. Whites should be employed in factories, J. H. Lumpkin of Georgia wrote in 1852, so that they can receive moral instruction under proper supervision.[31]

Hammond, as usual, spoke out bluntly in his address to the South Carolina Institute in 1849:

> But it has been suggested that white factory operatives in the South would constitute a body hostile to our domestic institutions. If any such sentiments could take root among the poorer classes of our native citizens, more danger may be apprehended from them, in the present state of things, with the facilities they now possess and the difficulties they now have to encounter, than if they were brought together in factories, with constant employment and adequate remuneration. It is well known that the abolitionists of America and Europe are now making the most strenuous efforts to enlist them in their crusade, by encouraging the use of what is called "free labor cotton," and by inflammatory appeals to their pride and their supposed interests. But all apprehensions from this source are entirely imaginary. The poorest and humblest freeman of the South feels as sensibly, perhaps more sensibly than the wealthiest planter, the barrier which nature, as well as law, has erected between the white and black races . . . Besides this, the factory operative could

not fail to see here, what one would suppose he must see, however distant from us, that the whole fabric of his fortunes was based on our slave system . . .[32]

Hammond's argument was echoed by others, but no one, not even Hammond himself, presented it so clearly as Gregg's associate, James H. Taylor. Taylor's words about "a great upbearing of our masses" have often been quoted, but too often out of context:

. . . Because an effort has been made to collect the poor and unemployed white population into our new factories, fears have arisen, that some evil would grow out of the introduction of such establishments among us. . . . I take the ground, that our institutions are safe if we are *true to ourselves;* and, *that truthfulness* must not only be manifest in our statesmen and politicians, but must be an abiding *principle* in the *masses* of our people. The poor man has a vote, as well as the rich man; and in our State, the *number* of the first will largely overbalance the last. So long as these poor, but industrious people, could see no mode of living, except by a degrading operation of work with the negro upon the plantation, they were content to endure life in its most discouraging forms, satisfied that they were *above* the slave, though faring, often worse than he. But the progress of the world is "onward," and though in some sections it is still slow, still it is "onward," and the great mass of our poor white population begin to understand that they have rights, and that they too, are entitled to some of the sympathy which falls upon the suffering. They are fast learning, that there is an almost infinite world of industry opening before them, by which they can elevate themselves and their families from wretchedness and ignorance to competence and intelligence. *It is this great upbearing of our masses that we are to fear, so far as our institutions are concerned.*

Let our slaves be continued where they have been, and where they are of immense value; let them raise from the earth the cotton, rice, corn, etc., which they are so well fitted to do, and then furnish the white population with employment in the manufactory and mechanical arts: and every man, from the deepest principle of self-interest, becomes a firm and uncompromising supporter of our institutions. But crowd from these employments the fast increasing white population of the South, and fill our factories and workshops with our slaves, and we shall have in our midst those whose very existence is in hostile array to our institutions.[33]

The full implications of this line of reasoning appeared, as might be expected, from the logical mind and facile pen of George Fitzhugh:

As ours is a government of the people, no where is education so necessary. The poor, too, ask no charity, when they demand universal education. They constitute our militia and our police. They protect men in possession of property, as in other countries; and do much more, they secure men in possession of a kind of property which they could not hold a day but for the supervision and protection of the poor. This very property has rendered the South merely agricultural, made population too sparse for neighborhood schools, prevented a variety of pursuits, and thus cut the poor off as well from the means of living, as from the means of education.[34]

Educate all Southern whites, employ them not as lacqueys, ploughmen, and menials, but as independent freemen should be employed, and let negroes be strictly tied down to such callings as are unbecoming white men, and peace would be established between blacks and whites.[35]

Finally, Fitzhugh made the point in language even dolts would understand: "The path of safety is the path of duty! Educate the people, no matter what it may cost."[36]

The arguments of the Hammonds, Taylors, and Fitzhughs made headway, but slowly and in the face of stubborn opposition and even more stubborn apathy. Much of the resistance to chartering Graniteville had arisen from displeasure with Gregg's plan to use white labor.[37] When Gregg defended his policy before the South Carolina Institute a few years later, he was sharply attacked by the *Charleston Mercury* and even denounced by an irresponsible gossip for allegedly advocating a doctrine identical with that of "Free Soil and Free Labor."[38] In a more rational vein, C. G. Memminger wrote to Hammond arguing that Negroes, not whites, ought to be employed in factories because a white proletariat would represent the greatest possible threat to the regime. These "Lowellers," he punned in a grim and worried letter, would soon all become abolitionists.[39]

Memminger's fears did not impress men like De Bow, who pointed out that Southern factory workers did not have contact with immigrants and foreign "isms."[40] The presence of four million slaves, according to one commentator, deterred immigration, for if foreigners did come, "it would probably be to starve."[41] Edmund Ruffin expressed the general feeling of the planters when he wrote: "One of the great benefits of the institution of African slavery to the Southern states is its effect in keeping away from our territory, and directing to the north and northwest, the hordes of immigrants now flowing from Europe."[42] Griffin attributes the docility and passivity of white workers in the textile mills to the newness of employment and to "the lack of European emigrants, who brought a more highly developed class consciousness with them to the North."[43]

Reliance on the isolation of native workers from foreign placed the advocates of increased manufacturing in a contradiction, for one of the effects of industrial expansion and the rising demand for skilled labor was certain to be greater immigration. C. T. James, to whom many Southern pro-industrial spokesmen looked for support and guidance, laid great stress on the certainty that the South would attract skilled labor just as soon as it could pay for it.[44] J. L. Orr, an advocate of industrial expansion, chose consistency over safety and advocated liberal naturalization procedures in the Confederacy, praising foreign mechanics as "everywhere useful citizens."[45]

Not many Orrs were to be found in the slave states. The foreign-born population of the Southern cities continued to cause apprehension among the rural slaveholders. With only 20 per cent of Charleston's population foreign-born in 1848, foreigners led natives by almost two to one in the race for poorhouse admission.[46] Elsewhere, except in New Orleans, conditions were about the same: unskilled Irish workers struggling to stay alive, Jewish peddlers and small merchants doing a necessary job but arousing considerable resentment by their mode of life, German artisans falling under the suspicion of antislavery feelings, and so forth.[47] Enthusiasm for manufacturing waned as it became clear that whites, not blacks, would be employed and that many foreigners would be joining the natives. The triumph of the Know-Nothings, in the streets and at the polls in the Southern cities, dealt a heavy blow to the industrial impulse, although ironically most Know-Nothings had been Whigs who were favorable to manufacturing. Even more ironically, the Know-Nothing upsurge tied the foreign-born workers more firmly to the Democratic party, which was rapidly becoming the party of the proslavery extremists.[48]

However docile the urban working class may have been relative to its Northern counterpart, it was becoming sufficiently rebellious to give pause to those who saw it as a political bulwark of the slave regime. Arthur C. Cole suggests that the class consciousness of the urban workers rose distinctly above that of the rural poor.[49] Labor organizations, although few, appeared with sufficient force and regularity to cause alarm. In the Upper South, unions grew more easily than further south. During the 1850s Baltimore, St. Louis, and Louisville gave rise to militant unions, which conducted strikes for higher wages and a ten-hour day.[50] Significant labor groups appeared sporadically in Virginia, South Carolina, and Louisiana during the 1830s.[51] At least two strong unions functioned in New Orleans during the 1850s: the Screwman's Association, which raised wages by 20 per cent by a successful strike in 1854; and the New Orleans Typographical Society, which successfully struck to defeat a wage-cutting campaign by the Associated Press during the same year.[52] Throughout the 1850s strikes and working-class demonstrations broke out, and the resort to slaves could not always be relied upon by employers to break a strike.[53]

Labor militancy disturbed the slaveholders on two counts: it indicated an unruliness among the lower class that offended their conservative sensibilities and made them apprehensive about the security of property in general; and it raised the specter of antislavery agitation. The direct and indirect workings of the slave system threatened the very freedom of the white workers. Richard B. Morris writes: "Confronted, on the one side, with competition from Negro labor and, on the other, with some influx of foreign immigrant and Northern labor, the position of white labor in South Carolina steadily deteriorated in the ante-bellum period. As labor controls in general tightened, many white workers suffered in fact a loss of their freedom of occupational choice, and their mobility, and suffered at law a denial of their right to take concerted action . . ."[54] The use of slaves, and even free Negroes, as mechanics, not to mention strikebreakers, led to serious and mounting agitation among urban white workers. It was only a short step from specific complaints about such practices to more general demands for social and political reform.[55] Anti-Negro feeling among the workers inhibited the growth of anti-slavery feeling, but the two were not incompatible and the latter did make strides. When the editor of the *Charleston Mercury* publicly approved George Fitzhugh's doctrine that slavery was the natural condition of all labor, the white mechanics burned him in effigy in a wrathful demonstration.[56] As organized Southern labor made steady, if slow and painful, progress during the 1850s, its leaders exhibited increasing hostility to the slave regime.[57] The use of Negro slaves to break strikes and of the state apparatus to imprison strike leaders pulled the white workers, however reluctantly, into fundamental opposition.

The pleas of the Hammonds, Taylors, and Greggs for the employment of white labor in factories must be evaluated in the light of these events. The growth of working-class consciousness, manifesting itself in conflicts with this or that feature of the slave regime, bore out the fears of those slaveholders who refused to yield to such pleas.[58] The sophisticated arguments of Hammond and Taylor, were, after all, mostly humbug. They rested on the assumption that the non-slaveholders would represent a greater danger to slavery under conditions of rural poverty than they would under conditions of urban industrial employment. Logic and experience suggested the reverse.

Taylor's famous remarks about a "great upbearing of our masses" are a case in point. A careful reading of his words reveals that he feared, or pretended to fear, that dissatisfaction would follow the inevitable rise in the expectations of the rural poor. He never did prove that expectations were in fact rising or about to rise. Whatever rise was occurring or was expected to occur might be traced to the impact of industrial expansion. Why then should slaveholders not conclude that industrialization, on any kind of a labor basis, would awaken their slumbering masses and cause trouble? Rural poverty and isolation, with its attendant cultural backwardness and absence of a direct and exploiting employer, generally produced acquiescence in the status quo. Urbanized workers, victimized by racism, might accept slavery in the abstract but were much more likely to collide with its political and social apparatus, and every such collision carried with it the danger of arousing a more profound consciousness of class interest.

Hammond and Taylor were really too clever. Industrialization would bind the workers to the regime by giving them jobs and flattering their feelings of racial superiority and would bind the industrialists to the regime by forcing them to rely on the slaveholders' black strikebreakers and political power to handle working-class unrest. Unfortunately, both workers and industrialists would benefit from public education, internal improvements to open new markets, increased urban political power, and a variety of other measures that the slaveholders could not easily accept. Unfortunately too, the workers could not be counted on to confine their class hostility to the manufacturers while the latter's dependence on the planters' power was so blatant.

Rural slaveholders had to view industrialization with either slave labor or free with misgivings. They needed more local manufacturing to supply the needs of the plantations and to guarantee the economic and military power of their states, but could not afford to permit too much. The exigencies of nineteenth-century life confronted the slaveholders with insoluble problems, with which they grappled as best they could. In the end, they could take no step along the industrial road without exposing themselves to perils so grave as to endanger their existence as a class.

N O T E S

1 Quoted by Thomas P. Jones, M. D., "The Progress of Manufactures and Internal Improvements in the United States and Particularly on the Advantages to be Derived from the Employment of Slaves in the Manufacturing of

Cotton and Other Goods," first published in the *American Farmer* (1827) and republished in *THR*, III (July 1962), 156. Original emphasis.

2 "Notes on the Arcadia (Florida) Manufacturing Company," Pensacola *Gazette*, Sept. 13, 1845, as reprinted in *THR*, II (July 1961), 163.

3 *South-Western Monthly*, II (Sept. 1852), 173–75.

4 Gregg, *Essays on Domestic Industry*, p. 48; *cf.* Mitchell, *William Gregg*, p. 23.

5 Brown, *Speeches, Congressional and Political*, p. 547.

6 See, *e.g.*, *DBR*, VIII (Jan. 1850), 25, 75–76; XII (Feb. 1852), 182.

7 *DBR*, XII (Feb. 1852), 185.

8 "A Brief Treatise on Manufacturing in the South," reprinted in *THR*, II (April 1962), 112.

9 Joseph R. Robert, *The Tobacco Kingdom* (Durham, N.C., 1938), p. 198.

10 *Cf.* Ernest M. Lander, Jr., "Slave Labor in the South Carolina Cotton Mills," *JNH*, XXXVIII (April 1953), 164–65 and *passim;* Richard W. Griffin, "Cotton Manufacture in Alabama to 1860," *AHQ*, XVIII (Fall 1956), 291–93.

11 Speech on the exemption bill, Sept. 20, 1862. *Proceedings of the Confederate Congress*, ed. Douglas Southall Freeman, *Southern Historical Society Papers*, XLVI, 192. For the iron industry see Lester J. Cappon, "Iron-Making—a Forgotten Industry of North Carolina," *NCHR*, IX (Oct. 1932), 341; Ernest M. Lander, Jr., "The Iron Industry in Ante Bellum South Carolina," *JSH*, XX (Aug. 1954), 350; Robert E. Corlew, "Some Aspects of Slavery in Dickson County," *Tennessee Historical Quarterly*, X (Sept. 1951), 229; Woodward, *Alabama Review*, VII (July 1954), 200. For the railroads see Black, *Railroads of the Confederacy*, pp. 29–30.

12 Leonard Price Stavisky, "Industrialism in Ante Bellum Charleston," *JNH*, XXXVI (July 1951), 319.

13 Richard W. Griffin, "The Origins of the Industrial Revolution in Georgia: Cotton Textiles, 1810–1865," *GHQ*, XLII (Dec. 1958), 363. According to John A. Chapman, Gregg's indifferent results at Vaucluse, in contrast to his later success at Graniteville, were due to his shift from slave to free labor. This opinion has not been corroborated. See his *History of Edgefield County*, p. 100.

14 *Economic Aspects*, p. 55.

15 Robert, *Tobacco Kingdom*, pp. 203 ff.

16 *Virginia Manufacture in the Slave Era* (New York, 1931), p. 252, n. 89.

17 Cf. James F. Hopkins, *A History of the Hemp Industry in Kentucky* (Lexington, Ky., 1951), p. 135; Black, *Railroads of the Confederacy*, p. 30; and Morris, *MVHR*, XLI (Sept. 1954), 231–35.

18 *DBR*, VIII (June 1850), 518.

19 *DBR*, XXVI (May 1859), 600.

20 Joseph G. Tregle, Jr., "Early New Orleans Society: A Reappraisal," *JSH*, XVIII (Feb. 1952), 34; Russel, *Economic Aspects*, p. 211.

21 Ulrich B. Phillips, "Slave Labor in the Charleston District," *PSQ*, XXII (Sept. 1907), 427, 429.

22 Smiley, *Lion of White Hall*, p. 261, n. 1.

23 Tarrant (ed.), *Daniel Pratt*, p. 26.

24 *DBR*, VIII (Jan. 1850), 27.

25 Walter E. Fleming, "Industrial Development in Alabama during the Civil War," *SAQ*, III (July 1904), 271.

26 Hutchins, *American Maritime Industries*, pp. 190–91.

27 Bonner, *AHR*, XLIX (July 1944), 670; T. P. Abernethy, *From Frontier to Plantation in Tennessee* (Durham, N.C., 1932), p. 286.

28 *DBR*, XXIV (May 1858), 383.

29 *THR*, II (July 1961), 1.

30 This argument had appeared as early as the *Essays on Domestic Industry* (see esp. pp. 105–13) and was developed in most of his writings thereafter.

31 *DBR*, IX (Jan. 1852), 249; *cf.* Richard W. Griffin, "Poor White Laborers in Southern Cotton Factories, 1789–1865," *SCHGM*, LXI (Jan. 1860), 32 ff.

32 *DBR*, VIII (June 1850), 519–20.

33 *DBR*, VIII (Jan. 1850), 25–26; also XXVI (April 1859), 477–78.

34 *Sociology for the South* (Richmond, Va., 1854), pp. 144–45.

35 *Ibid.*, p. 147.

36 *Ibid.*, p. 148.

37 Wallace, *THR*, I (Jan. 1960), 21.

38 Lander, *JNH*, XXXVIII (April 1953), 169.

39 Thomas P. Martin (ed.), *JSH*, XI (Aug. 1945), 414: letter dated April 28, 1849.

40 J. D. B. De Bow, *The Interest in Slavery of the Southern Non-Slaveholder* (Charleston, S.C., 1860), p. 8.

41 *SQR*, XXVI, 435.

42 *Address to the Virginia State Agricultural Society*, pp. 16–17.

43 *SCHGM*, LXI (Jan. 1960), 38.

44 C. T. James, *Practical Hints on the Comparative Costs and Productiveness of the Culture of Cotton* . . . (Providence, 1849), *passim;* and *Letters on the Culture and Manufacture of Cotton* (New York, 1850), p. 5.

45 Quoted in Ruth Ketring Nuermberger, *The Clays of Alabama* (Lexington, Ky., 1958), p. 201.

46 Benjamin Joseph Klebaner, "Public Poor Relief in Charleston, 1800–1860," *SCHGM*, LV (Oct. 1954), 218.

47 *Cf.* Herbert Weaver, "Foreigners in Ante-Bellum Towns of the Lower South," *JSH*, XIII (Feb. 1947), 62–73.

48 The foreign-born population of Natchez in 1860 was 25% of the total; Mobile, 24%; Louisville, 34%; Memphis, 36%; Charleston, 15.5% (but 36% of the whites). See Eaton, *Growth of Southern Civilization*, pp. 250 f, for a good discussion of the Southern cities in the 1850s.

49 *The Irrepressible Conflict* (New York, 1934), pp. 37–38.

50 John R. Commons, *et al.*, *History of Labour in the United States* (New York, 1918), I, 358–59, 386–87, 478.

51 Richard B. Morris, "Labor Militancy in the Old South," *Labor and Nation*, IV (May–June 1948), 33; *cf.* Wyatt, *William and Mary College Quarterly*, XVII (Jan. 1937), 20.

52 Philip S. Foner, *History of the Labor Movement in the United States from Colonial Times to the Founding of the American Federation of Labor* (New York, 1947), p. 249.

53 Herbert Aptheker, *The Labor Movement in the South during Slavery* (New York, 1955), pp. 12–14; *cf.* Eaton, *Growth of Southern Civilization*, pp. 165–66.

54 "White Bondage in Ante-Bellum South Carolina," *SCHGM*, XLIX (Oct. 1948), 194–95; and *MHVR*, XLI (Sept. 1954), 219–40.

55 *Cf.* Eaton, *Growth of Southern Civilization*, pp. 167–68; Fletcher M. Green, *Constitutional Development in the South Atlantic States, 1776–1860* (Chapel Hill, N.C., 1930), pp. 159–61.

56 Cole, *Irrepressible Conflict*, p. 55.

57 Bernard Mandel, *Labor: Free and Slave* (New York, 1955), Chap. II, esp. pp. 54–55; Foner, *Labor Movement*, pp. 262–63.

58 Russel, *Economic Aspects*, pp. 52–53; and "Economic History of Negro Slavery in the United States," *Agr. Hist.*, XI (Oct. 1937), 321.

PART FOUR ❧ THE GENERAL CRISIS OF THE SLAVE SOUTH

Matter does not have *but is* force or energy. *Only because it acts and acts on others is it actual. The expression of force is force itself, not an effect external to it. The externality of space-time relations in which this action and reaction or resistance takes place defines forces as natural.*

■ G. W. F. HEGEL, *Encyclopedia of Philosophy*

Ten ■ The Origins of Slavery Expansionism

Once upon a time in the happy and innocent days of the nineteenth century, men believed that Negro slavery had raised an expansionist slaveocracy to power in the American South. Today we know better. The revisionists have denied that slavery was expansionist and have virtually driven their opponents from the field. Their arguments, as distinct from their faith in the possibilities of resolving antagonisms peacefully, rest on two formidable essays. In 1926, Avery O. Craven published his *Soil Exhaustion as a Factor in the Agricultural History of Maryland and Virginia*, which sought to prove that the slave economy could reform itself, and three years later Charles William Ramsdell published his famous article on "The Natural Limits of Slavery Expansion,"[1] which constituted a frontal attack on the "irrepressible conflict" school.

I propose to restate the traditional view, but in such a way as to avoid the simplistic and mechanistic notions of Cairnes and his followers and to account for the data that has emerged from the conscientious and often splendid researches of the revisionist historians. Specifically, I propose to show that economics, politics, social life, ideology, and psychology converged to thrust the system outward and that beneath each factor lay the exigencies of the slaveholding class. Each dictated expansion if the men who made up the ruling class of the South were to continue to rule.

❂ Roots and Taproot

Antebellum Southern economic history reinforces rather than overturns the nineteenth-century notion of an expansionist slaveocracy. That notion undoubtedly suffered from grave defects and considerable crudeness, for it insisted on the lack of versatility of slave labor and the steady deterioration of the soil without appreciating the partially effective attempts to reform the slave economy. Yet the revisionist work of the Craven school, which has contributed so much toward an understanding of the economic complexities, has not added up to a successful refutation.

We may recapitulate briefly the main points of the preceding studies, which lead to the economic root of slavery expansionism. At the beginning we encounter the low productivity of slave labor, defined not according to some absolute or purely economic standard, but according to the political exigencies of the slaveholders. The slaves worked well enough in the cotton and sugar fields, when organized in gangs, but the old criticism of labor given grudgingly retains its force.

Slave labor lacked that degree and kind of versatility which would have permitted general agricultural diversification. Slaves could and did work in a variety of pursuits, including industrial, but under circumstances not easily created within the economy as a whole. Division of labor on the plantations and in society proceeded slowly and under great handicaps. The level of technology, especially on the plantations, was kept low by the quality and size of the labor force. Mules and oxen, for example, replaced faster horses principally because they could more easily withstand rough and perhaps vengeful handling. Negro laborers had been disciplined to sustained agricultural labor before being brought to the Americas. Their low productivity arose from the human and technological conditions under which they worked, and these arose from the slave system.

An analysis of Southern livestock and the attempts to improve it reveals the complex and debilitating interrelationships within the slave economy. The South had more than enough animals to feed its population but had to import meat. A shortage of liquid capital made acquisition of better breeds difficult, and the poor treatment of the animals by the slaves made maintenance of any reasonable standards close to impossible. As a further complication, the lack of urban markets inhibited attention to livestock by depriving planters of outlets for potential surpluses. The South boasted an enormous number of animals but suffered from their wretched quality.

Slavery provided a sufficient although not a necessary cause of soil exhaustion. It dictated one-crop production beyond the limits of commercial advantage and in opposition to the political safety of the slaveholders. Planters could not easily rotate crops under the existing credit structure, with a difficult labor force, and without those markets which could only accompany industrial and urban advance. The sheer size of the plantations discouraged fertilization. Barnyard manure was scarce, commercial fertilizers too expensive, and the care necessary for advantageous application unavailable. The shortage of good implements complicated the operation, for manures are easily wasted when not applied properly.

Craven insists that the existence of a moving frontier, north and south, brought about the same result, but as we have seen, the special force of slavery cannot so easily be brushed aside. The North confronted the devastating effects of soil exhaustion and built a diversified economy in the older areas as the frontier pushed westward. The South, faced with the debilitating effects of slavery long after the frontier had passed, had to struggle against hopeless odds.

These direct effects of slavery received enormous reinforcement from such indirect effects as the shortage of capital and entrepreneurship and the weakness of the market. Capital investments in slaves and a notable tendency toward aristocratic consumption had their economic advantages but inhibited the rise of new industries. The Southern market consisted primarily of the plantations and could not support more than a limited industrial advance. The restricted purchasing power of the rural whites, of the urban lower classes, and indirectly of the slaves hemmed in Southern manufacturers and put them at a severe competitive disadvantage relative to Northerners, who had had a head start and who had much wider markets in the free states to sustain production on an increasing scale. The barriers to industrialization also blocked urbanization and thereby undermined the market for foodstuffs.

Southern industrialization proceeded within the narrow limits set by the social milieu as well as by the market. The slaveholders controlled the state legislatures and the police power; they granted charters, set taxes, and ultimately controlled the lives of regional industries. So long as industry remained within safe limits the slaveholders offered no firm resistance, or at least no united front. Those limits included guarantees against the rise of a hostile and independent bourgeoisie and excessive concentrations of white workers of doubtful loyalty. Since the big slaveholders provided much of the capital for industry and since the plantations provided much of the regional market, the risks remained small, for even the nonslaveholding industrialists necessarily bound themselves to the rural regime and tried to do good business within the established limits. Industry made some progress; industrialization, understood as a self-propelling process, did not.

The South made one form of agricultural adjustment while slavery remained. The great agricultural revival in the Upper South overcame the most serious effects of slavery by reducing the size of slaveholdings, converting surplus slaves into cash, and investing the funds in the supervision, fertilization, and reconversion of smaller estates. This process threatened the economic and ideological solidity of the slaveholders' regime and had other drawbacks, but most important, it broke on an immanent contradiction. The sale of surplus slaves depended on markets further south, which necessarily depended on virgin lands on which to apply the old, wasteful methods of farming. Reform in one region implied exhaustive agriculture in another. Thus, the process of agricultural reform had narrow limits in a closed slave system and had to be reversed when it pressed against them. No solution emerged from within the system, but one beckoned from without. The steady acquisition of new land could alone guarantee the maintenance of that interregional slave trade which held the system together.

This economic root of slavery expansionism was only one of several roots, but itself grew strong enough to produce an ugly organism. If we begin with the economic process it is because the external threat to the slaveholders mounted so clearly, objectively and in their consciousness, with each new census report on the material conditions of the contending forces. The slaveholders might, of course, have resigned themselves to Lincoln's victory, accepted the essentials of the Wilmot Proviso, faced the impending crisis of their system, and prepared to convert to some form of free labor. Anything is possible where men retain the power to reason. Such a choice would have spelled their death as a ruling class and would have constituted moral and political suicide. Many contemporaries and many historians ever since have thought that they should have agreed to do themselves in. With this view I do not wish to argue. Neither did they.

The economic process propelling the slave South along expansionist paths had its political and social parallels, the most obvious being the need to re-establish parity in the Senate or at least to guarantee enough voting strength in Washington to protect Southern interests. In an immediate political sense the demand for more slave-state Congressmen was among the important roots of expansionism, but in a deeper sense it was merely a symptom of something more fundamental. Had the

South not had a distinct social system to preserve and a distinct and powerful ruling class at its helm, a decline of its political and economic power would have caused no greater alarm than it did in New England.

A second political root was the need to protect slavery where it was profitable by establishing buffer areas where it might not be. Just as the British had to spend money to secure ascendancy in Tibet so that they could make money in India, the South had to establish political control over areas with dubious potentialities as slave states in order to protect existing slave states. The success of the Texas cause removed the fear of Mexican tampering with slaves in Louisiana, much as annexation removed potential British-inspired tampering. "Texas must be a slave country," wrote Stephen F. Austin to his sister. "The interest of Louisiana requires that it should be; a population of fanatical abolitionists in Texas would have a very pernicious and dangerous influence on the overgrown population of the state."[2] In 1835, when a large Mexican force was reported near the Brazos River, the slaves apparently did attempt to rise. One hundred Negroes were severely punished, some executed.[3]

John A. Quitman, former governor of Mississippi, tried to organize a filibustering expedition to Cuba during 1853–1855, particularly because he feared that abolition there would present dangers to the South.[4] Samuel R. Walker and Albert W. Ely, among others, warned that Britain and France would force a weak Spain to sacrifice Cuban slavery and thereby isolate the South as a slaveholding country.[5] Many far-sighted Southerners understood the danger of permitting the isolation of Southern slavery. They desired Cuba in order to secure political control of the Caribbean, as well as for economic reasons.

Beyond Cuba and the Caribbean lay Brazil, the other great slaveholding country. "These two great valleys of the Amazon and the Mississippi," declared the *Richmond Enquirer* in 1854, "are now possessed by two governments of the earth most deeply interested in African slavery—Brazil and the United States . . . The whole intermediate countries between these two great valleys . . . is a region under the plastic hand of a beneficent Providence . . . How is it to be developed?" [*sic*] With black labor and white skill. Cuba and Santo Domingo, it continued, were potentially the bases for the control of the whole Caribbean. Such a political complex would cause the whole world to "fall back upon African labor."[6]

The warning of the Louisville *Daily Courier* in 1860 that Kentucky could afford to remain in the Union but that the Lower South could not touched the central issue. Suppose, it asked, Kentucky sold its slaves south. "And then what? Antislavery will not be content to rest. . . . The war will be transferred to the Cotton States."[7]

The need to push forward in order to ward off concentrations of hostile power arose from the anachronistic nature of the slave regime. By 1850, if not much earlier, world opinion could no longer tolerate chattel slavery, and British opposition in particular was both formidable and implacable. The transformation of the Caribbean into a slaveholders' lake and an alliance or understanding with Brazil held out the only hope of preventing a dangerous and tightening containment.

Slaveholders also sought additional territory to reduce the danger of internal convulsion. Lieutenant Matthew F. Maury, who helped bring about the American exploration of the Amazon Valley in the 1850s, discussed the eventual absorption of much of Latin America by the United States:

> I cannot be blind to what I see going on here. It is becoming a matter of *faith*—I use a strong word—yes a matter of faith among leading Southern men, that the time is coming, nay that it is rapidly approaching when in order to prevent this war of the races and all its horrors, they will in

self-defense be compelled to conquer parts of Mexico and Central America, and make slave territory of that—and that is now free.[8]

Representative Thomas L. Clingman of North Carolina told the House that Northerners were "too intelligent to believe that humanity, either to the slave or the master, requires that they should be pent up within a territory which after a time will be insufficient for their subsistence, and where they must perish from want, or from collision that would occur between the races."[9] Southerners always kept the West Indian experience in front of them when they discussed the racial proportions of the population.

Probably, steady infusions of new land were also needed to placate the nonslaveholders, but we know little about slaveholder-nonslaveholder relationships as yet and little can be said with certainty.

The psychological dimension of slavery expansionism has been the subject of various essays and has, for example, emerged from interpretations of Southern frustration and resultant aggression. We need not pursue esoteric lines of inquiry, especially with formulas so broad as to be able to encompass almost every society in any age, to appreciate that a psychological dimension did exist. As Southerners came to regard slavery as a positive good and as they came to value the civilization it made possible as the world's finest, they could hardly accept limits on its expansion. To agree to containment meant to agree that slavery constituted an evil, however necessary for the benefit of the savage Africans. That sense of mission so characteristic of the United States as a whole had its Southern manifestation in the mission of slavery. If slavery was making possible the finest society the world had ever known, the objections to its expansion were intolerable. The free-soil argument struck at the foundations of the slaveholder's pride and belief in himself.

It is difficult but unnecessary to assess the relative strength of the roots of slavery expansionism. Each supported and fed the taproot—the exigencies of slaveholder hegemony in a South that fought against comparative disadvantages in the world market and that found itself increasingly isolated morally and politically. From another point of view, each was a manifestation of those exigencies. Although some appear to be objective, or matters of social process, whereas others appear to be subjective, or matters of psychological reaction to possibly imaginary dangers, the difference becomes unimportant when each is related to the fundamental position of the slaveholders in Southern society. The existence of a threatening economic process, such as has been described, would have been enough to generate fear and suspicion, even without the undeniable hostility arising in the North on political and moral grounds.

✖ The "Natural Limits" Thesis

With these observations on the origins of slavery expansionism aside, we may consider the revisionists' objections. Since Ramsdell's article, "The Natural Limits of Slavery Expansion," most cogently presents the opposing view, let us summarize it as much as possible in his own words:

[1] Slavery in the territories was the most persistent issue of the 1840s and 1850s. "It seems safe to say that had the question been eliminated or settled amicably there would have been no secession and no Civil War."

[2] Free-soilers demanded that slave labor and the plantation system should be excluded from the Western plains to guarantee the predominance there of the free farmer and to prevent any extension of the political power of the

slaveholders. Southerners sought to uphold their constitutional rights in the territories and to maintain sufficient political strength to repulse "hostile and ruinous legislation."

[3] Slavery expanded "in response to economic stimuli." No conspiracy or political program brought about expansion; in fact, Southerners were too individualistic ever to have agreed on such a program.

[4] By 1849–1850, "The westward march of the cotton plantations was evidently slowing down." Only in Texas was the Cotton Belt advancing; elsewhere it stopped at given geographic lines.

[5] Even in Texas there were geographical limits. "Therefore, in the early fifties, the cotton plantations tended to cluster in the river counties in the eastern and southern parts of the state." Elsewhere, small farmers and herdsmen were establishing a free-labor economy, for slavery was unprofitable and could not take root.

[6] Railroads, if capital could have been raised, would have guided cotton westward up to the black-land prairies of central Texas or the semi-arid plains of western Texas. Beyond that cotton could not go. Woodlands were lacking, and fencing was impossible until the invention of barbed wire in the late 1870s. Here, then, was a temporary barrier.

[7] Beyond it lay a permanent barrier. "The history of the agricultural development of the Texas plains region since 1880 affords abundant evidence that it would never become suitable for plantation slave labor." Twenty years of experimentation with windmills, dry farming, and drought-resistant food crops were required before cotton farmers could conquer the plains. The experimental

period involved much capital and great risks of a type hard to associate with the plantation system. Labor-saving machinery, not gang labor, was needed.

[8] Even in the 1850s, Mexican labor was cheaper than Negro slave labor, and the Germans of southwestern Texas had an antipathy to slavery.

[9] Slavery had less chance beyond Texas. "Possibly, southern California could have sustained slavery, but California had already decided that question for itself. . . . As to New Mexico, the census of 1860, ten years after the territory had been thrown open to slavery, showed not a single slave . . ."

[10] In Kansas-Nebraska, slavery at best would have come to dominate the hemp regions of eastern Kansas, "but the infiltration of slaves would have been a slow process."

[11] "To say that the individual slaveowner would disregard his own economic interest and carry valuable property where it would entail loss merely for the sake of a doubtful political advantage seems a palpable absurdity." Southerners knew that slavery would not take root in the Southwest but considered establishment of the principle necessary to a defense against abolitionist attacks on the institution itself.

[12] "The one side fought rancorously for what it was bound to get without fighting; the other, with equal rancor, contended for what in the nature of things it could never use."

[13] On expansion into Latin America: there were mixed motives for desiring more annexations, most of them having nothing to do with slavery. In particular, Scroggs has shown that "had [William] Walker succeeded, those

pro-slavery expansionists who had applauded him would most certainly have been sorely disappointed in him." Walker sought a private empire, not annexation by the United States.

[14] The proposal to reopen the slave trade, which was often linked to expansion, failed to arouse necessary support even in the South.

[15] Ramsdell concludes by suggesting that without such expansion slavery slowly would have declined in profitability and would have given way to an alternative system. The great obstacle to peaceful reform would have been the problem of the place of the free Negro in Southern society.

With due respect for Ramsdell's scholarship and with full appreciation for the workmanlike manner in which he presented the essentials of the revisionist argument, I submit that the thesis is self-contradictory, that it confuses slavery expansionism with the prospects for cotton expansion, and that it rests on the untenable assumption that slaveholders were merely ordinary capitalists who happened to have money in slaves but who might have come to see the advantage of investing differently—the assumption, that is, that no deep identification was made by the slaveholders of slavery with civilization, that slave ownership imbued the master class with no special set of values and interests incapable of being compromised.

❧ The Contradictory Nature of the "Natural Limits" Thesis

The "natural limits" thesis is self-contradictory—and, in one important sense, irrelevant—for it simultaneously asserts that slavery was nonexpansionist and that it would have perished without room to expand. The only way to avoid judging the thesis to be self-contradictory is to read it so as to state that slavery needed room to expand but that, first, it needed room only in the long run and, second, that it had no room. This reading removes the contradiction but destroys the thesis.

If the slave states would eventually need room to expand, they had to set aside new territory when they could get it or face a disaster in a few years or decades. Hence, wisdom dictated a fight for the right to take slaves into the territories, for ultimately that right would be transformed from an abstraction into a matter of life and death. W. Burwell of Virginia wrote in 1856 that the South needed no more territory at the moment and faced no immediate danger of a redundant slave population. "Yet statesmen," he concluded, "like provident farmers, look to the prospective demands of those who rely upon their forethought for protection and employment. Though, therefore, there may be no need of Southern territory for many years, yet it is important to provide for its acquisition when needed . . ."[10]

To establish that slavery had no room to expand is not to refute the theory of slavery expansionism. If it could be firmly established that slavery needed room to expand but had none, then we should have described a society entering a period of internal convulsion. The decision of most slaveholders to stake everything on a desperate gamble for a political independence that would have freed them to push their system southward emerges as a rational, if dangerous, course of action.

❧ The Territorial Question

One of the most puzzling features of Ramsdell's essay is the virtual equation of cotton and slavery. Only occasionally and never carefully does he glance at the prospects for using slave labor outside the cotton fields. To identify any social system with a single commodity is indefensible, and in any case, Southern slavery had much greater flexibility. Ramsdell's essay is puzzling with respect to these general considerations but even more so with respect to his specific contention that contemporary Southerners viewed the territorial question as a cotton question. They did not.

When the more intelligent and informed Southerners demanded the West for slavery they often, perhaps most often, spoke of minerals, not cotton or even hemp. Slavery, from ancient times to modern, had proved itself splendidly adaptable to mining. Mining constituted one of the more important industries of the Negroes of preconquest Africa, and slave labor had a long history there. The Berbers, for example, used Negro slaves in West Africa, where the salt mines provided one of the great impetuses to the development of commercial, as opposed to traditional and patriarchal, forms of slavery.[11] Closer in time and place to the South, Brazil afforded an impressive example of the successful use of slave labor in mining. In the middle of the eighteenth century diamond mining supplemented gold mining in Minas Gerais and accounted for a massive transfer of masters and slaves from the northeastern sugar region.[12] Southern leaders knew a good deal about this experience. "The mines of Brazil," reported De Bow's Review in 1848, "are most prolific of iron, gold, and diamonds. . . . The operation is performed by negroes . . . 30,000 negroes have been so employed."[13] The eastern slave states had had experience with gold mining, and although the results were mixed, the potentialities of slave labor had been demonstrated.[14] Planters in the Southwestern states expressed interest in gold mines in Arkansas and hopefully looked further west.[15] "If mines of such temporary value should, as they may, be found in the territories, and slaves could be excluded from these," wrote A. F. Hopkins of Mobile in 1860, "it would present a case of monstrous injustice."[16]

During the Congressional debates of 1850, Representative Jacob Thompson of Mississippi, later to become Secretary of the Interior under Buchanan, expressed great concern over the fate of the public domain of California if she were to be hastily admitted to the Union and expressed special concern over the fate of the gold mines.[17] Ten years later, after a decade of similar warnings, pleas, hopes, and threats, S. D. Moore of Alabama wrote that the South was "excluded from California, not pretendedly even by 'isothermal lines,' or want of employment for slave labor, for in regard to climate and mining purposes the country was admirably adapted to the institution of African slavery."[18] Had it not been for the anti-slavery agitation, Representative Clingman told the House in 1850, Southerners would have used slaves in the mines of California and transformed it into a slave state.[19] Albert Gallatin Brown, one of the most fiery and belligerent of the pro-slavery extremists, wrote his constituents that slave labor was admirably suited to mining and that California could and should be made into a slave state.[20] Even as a free state California demonstrated the usefulness of slave labor. In 1852 the state legislature passed a mischievous fugitive slave law that could be and was interpreted to allow slaveholders to bring slaves into the state to work in the mines and then send them home.[21]

Similarly, a Texan wrote in 1852 that a Mississippi and Pacific railroad would secure the New Mexico territory for the South by opening the mining districts to slave labor.[22] During the War for Southern Independence, Jefferson Davis received a communication from his Southwestern field commander that a successful drive to California would add "the most valuable agriculture and grazing lands, and the richest mineral region in the world."[23]

Southerners had long cast eyes toward Mexico and looked forward to additional annexations. "I want Cuba," roared Albert Gallatin Brown. "I want Tamaulipas, Potosí, and one or two other Mexican states; and I want them all for the same reason—for the planting or spreading of slavery."[24] Throughout the 1850s, De Bow's Review printed articles about Mexico and particularly about Mexican mines. In 1846, Joel R. Poinsett reviewed Waddy Thompson's Reflexions on Mexico and noted the extensive mineral wealth in an article that struck no bellicose note.[25] During the same year Gustavus Schmidt, in a humane, nonracist, nonchauvinist account, wrote of Mexico's "inexhaustible deposits of gold and silver."[26] In 1850, Brantz Mayer of Baltimore estimated that one-fifth of Mexican territory contained excellent mineral resources.[27] Covetous eyes and bellicose projects appeared soon enough.

> The mineral resources of Mexico are unquestionably immense. . . . The moment Mexico falls into the hands of the Anglo-Saxon race, every inch of her territory will be explored. . . . The mines of Mexico, which have now been worked near three hundred years, are inexhaustible; and they only need the protection of a good government and the skill of an intelligent and industrious people, to render them productive of the most astonishing quantities of the precious metals.[28]

George Frederick Holmes, in a long, rambling article on gold and silver mines, wrote glowingly of Chile as well as Mexico.[29] H. Yoakum ended an article on Mexico with the warning, "You must make progress, or you will be absorbed by a more energetic race."[30] Southerners and Mexicans took these designs seriously. Confederate troops marched into New Mexico with the intention of proceeding to Tucson and then swinging south to take Sonora, Chihuahua, Durango, and Tamaulipas.[31] The Confederate government tried to deal with Santiago Vidaurri, the strong man of Coahuila and Nuevo León, to bring northern Mexico into the Confederacy, and Juárez was so alarmed that he was ready to go to great lengths to help the Union put down the rebellion.[32]

It is one thing to note that Southerners sought to expand

slavery into Mexico's mining districts or that they lamented
the political barriers to the expansion of slavery into New
Mexico's; it is another for us to conclude that their hopes and
desires were more than wishful thinking. Allan Nevins has
presented a formidable case to suggest that slavery had little
room even in the mining districts of the Southwest and
Mexico. He shows that even in the Gadsden Purchase the
economic exigencies of mining brought about the quick sup-
pression of the enterprising individual by the corporation.
Western mining, as well as transportation, lumbering, and
some forms of agriculture, required much capital and became
fields for big business. High labor costs led to a rising demand
for labor-saving machinery, but Nevins does not consider that
this very condition might, under certain circumstances, have
spurred the introduction of slave labor.[33] He writes:

> For three salient facts stood out in any survey of the Far
> West. First, this land of plain and peak was natural soil for
> a free-spirited and highly competitive society, demanding
> of every resident skill and intelligence. It was, therefore,
> even in that Gadsden Purchase country which had been
> bought at the behest of the slave states, a country naturally
> inhospitable to slavery. Second, when so much energy was
> steadily flowing into western expansion, and such wide
> outlets for more effort existed there, it was impossible to
> think of the country turning to Caribbean areas for a
> heavy thrust southward. Its main forces moved naturally
> toward the sunset, where rich opportunities were hardly
> yet sampled. The cotton kingdom, which realized that the
> West gave little scope for its peculiar culture, might plan
> grandiose Latin American adventures; but it would get
> little support from other regions. And in the third place,
> conditions in the West demanded capital and organization
> on a broad scale; if it was a land for individualists, it was
> even more a land for corporate enterprise—a land for the
> businessman. Those who pondered these three facts could
> see that they held an ominous meaning for the South.
> The nearer Northwest had already done much to upset

the old sectional balance, and the Far West, as it filled up, would do still more.[34]

On economic grounds Nevins' analysis has much to offer, but his remarks on the competitive struggle in the Southwest and on the inability of Southerners to get national support for Caribbean adventures do not prove nearly so much as he thinks. At most, they suggest that the North was strong enough to block slavery expansionism into the Southwest and frustrate Southern ambitions elsewhere. If so, the case for secession, from the proslavery viewpoint, was unanswerable.

Nevins' remarks illustrate the wisdom of other Southern arguments—that the South had to secure new land politically, not by economic advance, and that the South had to have guarantees of positive federal protection for slavery in the territories.[35] The *Charleston Mercury*, climaxing a decade of Southern complaints, insisted in 1860 that slavery would have triumphed in California's gold-mining areas if Southerners had had assurances of protection for their property. It singled out the mineral wealth of New Mexico as beckoning the South and even saw possibilities for slave-worked mining in Kansas.[36] With fewer exaggerations De Bow, a decade earlier, had pointed to the political aspect of the problem: "Such is the strength and power of the Northern opposition that property, which is ever timid, and will seek no hazards, is excluded from the country in the person of the slave, and Southerners are forced, willingly or not, to remain at home. Emigrants, meanwhile, crowd from the North."[37] During the bitter debate in Congress over the admission of California, Senator Jeremiah Clemens of Alabama replied heatedly to Clay in words similar to those used by De Bow. Free-soil agitation, he said, had kept slavery from the territories. "Property is proverbially timid. The slaveholder would not carry his property there with a threat hanging over him that it was to be taken away by operation of law the moment he landed."[38] Representative Joseph

M. Root of Ohio, Whig and later Republican, commented on such charges by boasting that if the Wilmot Proviso had accomplished nothing more than to create a political climate inimical to slavery expansion, it had accomplished its purpose.[39]

The Southern demand for federal guarantees made sense, but even that did not go far enough. Ultimately, the South needed not equal protection for slave property but complete political control. If a given territory could be organized by a proslavery party, then slaveholders would feel free to migrate. Time would be needed to allow the slave population to catch up; meanwhile, free-soil farmers had to be kept out in favor of men who looked forward to becoming slaveholders. Under such circumstances the territory's population might grow very slowly, and the exploitation of its resources might lag far behind that of the free territories. Nothing essential would be lost to the South by underdevelopment; the South as a whole was underdeveloped. In short, the question of political power necessarily had priority over the strictly economic questions.

Even if the South had looked forward to extending the cotton kingdom, the political question would have had to take priority. Douglass C. North has incisively described the rhythm of such extensions:

> Long swings in the price of cotton were the result of periods of excess capacity with a consequent elastic supply curve of cotton over a substantial range of output. Once demand had shifted to the right sufficiently to use all available cotton land, the supply curve became rather inelastic. A rise in cotton prices precipitated another move into new lands of the Southwest by planters and their slaves. Funds from the Northeast and England financed the transfer of slaves, purchase of land, and working capital during the period of clearing the land, preparing the soil and raising a cotton crop. There was a lag of approximately four or five years between the initial surge and the resulting large increase in output which caused a tremendous shift to the right in the supply curve and the beginning of another lengthy period of digesting the increased capacity.[40]

Under such circumstances the political safety of slavery, especially during the difficult interlude North describes, always had to be assured before any significant economic advance could occur. Significantly, even the long-range possibility of irrigating the Southwest was noted in *De Bow's Review* as early as 1848.[41]

Slavery certainly would have had a difficult time in Kansas, although as Nevins has shown, greater possibilities existed than Stephen Douglas or many historians since have been prepared to admit. The proslavery leaders there, Atchison and Stringfellow, fully appreciated the importance of the prior establishment of political power, as their rough tactics and ingenious scheme to monopolize the timber and water resources showed.[42] Nevins, on the other hand, questions the ability of the South to provide settlers. We shall return to this objection.

For the moment let us consider Kansas as solely and inevitably a wheat state. Large slave plantations have not proved well adapted to wheat growing, but small plantations were doing well in the Virginia tidewater. In open competition with Northwestern farmers the slaveholders probably would have been hurt badly. They knew as much. When, for example, Percy Roberts of Mississippi maintained that Negro slavery could thrive in the Northwest grain belt, he simultaneously maintained that the African slave trade would have to be reopened to drive down the cost of labor and put the slaveholders in a favorable competitive position.[43] Historians like Nevins and Paul W. Gates have expressed confidence that slavery could not have triumphed in Kansas even if it had been allowed a foothold. They may be right, but only if one assumes that the South remained in the Union. Slavery expansionism required fastening proslavery regimes in such territories, but ultimately it required secession to protect the gains. Had Kansas joined a Southern Confederacy as a slave state, its wheat-growing slaveholders could have secured the same internal advantages as the sugar planters of Louisiana, and Union wheat could effectively have been placed at a competitive disdvantage in the Southern market.

Ramsdell's dismissal of Southern interest in Cuba and Central America, however necessary for his argument, does not bear examination. Southern sugar planters, who might have been expected to fear the glutting of the sugar market should Cuba enter the Union, spoke out for annexation. They seem to have been convinced that suspension of the African slave trade to Cuba would raise the cost of production there to American levels and that they would be able to buy Cuban slaves cheaply.[44] Besides, as Basil Rauch points out, Louisiana sugar planters were moving to Cuba during the 1850s and looking forward to extending their fortunes.[45] Southerners, like Northerners, often spoke of annexation in nationalist terms and sometimes went to great lengths to avoid the slavery question. J. J. Ampère heard that Cuba had been detached from the mainland by the Gulf Stream and rightfully belonged to the United States. He recommended that France reclaim Britain on the same grounds. He also heard that Cuba had to be annexed to provide a rest home for American consumptives.[46] J. C. Reynolds, writing in *De Bow's Review* in 1850, described appalling losses in the illegal slave trade to Cuba and urged annexation to bring American law enforcement there and to end the terrible treatment of the Negroes.[47] More sweepingly, some argued that without more territory the Negroes of the United States would be extinguished by overpopulation and attendant famine.[48] All for the poor Negroes! Others, like Soulé and Albert Gallatin Brown, bluntly demanded Cuba and Central America to strengthen and defend slavery.[49]

As for William Walker, he said enough to refute the Scroggs-Ramsdell interpretation. His *War in Nicaragua* makes clear that American politics made it necessary for him to appear to renounce annexation and that he was biding his time. No matter. His purpose there, as he boldly proclaimed, was to expand slavery as a system.

Opposition to territorial expansion by many Southerners has led some historians to deny the existence of an "aggressive slaveocracy" or to assert, with Ramsdell, that Southerners were too individualistic to be mobilized for such political adventures, which were often contrary to their private interests. No conspiracy theory is required. That there were many Southern leaders who sensed the need for more territory and fought for it is indisputable. That individual Southerners were not always willing to move when the interests of their class and system required them to merely indicates one of the ways in which slavery expansionism proved a contradictory process. Southerners opposed expansion for a variety of reasons, but mostly because they feared more free states. Expansion southward had the great advantage of not being cotton expansion, and the economic argument against it was weak. On the other hand, many feared that the annexation of Cuba would provide an excuse for the annexation of Canada or that the annexation of Mexico would repeat the experience of California. This opposition should be understood essentially as a preference for delaying expansion until secession had been effected, although there were, of course, many who opposed both.[50]

❧ *The Anguish of Contradiction*

If the slave South had to expand to survive, it paradoxically could not do so when given the opportunity. Unsettled political conditions prevented the immigration of slave property, much as the threat of nationalization or of a left-wing or nationalist coup prevents the flow of American capital to some underdeveloped countries to which it is invited.

"Where," asks Allan Nevins when discussing Kansas, "were

proslavery settlers to come from? Arkansas, Texas, and New Mexico were all calling for slaveholding immigrants, and the two first were more attractive to Southerners than Kansas."[51] Slave property necessarily moved cautiously and slowly. So long as it had to move at the pace set by Northern farmers, it would be defeated. The mere fact of competition discouraged the movement of slaveholders, and if they were willing to move, they could not hope to carry enough whites to win.

An area could be safely absorbed by the slave regime only by preventing Northern free-soilers from entering. Danhof has demonstrated that farm making was an expensive business.[52] Northern farmers had a hard time; Southern farmers, without slaves or minimal savings, found it much harder. Traditionally, the more energetic nonslaveholders moved into new land first and cleared it; the planters followed much later.[53] If those early settlers had to secure the territory against free-soilism before the planters and slaveholders moved in, the struggle could not ordinarily be won. Many Southern nonslaveholders could be and were converted to the antislavery banner once they found themselves away from the power and influence of the slaveholders. Charles Robinson bitterly criticized John Brown for his inability to appreciate the possibilities of persuasion: "While our free state colonies were trying to convert the whites from the South and make them sound free-state men, John Brown thought it better to murder them."[54]

Missouri and Kansas, therefore, were worlds apart. W. A. Seay, in an article entitled "Missouri Safe for the South," dismissed suggestions that Missouri would abolish slavery. The nonslaveholding counties, he noted, lay in the southern part of the state and were inhabited by men from other parts of the South who owned no slaves only because they were as yet too poor.[55] Their allegiance to the system rested ultimately on the ability of the slaveholders to retain political power and social and ideological leadership and to prevent these men of the lower classes from seeing an alternative way of life. Yet, by 1860 even Missouri had become a battleground because of its special geographic position and Northern and foreign immigration. Kansas could never be secured for slavery unless the slaveholders had political control and the migrating Southern farmers were isolated from corrupting influences. As it was, Northerners, according to Representative William Barksdale of Mississippi, went as families, whereas Southerners often went as young adventurers who had no intention of remaining once the excitement was over.[56]

The South's anguish arose from having to expand and being unable to meet the tests of expansion set by life in mid-nineteenth-century America. Like T. S. Eliot's Hollow Men, it found that

> Between the desire
> And the spasm
> Between the potency
> And the existence
> Between the essence
> And the descent
> Falls the shadow

Only if a territory shut out free-soil immigration, quickly established the political hegemony of the slaveholders, and prepared for a much slower development than Northerners might give it, could it be secured for slavery. These conditions negated slavery expansionism, but only so long as the South remained in the Union.

✖ Invitation to a (Self-Inflicted) Beheading

The South had to expand, and its leaders knew it. "There is not a slaveholder in this House or out of it," Judge Warner of Georgia declared in the House of Representatives in 1856, "but who knows perfectly well that whenever slavery is confined within certain specified limits, its future existence is doomed."[57] The Republican party, said an editorial in *The Plantation* in 1860, denies that it wants to war on slavery, but it admits that it wants to surround it with free states. To do so would be to crush slavery where it now exists.[58] Percy L. Rainwater's study of sentiment in Mississippi in the 1850s shows how firmly convinced slaveholders were that the system had to expand or die.[59] Lincoln made the same point in his own way. He opposed any compromise on slavery expansion in 1860 because he feared new and bolder expansionist schemes and because he wished to contain slavery in order to guarantee its ultimate extinction.

Nevins' discussion of Lincoln's view illuminates one of the most tenacious and dubious assumptions on which many historians have based their interpretations of the origins of the war:

> In view of all the trends of nineteenth century civilization, the terrible problem of slavery could be given a final solution only upon the principle . . . of gradual emancipation. . . . The first step was to stop the expansion of slavery, and to confine the institution within the fifteen states it already possessed. Such a decision would be equivalent to a decree that slavery was marked for gradual evolution into a higher labor system. Slavery confined would be slavery under sentence of slow death. The second step would be the termination of slavery in the border states. Missouri by 1859 stood near the verge of emancipation . . .[60]

The assumption on which these notions rest is that the South, faced with containment, could have accepted its consequences. On the further assumption that men may agree to commit suicide, the assumption is plausible.

If instead of speaking of the South or of the system of slavery, we speak of the slaveholders who ruled both, the assumption is less plausible. [The extinction of slavery would have broken the power of the slaveholders in general and the planters in particular. Ideologically, these men had committed themselves to slaveholding and the plantation regime as the proper foundations of civilization. Politically, the preservation of their power depended on the preservation of its economic base. Economically, the plantation system would have tottered under free labor conditions and would have existed under some intermediary form like sharecropping only at the expense of the old ruling class. The "higher" forms depended on the introduction of commercial relations that would have gradually undermined the planters and guaranteed the penetration of outside capital. We have the postbellum experience to cite here, although it took place at a time when the planters had suffered hard blows, but slaveholders saw the dangers before the war and before the blows. "Python," in a series of brilliant articles in *De Bow's Review* in 1860, warned that emancipation, even with some form of "apprenticeship" for the Negroes, would open the way for Northern capital to command the productive power of the South. Once Negro labor is linked to capital in the open market, he argued, rather than through the patriarchal system of plantation slavery, it will fall prey to a predatory, soulless, Northern capitalism. There will be no place left for the old master class, which will be crushed by the superior force of Northern capital and enterprise or absorbed into them.[61] "Of what advantage is it to the South," he asked, "to be destroyed by Mr. Douglas through territorial sovereignty to the exclusion of Southern institutions, rather than by Mr. Seward through Congressional sovereignty to the same end? What difference is there to the South whether they are forcibly led to immolation by Seward, or accorded, in the alternative, the Roman privilege of selecting their own mode of death, by Douglas? Die they must in either event."

These words demonstrate that the probable effect of a "higher labor system" on the fortunes of the slaveholding class was not beyond the appreciation of its intellectual leaders. We need not try to prove that so specific an appreciation was general. The slaveholders knew their own power and could not help being suspicious of sweeping changes in their way of life, no matter how persuasively advanced. Their slaveholding psychology, habit of command, race pride, rural lordship, aristocratic pretensions, political domination, and economic strength militated in defense of the status quo. Under such circumstances an occasional voice warning that a conversion to tenantry or sharecropping carried serious dangers to their material interests sufficed to stiffen their resistance.

No demagogy or dogmatic speculation produced "Python's" fears. Even modest compensation—paid for by whom?—would have left the planters in a precarious position. At best, it would have extended their life as a class a little while longer than postbellum conditions permitted, but Northern capital could not long be kept from establishing direct relationships with tenants and sharecroppers. The planters would have steadily been reduced to middlemen of doubtful economic value or would have merged imperceptibly into a national business class. The change would have required, and eventually did require under disorderly postbellum conditions, extensive advances to laborers in the form of additional implements, fertilizer, household utensils, even food, and innumerable incidentals. This process guaranteed the disintegration of the old land-owning class, however good an adjustment many of its members might have made to the new order.

Those who, like Max Weber, Ramsdell, even Phillips, and countless others, assume that the South could have accepted a peaceful transition to free labor gravely misjudge the character of its ruling class. The question of such a judgment is precisely what is at issue. As noted in the Introduction to this volume, a revisionist historian might accept the empirical findings reported here and even the specific interpretations of their economic significance and still draw different conclusions on the larger issues. The final set of conclusions, and the notion of a general crisis itself, eventually must rest on agreement that the slaveholders constituted a ruling class and that they displayed an ideology and psychology such as has merely been suggested in these studies.

The slaveholders, not the South, held the power to accede or resist. To these men slaves were a source of power, pride, and prestige, a duty and a responsibility, a privilege and a trust; slavery was the foundation of a special civilization imprinted with their own character. The defense of slavery, to them, meant the defense of their honor and dignity, which they saw as the essence of life. They could never agree to renounce the foundation of their power and moral sensibility and to undergo a metamorphosis into a class the nature and values of which were an inversion of their own. Slavery represented the cornerstone of their way of life, and life to them meant an honor and dignity associated with the power of command. When the slaveholders rose in insurrection, they knew what they were about: in the fullest sense, they were fighting for their lives.

N O T E S

1 *AHR*, XVI (Sept. 1929), 151–71.

2 Quoted in Herbert Aptheker, *American Negro Slave Revolts* (New York, 1963), pp. 32–33.

3 *Ibid.*, p. 93.

4 C. Stanley Urban, "The Abortive Quitman Filibustering Expedition, 1853–1855," *JMH*, XVIII (July 1956), 177.

5 William Walker, *The War in Nicaragua* (Mobile, Ala., 1860), Chap. VIII; Ely, "Spanish and Cuban Views of Annexation," *DBR*, XVIII (March 1855), 305–11, esp. 311.

6 "The Destiny of the Slave States," reprinted in *DBR*, XVII (Sept. 1854), 281, 283.

7 Dec. 20, 1860 in Dwight L. Dumond (ed.), *Southern Editorials on Secession* (New York, 1931), p. 360.

8 Quoted in Aptheker, *Slave Revolts*, p. 34.

9 Clingman, *Speeches*, p. 239.

10 "The Policy of the South—Suggestions for the Settlement of Our Sectional Differences," *DBR*, XXI (Nov. 1856), 478.

11 J. D. Fage, *An Introduction to the History of West Africa* (3rd ed.; Cambridge, Eng., 1962), p. 14; Cline, *Mining and Metallurgy in Negro Africa, passim.*

12 João Pandía Calógeras, *A History of Brazil* (tr. Percy Alvin Martin; Chapel Hill, N.C., 1939), pp. 40–41; C. R. Boxer, *The Golden Age of Brazil, 1695–1750* (Berkeley, Cal., 1962) devotes a chapter and additional space to a splendid discussion.

13 "The South American States," *DBR*, VI (July 1848), 14.

14 *Cf.* Fletcher M. Green's articles on gold mining in Georgia, North Carolina, and Virginia: *GHQ*, XIX (June 1935), 93–111 and (Sept. 1935), 210–28; *NCHR*, XIV (Jan. 1937), 1–19 and (Oct. 1937), 357–66. Significantly, the Southeastern developments were discussed in relation to California. See *DBR*, XVIII (Feb. 1855), 241–50.

15 See, *e.g.*, Francis Terry Leak Diary, July 7, 1855.

16 *DBR*, XXVIII (March 1860), 281.

17 *Congressional Globe*, XIX, Part 2, 31st Congress, 1st Session, HR, Sept. 7, 1850.

18 "The Irrepressible Conflict and the Impending Crisis," *DBR*, XXVIII (May 1860), 535.

19 Clingman, *Speeches*, p. 239 (Jan. 22, 1850).

20 *Speeches, Messages, and Other Writings* (ed. M. W. Cluskey; Philadelphia, 1859), p. 181.

21 Delilah L. Beasley, "Slavery in California," *JNH*, III (Jan. 1918), 40–41.

22 "Public Lands of Texas," *DBR*, XIII (July 1852), 54.

23 Quoted in W. H. Watford, "Confederate Western Ambitions," *SHQ*, XLIV (Oct. 1940), 168.

24 Brown, *Speeches, Messages*, p. 595; speech at Hazlehurst, Miss., Sept. 11, 1858.

25 "Mexico and the Mexicans," *DBR*, II (Sept. 1846), 164–77.

26 "Mexico, Its Social and Political Condition," *DBR*, I (Feb. 1846), 117.

27 "Mexican Mines and Mineral Resources in 1850," *DBR*, IX (July 1850), 34.

28 "Mexico in 1852," *DBR*, XIII (Oct. 1852), 325–54, quotes on pp. 336 and 338.

29 "Gold and Silver Mines," *DBR*, XXI (July 1856), 55.

30 "The Republics of Mexico and the United States," *DBR*, XXI (Oct. 1856), 361. Original emphasis.

31 Watford, *SHQ*, XLIV (Oct. 1940), 167.

32 J. Fred Rippy, "Mexican Projects of the Confederates," *SHQ*, XXII (April 1919), 294, 298–99.

33 *The Emergence of Lincoln* (2 vols.; New York, 1950), I, 330–31.

34 *Ibid.*, I, 342.

35 I find it strange that Nevins attacks this late antebellum demand as an abstraction; his own evidence indicates that it was of central importance to the slavery cause.

36 Editorials, Feb. 28 and March 31, 1860, in Dumond (ed.) *Southern Editorials*, pp. 41, 45, 65.

37 J. D. B. De Bow, "California—The New American El Dorado," *DBR*, VIII (June 1850), 540.

38 *Congressional Globe*, XIX, Part 1, 31st Congress, 1st Session, Senate, Feb. 20, 1850, p. 397.

39 *Congressional Globe*, XIX, Part 2, 31st Congress, 1st Session, HR, June 7, 1850, p. 1149.

40 *Economic Growth*, pp. 128–29.

41 Dr. Wislizenus' report as extracted and printed in J. D. B. De Bow, "California, New Mexico and the Passage Between the Atlantic and Pacific Oceans," *DBR*, VI (Sept. 1848), 223.

42 Allan Nevins, *Ordeal of the Union* (2 vols.; New York, 1947), II, 116–17, 310.

43 "African Slavery Adapted to the North and Northwest," *DBR*, XXV (Oct. 1858), 379–85.

44 J. S. Thrasher, "Cuba and the United States," *DBR*, XVII (July 1854), 43–49.

45 *American Interest in Cuba, 1848–1855* (New York, 1948), p. 200; James Stirling, *Letters from the Slave States* (London, 1857), pp. 127 ff; John S. C. Abbott, *South and North; or Impressions Received during a Trip to Cuba* (New York, 1860), pp. 52, 53. Texans, too, wanted Cuba. See Earl W. Fornell, "Agitation in Texas for Reopening the Slave Trade," *SHQ*, LX (Oct. 1956), 245–59.

46 Ampère, *Promenade en Amérique* (Paris, 1855), II, 223–24.

47 "Cuba—Its Position, Dimensions and Population," *DBR*, VIII (April 1850), 13–23.

48 Dr. Van Evne, "Slavery Extension," *DBR*, XV (July 1853), 10.

49 J. Preston Moore, "Pierre Soulé: Southern Expansionist and Promoter," *JSH*, XXI (May 1855), 206; Brown, *Speeches, Messages*, p. 329.

50 *SQR*, XXI (Jan. 1852), 3; see the arguments advanced by William Walker for avoiding an attempt to link Nicaragua with the Union, *The War in Nicaragua*, Chap. VIII.

51 *Ordeal of the Union*, II, 304.

52 Clarence H. Danhof, "Farm-making Costs and the 'Safety Valve,'" *JPE*, XLIX (June 1941), 317–59. Cf. Nevins, *Emergence of Lincoln*, I, 159, on Kansas in the 1850s.

Thomas Le Duc has argued that many farmers could and did squat in squalor while slowly building a farm: "Public Policy, Private Investment and Land Use in American Agriculture, 1825–1875," *Agr. Hist.*, XXXVII (Jan. 1963), 3–9. Even with this qualification, capital and resources were a big factor, and the competitive advantage of Northern farmers over Southern is beyond doubt. Only when circumstances permitted the massive movement of planters and slaves could the result be different.

53 Yarbrough, *Economic Aspects of Slavery*, p. 104.

54 Quoted in Nevins, *Emergence of Lincoln*, II, 24, n. 37.

55 *DBR*, XXIV (April 1858), 335–36.

56 Nevins, *Emergence of Lincoln*, I, 160.

57 Quoted in George M. Weston, *The Progress of Slavery in the United States* (Washington, D.C., 1857), p. 227.

58 *The Plantation* (March 1860), pp. 1–2.

59 "Economic Benefits of Secession: Opinions in Mississippi in the 1850's," *JSH*, I (Nov. 1935), 459 and *passim*.

60 *Emergence of Lincoln*, I, 344.

61 "The Issues of 1860," *DBR*, XXVIII (March 1860), 245–72.

A Note on the Place of Economics in the Political Economy of Slavery

⬛ *On Recent Contributions to an Endless Debate*

In 1958 the debate on the profitability of slavery, which has raged since antebellum days, took a new turn with the publication of the now famous Conrad-Meyer study.[1] Their paper has been followed by several others by economists who have used somewhat different routes to the same place. They conclude that slavery generated a high level of profits and that investments in slave plantations yielded as high a return as investments in alternative industries.[2] Had matters been left there, no great issue would be involved, but the most sweeping social and political questions have been thought to be hanging on the calculation of profit and loss.

No sooner had the old question of profitability ostensibly been laid to rest, with appropriate hosannas to the wonderful achievements of the "new economic history," as some econometric historians modestly style their discipline, than the counterattack began. On the technical level Edward Saraydar, in an able reply, presented alternative calculations based on better data and the correction of errors. He concluded that slavery had not at all been significantly profitable.[3] The problem of data goes far beyond what even Saraydar suggests: there is hardly a figure in the Conrad-Meyer article, as well as the alternative studies, that cannot effectively be challenged. To cite a few cases, not previously examined by critics:

(1) *Medical care.* Conrad and Meyer have made a guess based on the previous guessing of historians and set the annual cost at $1.50–2.00. Let us put aside Saraydar's insistence that they confuse costs per hand with costs per slave. An inspection of plantation manuscripts, medical journals, and physicians' accounts does not settle the matter but does suggest that their figures are probably half what they should be. A study of the sources, still involving more guesswork than we would like, suggests about $3.00 per slave.[4]

(2) *Supervision.* A planter with twenty slaves in Mississippi in the 1850s could hardly expect to get a suitable overseer for $15 per hand, or $150. Even at $15 per slave, or $300, the figure is about 50 per cent too low. My estimate would be $450; John Hebron Moore gives an estimated range of $350–500 for the period 1830–1860.[5] William K. Scarborough, whose book on the Southern overseer will appear soon and who qualifies as our best authority on this subject, independently arrived at a range of $200–1,000 with an average of $450 for the Cotton Belt. He provides these figures under some protest, for "there are so many variables—size of plantation, length of tenure with current employer, age and experience of overseer."[6] Thus, the cost should be $22.50 per slave, exclusive of an entrepreneurial salary for the planter himself.

(3) *Work Animals.* Conrad and Meyer, in their capital costs, provide a figure for the initial cost of work animals and assume that they were thereafter self-reproducing. Since the great bulk of the work animals consisted of mules and oxen,

the assumption is regrettable. Equally distressing, competent observers agreed that even the horses were so abused by slaves that replacement costs proved a recurring headache.

(4) *Food and Clothing*. Their figures ($7.00–10.00 per slave, which Saraydar corrects to $14.00–20.00) are much too low. Little clothing was produced at home, as we have seen, and the cost of such minor items as shoes and blankets alone was at least $2.00 per slave. Total clothing costs were probably about $16.00, and food costs varied enormously according to the size of the estate but were certainly much higher than Conrad and Meyer imagine.[7] An estimate with which we can work with safety will be established only after much work has been done with the data in the manuscript census returns and only if certain technical difficulties are removed. For example, if we can get a solid figure for the average weight of hogs on the plantations, we could estimate pork production from the number of hogs reported and use that figure, together with corn output, to measure plantation self-sufficiency. Until then, everyone's guess is equally valuable, and all can play the game. If these or other figures are shifted upward a little, the results will be substantially altered. Surely, we cannot continue to work along these lines and think we are solving anything.

The Conrad-Meyer study, and the other economic studies as well, turn decisively on estimates of slave longevity, but the data problem here is especially grave. Those who think they can use census statistics on slave ages for close quantitative work ought to consider the testimony of innumerable planters. George S. Barnsley of Georgia took a slave to a Major Wooley for an estimate, but the two men differed by seven years.[8] Slave ages in plantation books were often recorded as "about" without pretense of accuracy.[9] Ernest Haywood of North Carolina had lists of slaves "with their supposed ages."[10] The following note from a planter to an overseer reveals a common situation: "There are also others whose names and ages are misplaced. You must try to find them out and guess at their ages if you can not ascertain from the fathers or mothers of them."[11] A perusal of manuscript census returns strongly suggests that slave ages were recorded haphazardly and that great variations in the ages of the same slaves appeared from one census to another. The use of such data in close computations can only lead to gross distortion. The census statistics on mortality, which normally would have been helpful and have been relied upon often by historians, are almost useless. J. D. B. De Bow, who directed the census of 1850, said as much; and in any case, the underreporting of deaths by one-third, under conditions in which no assumption of equal effects on whites and blacks is tenable, makes all calculations guesswork.[12]

Other kinds of costs slide from view. Many and probably most planters gave their slaves Christmas presents at a cost of several dollars per slave. On a broader social level, they had to spend large sums to educate their children by tutors and at academies, finishing schools, and colleges, not to mention the additional sums necessary to permit their children to live in the appropriate manner. Such items extend in many directions and suggest two conclusions. First, such incidentals as Christmas presents must be included in any assessment of plantation costs. Second, we must not confuse profits, nicely defined to fit some scheme developed to accommodate bourgeois practices, with capital accumulation in a system in which the social leakages alone were enormous. (Those regular and expensive vacations in watering places, Northern resorts, and abroad were not so much evidence of household affluence or some alleged rural indifference to thrift as they were vital parts of a total social setting.) If an economist objects that the cost of education in a society incapable of producing adequate public facilities or the cost of Christmas presents and other incidentals for slaves cannot be considered "business expenses," we must answer that plantation slavery was no mere business and that a system of accounting that limits itself to "business expenses" is a waste of time.

If the investigation of broad social and political issues did in fact rest on the solution of the profitability question, strictly defined, we should be in a sorry state, for no such solution has been offered or may ever be. Fortunately, we are not so badly off. Harold D. Woodman has come to the rescue and helped to restore order.[13] We are indebted to him for, among other things, making it unnecessary to review the whole irritating debate, which has gone on since antebellum days. He has patiently done it for us, and those interested may consult his article with the assurance that he has done it fairly.

The burden of Woodman's critical analysis rests on his correct insistence that two separate issues have been confused. First, some have asked: Did planters make money and did they make as much as they might have elsewhere? Considered thus: "Profitability relates only to the success or failure of slave production as a business and ignores the broader questions of the effects of this type of enterprise on the economy as a whole." Second, some have viewed slavery as an economic system. "The issue of profits earned by individual planters is subordinated to the larger problems of economic growth, capital accumulation, and the effects of slavery on the general population." He properly notes that Ulrich B. Phillips—let us add, the much-maligned Phillips, whose work remains the best starting point for any study of slavery in the United States—never let himself be confused but that after his death "a subtle shift" occurred from a primary concern with the second problem to a primary concern with the first. This shift, which the Conrad-Meyer article, with its brilliant technical apparatus and sophisticated discussion, completed, has carried with it a potential disaster for efforts to understand the slave South.

Woodman's article has helped immeasurably to bring the

debate back to reality, but it is not altogether free of the confusion against which he has struggled so well:

> Those who argue that slavery prevented diversification must prove (1) that economic diversification did take place in nonslave agricultural areas and (2) that it was slavery and not other factors which prevented diversified investment in the South.[14]

If Woodman means "nonslave agricultural areas" within the South, then he has missed the very point he previously saw so clearly, for slavery wrought its worst devastation precisely there. If he means outside the South, then there is nothing left to prove. When he writes that we must prove that "slavery and not other factors" prevented diversified investment, he again misses the point, for to us slavery was no mere factor but the foundation of the social system in which the various factors operated and by which they were shaped. Having argued these matters explicitly and implicitly throughout these studies, I shall not belabor them here.

❧ From Economics to Political Economy: Eight Theses

I. *In a strict accounting sense farms and plantations must have been profitable, for, considered as a whole, they survived for decades.*

II. *Slave farms and plantations might and probably would have continued to produce earning less than the rate of interest.*

The qualifying phrase, "in a strict accounting sense," in Thesis I is necessary for two reasons. First, slaveholding determined status and social power. Second, however brisk the slave trade, considerable sentimental pressure existed to inhibit a purely rational approach to buying and selling slaves. Any notion that the slaveholders as a class could or would have abandoned their estates to invest in more remunerative pursuits in the free states or even within the South—in other words, to transform themselves into ordinary capitalists—rests on a vulgar economic determinist outlook, contradicts the actual historical experience, and ignores the essential qualities of slave-based Southern life.

III. *The question of whether or not the slaveholders earned a return equal to that accruing to Northern capitalists is not an especially significant political or social question.*

Economists have assumed that an affirmative answer would prove slaveholding to have been just another business. Such a conclusion would be a nonsequitur; as Schumpeter warns us, statistics can never disprove what we have reason to know from simpler and more direct methods.

IV. *The question of profitability, strictly considered, can and should be approached as an empirical economic problem having only tangential relation to the large political and social issues. Both the traditional and revisionist interpretations of the origins of the war can absorb either positive or negative findings.*

Irrepressible Conflict Case A. The existence of an economically profitable plantation system made the slaveholders anxious to protect their valuable property against outside interference and made them especially furious with ignorant criticisms of their system of economy. It emboldened them to strike out on their own rather than to tolerate Northern criticism and encirclement. *Ergo,* secession and the risk of war were necessary to the defense of a healthy society.

Irrepressible Conflict Case B. Faced with an inability to earn a decent living under conditions of deteriorating soil and falling profit rates, the slaveholders had to stake everything on a political independence that could lead to the acquisition of virgin soils. *Ergo*, secession and the risk of war were necessary to shore up a faltering economy.

Repressible Conflict Case A. With a prosperous economy strengthening the conservative tendencies of the planters and giving them too much to risk on foolish adventures, the South would have faced the moral issue of slavery in due time. Since the whole country benefited from Southern prosperity, both North and South had an interest in resolving the slavery issue in such a way as to prevent the slaveholders from suffering economically and to maintain the Negroes in a system within which their labor could be guaranteed and their behavior properly controlled. With time and good will slavery would have gradually yielded to a more humane system without convulsions and without any interruption in the economic process. *Ergo*, demagogy and blundering produced a needless bloodbath.

Repressible Conflict Case B. With a low or negative profit rate Southerners would have had to rid themselves of slavery before long. It was time for Northerners to come forward with sympathetic and constructive proposals designed to compensate the slaveholders and help them re-establish a healthy economy under their own experienced direction. *Ergo*, a bloody and destructive war was fought to gain what necessarily had to come about peacefully in the near future.

Any reader could, with a little effort, double or triple the number of possibilities within each case. Great social transformations do not come about as a result of a kind of popular income accounting. An accurate knowledge of profit or loss will not tell us much about the origins of the secession crisis.

V. *Even if it could be established that plantation profit levels did stay high and that long-range prospects looked good, it would not follow that capital was being accumulated in a manner guaranteeing a politically viable economic development.*

A. To speak of the viability of the South is meaningless; of slavery, misleading. It is the political viability of the slaveholders, and the necessary economic basis of that viability, that are in question.

B. The structure of income distribution needs to be more closely analyzed, but we already know that slaveholders in general, and planters in particular, got a disproportionately high share. Planters siphoned off much of the yeomen's cotton profits by charges for ginning and other services and through a cotton market that operated to give big producers higher prices than small producers. Average cotton prices disguised a big spread in the returns to social groups.

C. Therefore, even if general profit levels remained high, the level of capital accumulation would have been seriously undermined by a high propensity to consume and a tendency toward seigneurial display.

D. On a strictly economic plane, the continued capitalization of labor may have paid and may be considered part of the process of capital accumulation; but it necessarily restricted the accumulation of capital for broad regional development.

E. The high propensity to consume—and squander—presents no mystery or metaphysical problem. Precapitalist landowning classes generally exhibit such a propensity, which arises naturally from their relationship to labor and other classes. An ideological and psychological assessment of the Southern slaveholders is essential to an understanding of Southern political economy.

VI. *The economic prospects facing the slaveholders in 1860 contained serious dangers to their hegemony.*

    A. The long-range prospects for cotton planters do not seem to have been bright. Increasingly, their region would have found itself in the position of those underdeveloped countries whose problems Raúl Prebisch and others have recently brought to the attention of the United Nations and world opinion. Those countries must sell their agricultural and primary products in markets in which prices are set under conditions of vigorous competition but must buy finished goods in markets in which prices are set under conditions of oligopolistic manipulation.

    B. Southerners had not anticipated Prebisch's thesis during the 1850s but had begun to worry about the permanence of their near-monopoly of raw cotton and, in a general way, about their long-range prospects for dealing with European and Northern business.

    C. Short-range prospects underscored their fears. The English textile depression of 1861–1865 had long been attributed to the wartime cotton famine, but recent work suggests a crisis of overproduction.[15]

    D. Therefore, objective and subjective data suggest some Southern uneasiness about economic prospects at a moment of great political agitation. Even if profit levels had been as high during the 1850s as many now believe, the memory of the 1840s and the doubts about the future might have had considerable political effect. These considerations cannot explain the origins of the secession crisis but do suggest the need for further study to determine to what extent economic pressures affected the pace of political events.

VII. *The South moved steadily into a crisis as its slave system matured, but this crisis must not be confused with economic crises of either a cyclical or secular type.*

A. There is no necessary relationship between the unfolding crisis of the slave South and any cyclical economic crisis. Even if cotton prices and profits had remained permanently at their average levels for the 1850s, the crisis would have continued to deepen. Yet, the specific cyclical conditions of the 1850s might and probably did affect the pace and quality of the political response of the slaveholding class.

B. A prospective secular decline in the price of cotton and other Southern staples relative to the price of Southern imports, even if such a decline could be firmly established, should not be confused with the general crisis described here. Such a decline under other social conditions might merely have occasioned the shift of capital to alternative pursuits. Yet, a secular decline would necessarily be indistinguishable from the economic aspect of a general crisis.

VIII. *The general crisis manifested itself in all spheres of life.*

A. The political, economic, and ideological barriers to capital accumulation, to the development of a home market, and to the rise and consolidation of independent middle classes effectively prevented the South from keeping pace with Northern material development.

B. The attendant sapping of Southern political power in the Union threatened to sap slaveholder hegemony in the South.

C. The declining power of the South made the defense of Southern values especially difficult in a world in which they were already under widespread attack.

D. Therefore, the general crisis had its economic as well as political, social, ideological, and psychological aspects, but was not essentially an economic crisis. It was the crisis of a social class and of the civilization it was painfully struggling to build.

N O T E S

1 "The Economics of Slavery in the Ante Bellum South,"
JPE, LXVI (April 1958), 95–130; reprinted in Conrad and
Meyer, *The Economics of Slavery and Other Econometric
Studies* (Chicago, 1964). Their book includes criticisms of
their paper by Douglas F. Dowd and John E. Moes and
rejoinders, as well as a "Polemical Postscript on Economic
Growth," which replies to a paper by Moes, "The Absorption of Capital in Slave Labor in the Ante Bellum South
and Economic Growth," *American Journal of Economics
and Sociology*, XXI (Oct. 1961), 535–41, and also to the
paper that constitutes Chapter VII of this book.

   In that "Polemical Postscript" they write: "Insofar as
income increases are both a measure of and a potential support for growth—we could say that slavery was not incon-
sistent with growth in purely economic terms. Finally, in-
ferring from the effectiveness of the interregional capital
market and some evidence of the use of slave labor outside
of staple agriculture, we argued that slavery was not incon-
sistent with economic diversification."

   Although a full discussion of their essay would not be in
order here, I should like to make a brief reply. It is precisely
the "purely economic terms" with which I should quarrel.
Absolute growth is not in question; a politically viable
growth is. In short, a strictly economic approach is not
helpful, however valid it might be in its own terms. On the
broader questions, I must stand on this essay and the others
in this volume.

2 See esp. Robert Evans, Jr., "The Economics of American
Negro Slavery," National Bureau of Economic Research,
Aspects of Labor Economics (Princeton, N.J., 1962), pp.
183–256, including critical comments by Thomas P. Govan
and John E. Moes. Of the three items by Moes mentioned
in these notes, this is his strongest and deserves careful atten-

tion. He argues, in effect, that the natural economic tendency was toward gradual emancipation but recognizes that such a tendency was inhibited by noneconomic factors.

3 "A Note on the Profitability of Ante Bellum Slavery," *SEJ*, XXX (April 1964), 325–32.

4 Eugene D. Genovese, "The Medical and Insurance Costs of Slaveholding in the Cotton Belt," *JNH*, XLV (July 1960), 141–55. Joe Gray Taylor, *Negro Slavery in Louisiana* (Baton Rouge, La., 1962), p. 104, independently arrived at a similar figure.

5 "Two Documents Relating to Plantation Overseers of the Vicksburg Region, 1831–1832," *JMH*, XVI (Jan. 1964), 32.

6 Personal correspondence, Oct. 1, 1964, quoted with permission.

7 See the appendix to my unpublished doctoral dissertation, "The Limits of Agrarian Reform in the Slave South," Columbia University, 1959.

8 Barnsley Papers, Jan. 9, 1860, University of North Carolina.

9 See, *e.g.*, Bruce Papers, Box II, Folder 1855.

10 Ernest Haywood Papers, *passim*.

11 A. H. to Joseph Arrington, March 12, 1860.

12 *Mortality Statistics of the Seventh Census of the United States*, esp. pp. 8–9.

13 "The Profitability of Slavery: A Historical Perennial," *JSH*, XXIX (Aug. 1963), 303–25.

14 *Ibid.*, p. 324.

15 Eugene A. Brady, "A Reconsideration of the Lancashire 'Cotton Famine,'" *Agr. Hist.*, XXXVII (July 1963), 156–62.

Bibliographical Note

In the hope that the notes will serve as an adequate guide to the primary and contemporary sources, I should like to draw the nonspecialists' attention to the more important secondary works.

Of the enormous number of general works on the slave South, three are especially valuable as introductions. Chapters II and III of J. G. Randall and David Donald, *The Civil War and Reconstruction* (Boston, 1961) present a carefully balanced and remarkably substantial sketch of the South and of slavery. Still valuable are Chapters II and III of Arthur C. Cole, *The Irrepressible Conflict* (New York, 1934). Clement Eaton, *The Growth of Southern Civilization* (New York, 1961) suffers from an undue urban Whig bias but has much to offer in fresh material and the mellowed reflections of a mature scholar. Of special interest is Douglas F. Dowd, "A Comparative Analysis of Economic Development in the American West and South," *JEH* (Supplement), XVI (Dec. 1956), 558–74.

The literature on slavery is large and growing, and much of it bears on the problems discussed here. The writings of Ulrich B. Phillips, embracing a lifetime of research and reflection, remain the best introduction despite his debilitating race prejudice. Frank Tannenbaum, *Slave & Citizen* (New York, 1947) is one of those rare little books that get better with each reading. Of the various state studies, Charles Sackett Sydnor, *Slavery in Mississippi* (New York, 1933) enjoys pride of place.

Since agriculture constituted the heart of the Southern economy, we are fortunate in having many creditable and some outstanding studies. Lewis C. Gray, *History of Agriculture in the Southern United States to 1860* (2 vols.; Gloucester, Mass., 1958) remains indispensable, but Paul W. Gates, *The Farmer's Age, 1815–1860* (New York, 1960) has a great deal to offer. Gates's chapters on the Southern states are inferior to those on the Northern, but what is inferior for Gates might be considered outstanding for most others. If his discussion has not supplanted Gray's, it has provided a large and necessary supplement. The starting point for a consideration of agricultural reform is Avery O. Craven, *Soil Exhaustion as a Factor in the Agricultural History of Virginia and Maryland, 1606–1860* (Urbana, Ill., 1926). The subsequent literature on agricultural history in general and reform in particular grows larger with each passing year. Certain items are invaluable even for a nonspecialist who wants to get beneath the surface. Weymouth T. Jordan's many books and articles must be consulted, especially his *Ante-Bellum Alabama: Town and Country* (Tallahassee, Fla., 1957). John Hebron Moore, *Agriculture in Ante-Bellum Mississippi* (New York, 1958) and Cornelius O. Cathey, *Agricultural Developments in North Carolina, 1783–1860* (Chapel Hill, N.C., 1956) are the kind of studies we need for every state. The articles of James C. Bonner, especially his "Profile of a Late Ante-Bellum Community," *AHR*, XIX (Jan. 1944), 663–80, deserve special note. These men have set a high standard of performance and have placed all students of the subject deep in their debt.

Several works on Southern economic history are essential introductions to industrial as well as agricultural development. Robert R. Russel, *Economic Aspects of Southern Sectionalism, 1840–1861* (New York, 1924, 1960) contains a startling amount of data and insights and remains the best introduction to the most politically pregnant questions in Southern economic life.

It has stood up for forty years and is likely to stand up for forty years more. Alfred Glaze Smith, Jr., *Economic Readjustment of an Old Cotton State: South Carolina, 1820–1860* (Columbia, S.C., 1958) and Milton S. Heath, *Constructive Liberalism: The Role of the State in Economic Development in Georgia to 1860* (Cambridge, Mass., 1954) both contain important material and useful discussions but suffer from a narrow economic perspective.

The history of Southern industry needs to be written. The many articles of Richard W. Griffin (see the notes to Chapters VIII and IX of this book) are of great value and will hopefully be collected before long. Griffin has also done a remarkable job with the *Textile History Review*, which he edits. Like all new and small journals, it has its problems and is uneven, but it brings together some fine articles and reprints much useful source material. Griffin's articles and those of Ernest M. Lander, Jr., are especially valuable. Lander has contributed important articles on several phases of Southern industry to other journals (see notes to Chapters VIII and IX). A fresh study of William Gregg is in order, but Broadus Mitchell, *William Gregg, Factory Master of the Old South* (Chapel Hill, N.C., 1928) may still be consulted with profit. A good biography of Daniel Pratt has yet to be written. Three articles by Richard B. Morris contain perspectives and material that others have missed: "Labor Militancy in the Old South," *Labor and Nation*, IV (May–June 1948), 32–36; "The Measure of Bondage in the Slave States," *MVHR*, XLI (Sept. 1954), 219–40; and "White Bondage in Ante-Bellum South Carolina," *SCHGM*, XLIX (Oct. 1948), 191–207.

On Southern commercial relations see Douglass C. North, *The Economic Growth of the United States, 1790–1860* (Englewood Cliffs, N.J., 1961) for new perspectives. A standard work is Herbert Wender, *Southern Commercial Conventions, 1837–1859* (Baltimore, 1930). Robert G. Albion's studies are indispensable: *The Rise of New York Port, 1815–1860* (New York, 1939) and *Square-Riggers on Schedule* (Princeton, N.J., 1938). Several new studies of the factorage system have been under way and will hopefully appear soon.

On the vexing profitability question see Harold D. Woodman, "The Profitability of Slavery: A Historical Perennial," *JSH*, XXIX (Aug. 1963), 303–25, for a good critical survey of the literature.

Since World War II a great many excellent studies of economic development in general and of underdeveloped areas in particular have appeared. Used carefully, they have much to offer a student of the slave South. Of special value are: Maurice Dobb, *Studies in the Development of Capitalism* (New York, 1947); Gunnar Myrdal, *Rich Lands and Poor* (New York, 1957); H. J. Habakkuk, "The Historical Experience on the Basic Conditions of Economic Progress," pp. 149–69 of Léon H. Dupriez (ed.), *Economic Progress* (Louvain, 1958); and Paul A. Baran, *The Political Economy of Growth* (New York, 1957).

Index